CW00502229

GULCHEHRA HOJA is a Uygh DC. Her reporting on what the the 'genocide and crimes agains Radio Free Asia has been widel and has led to honours such as the 2019 Magnitsky Human Rights Award; the 2020 Courage in Journalism Award; her recognition as one of the '500 Most Influential Muslims' in the world every year since 2016; and platforms at Tina Brown's Women in the World summit and the Oslo Freedom Forum.

Working closely with the *New York Times* and *Guardian*, as well as directly with the US State Department, she has also been central to bringing to light both the stories of escapees from East Turkestan's concentration camps, and exposing China's use of Uyghurs for forced labour in their cotton and wig-making industries.

'We said "never again" after millions of Jews were killed in the Holocaust, but here we are in 2023 and another genocide is taking place in front of our eyes. Gulchehra Hoja bravely exposes this new holocaust perpetrated by the Chinese communist party in her brilliantly written book, *A Stone is Most Precious Where it Belongs*. The suffering of the Uyghur people that she documents is a must read. We owe Gulchehra Hoja an enormous debt of gratitude to bear witness and share this horrifying story' Bill Browder, author of *Red Notice*

'Gulchehra's story, and her work to shed light on the Chinese Communist Party's genocide of the Uyghurs, has been carried out at a high price. This book offers a valuable look at the experiences that led to her dedicated journalism, and her fight to preserve and live out Uyghur culture' Nury Turkel, author of *No Escape: The True Story of China's Genocide of the Uyghurs*

'I found this heart-rending book impossible to put down and hope it finds the global audience it deserves' Peter Oborne, author of *The Fate of Abraham: Why the West is Wrong about Islam*

'A *Stone is Most Precious Where it Belongs* is a brave and brilliant book. It is a window into topics ranging from efforts to maintain Uyghur culture in the face of suffocating propaganda in Chinese state media through to the opportunities and agonies of exile. But most gripping is Gulchehra Hoja's willingness to share not just her story but herself – humour and humility, pain and love and faith' Sophie Richardson, China Director at Human Rights Watch

'We are lucky to have this important historical record of what she – and so many others – endured. A heartfelt, accessible story of a determined warrior for her oppressed people' *Kirkus Reviews*

'Gulchehra Hoja has given the world that rarest of treasures: a true account that magnificently tells the story of a whole people – the Uyghur nation – while simultaneously telling the most personal and powerful chronicle of one heroic woman's life. Readers will not be able to put down this beautifully written chronicle of Gulchehra's devotion to her family, her people, her faith and to her conscience' Dr Katrina Lantos Swett, President of the Lantos Foundation, past Chair of the US Commission on International Religious Freedom

GULCHEHRA HOJA

A Stone is Most Precious Where it Belongs

A Memoir of Uyghur Loss, Exile and Hope

virago

VIRAGO

First published in the United States in 2023 by Hachette Books
First published in Great Britain in 2023 by Virago Press
This paperback edition published in 2024 by Virago Press

1 3 5 7 9 10 8 6 4 2

A CIP catalogue record for this book is available from the British Library.

ISBN 978-0-349-01598-9

Printed and bound in Great Britain by
Clays Ltd, Elcograf S.p.A

Papers used by Virago are from well-managed forests and other responsible sources.

FSC www.fsc.org MIX Supporting responsible forestry FSC® C104740

Virago Press
An imprint of
Little, Brown Book Group
Carmelite House
50 Victoria Embankment
London EC4Y 0DZ

An Hachette UK Company
www.hachette.co.uk

www.virago.co.uk

I dedicate this book to my father, Abdulqeyyum Hoja,
who taught me to love myself and my people, my homeland,
the world and all of humanity, and most importantly, freedom

Contents

R U S
KAZAKHSTAN
UZBEKISTAN
TURKMENISTAN
KYRGYSTAN
TAJIKISTAN
AFGHANISTAN
PAKISTAN
M
Altay
Yining
Ghulja
Ürümqi
Tengritagh Mountains
Turpan
Ham
EAST TURKESTAN
Upal
Kashgar
Baren
Täklimakan
Desert
Hotan
C H
TIBET
Lhasa
NEPAL
BHUTAN
INDIA
BANGLADESH
MY
500 miles
Tropic of Cancer
70°
80°
90°

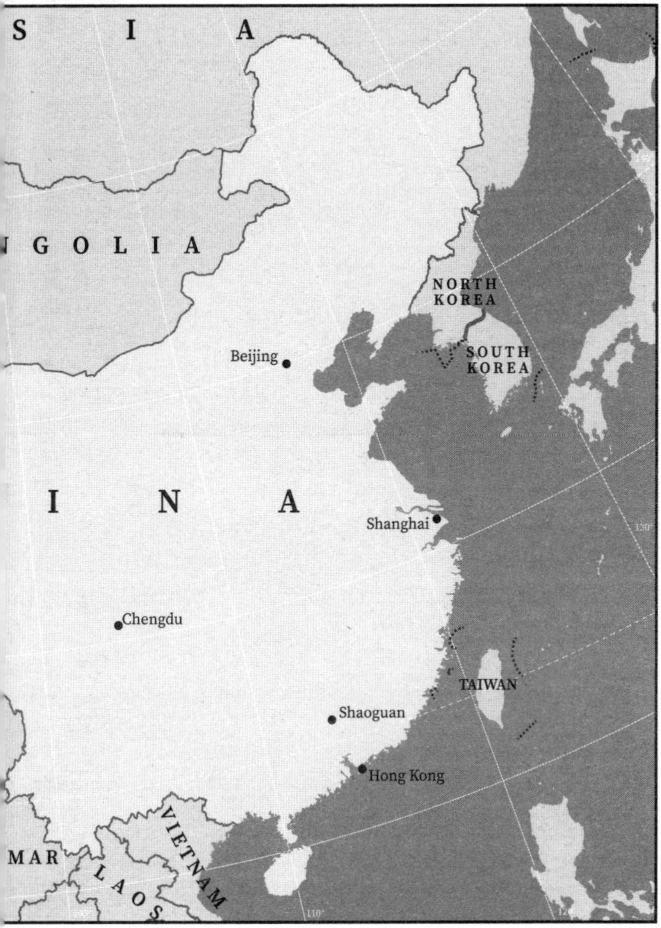
S I A
G O L I A
NORTH
KOREA
SOUTH
KOREA
Beijing
I N A
Shanghai
Chengdu
TAIWAN
Shaoguan
Hong Kong
MAR
LAOS
VIETNAM
130°
110°

Prologue

Late in the evening on February 1, 2018, twenty-four members of my extended family were arrested in the course of a single night. Among them were my elderly father and mother, along with aunts, uncles, cousins and their spouses. Although my younger brother wasn't arrested with them, that wasn't because of any kind of luck. The previous year, he had already been detained without cause and had been disappeared into an internment camp.

On that terrible night, two police officers, one Uyghur and one Han Chinese, barged through my mother's front door under cover of darkness. With my brother interned and my father in the ICU after suffering a stroke, she was alone in the house. They slapped handcuffs on her and threw a hood over her head. Because of her high blood pressure (among other serious health issues), the thick black cloth over her face left her fighting for breath. She begged the police officers to take it off.

The Uyghur policeman leaned down close to her. "I'm sorry. We have to take you like this. Those are our orders." But as he spoke, he lifted the bottom of the hood slightly so her mouth was exposed.

The other policeman noticed what he was doing and said harshly, "What, is she your mother or something?" He pulled the hood back down tightly over my mother's face and led her to a waiting police car.

She was taken first to the local jail, where she met my elderly aunt, who had also just been detained. By this point my mother's blood pressure was dangerously high. Jail officials examined her, but because the jail didn't have any medical facilities, they wouldn't accept her. So my mother was separated once more from her sister and taken to the Ürümchi No. 1 Prison, a notorious facility for hardened criminals. Although this prison did have medical facilities, my mother never received any care. When she asked for her blood pressure medication, she was given cough drops. As a professor of pharmacology, she knew the difference.

At the prison, they made her strip off her clothes and change into a dirty uniform, still stinking of the sweat and fear of the last prisoner to wear it. She was thrown into a small room with thirty other women and kept chained to a pipe for days on end. It was just one of many humiliations visited upon her. And she is very far from the only person to undergo such degradations. In the twenty-first century, my beautiful homeland has become the site of terror. The wholesale destruction of the ancient Uyghur culture and way of life has proceeded at an unimaginable pace. My story, and the story of my family, is very much part of that cultural genocide.

The city of Ürümchi where I grew up is flanked to the west by the breathtaking mountains of the Tengri Tagh and surrounded by vast desert landscapes punctuated with startling green oases filled with grape and melon vines. It is an ancient city situated much closer to Kazakhstan than to Beijing. Long a major trading center on the Silk Road, Ürümchi is now the bustling capital of an area that has been known to its indigenous inhabitants as East Turkestan since the nineteenth century. The Uyghur people and our ancestors have thrived for thousands of years amid this harsh and spectacular natural beauty, and along the way developed a complex and rich culture of music, dance, architecture, visual arts, language, and a unique form of Islam. Many elements of the culture can be traced back to ancient Turkic and Central Asian influences from which descended our Sufi-inflected musical tradition, the *muqam*, and many of our local foods—from the fragrant flatbreads known as nan to the cumin-spiced skewered kebabs cooked over an open flame.

To the south of Ürümchi is the great Taklamakan Desert, the second largest shifting sand desert in the world, in whose oases for more than a millennium the Uyghur people have grown millet, wheat, cotton, figs, persimmons, and other small-scale crops using clever underground systems of irrigation known as *kariz*. Along the edges of that enormous expanse of sand, the Uyghur people and our ancestors have mainly ruled ourselves under various Turkic, primarily Muslim, potentates. Around 1755, the Manchu-led Qing Dynasty invaded the Uyghur area—which is about the size of the state of Alaska and which today comprises one-sixth of what is now known as the People's Republic of China—and brought it under the umbrella of imperial China. Local rebellions proliferated and the area increasingly became subject to Chinese military control. It was not named Xinjiang (meaning New Territory) by the Chinese until 1884, while my great-grandparents were alive.

Our cultural memories are long. My father still remembers marching in a parade celebrating East Turkestan when he was seven years old, while his older brother rode on horseback in the local Uyghur cavalry, flying our blue flag with its distinctive star and crescent moon.

Up until 1949, East Turkestan proudly waved its own flag, and came as much within the cultural sphere of the Soviet Union as of the Chinese state. Although it was a majority Uyghur area, with Uyghurs constituting 75 percent of the population until the mid-twentieth century, there was also a sizable population of Kazakhs, Tajiks, Uzbeks, Tatars, and Kirgiz, most of whom follow some form of Islam. It was a delicate balance, one that in the mid-1900s the Chinese government began to systematically destroy.

With the official founding of the People's Republic of China in 1949 and the establishment of the Communist Party of China as the government, a new policy with respect to East Turkestan came into effect. Instead of nominally ruling from afar, the young CCP decided that a full-scale occupation was necessary to control the Uyghur area and, just as importantly, the Uyghur people. The 1950s saw a massive movement of Han citizens—the Han being the dominant ethnic group in China, and what people may generally picture when they think of a "Chinese person"—mostly former soldiers, into the northern part of East Turkestan. The government sent them there to farm wild lands as well as to provide an enormous paramilitary presence in the region. These people constituted the Xinjiang Production and Construction Corps, or the *bingtuan*, and they were there to exploit the land and natural resources as much as possible. Simply put, the situation became one of a colonized people and a colonial overlord, with all the shots called by the communist powers in Beijing. Within a few decades, the ethnically Uyghur population in the region dropped to below 50 percent. A vast and terrifyingly accelerating program of colonization and cultural annihilation had begun.

The CCP designated East Turkestan the "Xinjiang Uyghur Autonomous Region" in the 1950s, but just like the "Tibet Autonomous Region," almost no political or cultural autonomy followed from the name. The Uyghurs, like the Tibetans, were considered by the Han authorities to be a backward people, and few Han Chinese knew anything about our traditions or way of life. Travel was made difficult for Uyghurs—many hotels outside the region even refused to give rooms to Uyghurs—and many Han increasingly considered the Uyghur region to be the "wild west," full of violence, lawlessness, and primitive conditions. Prejudice against Uyghurs, largely stemming from longstanding CCP propaganda about the necessity of "opening up" the Uyghur region and teaching Uyghurs how to be modern and "civilized," ran rampant.

In 2017, this campaign was ramped up in horrifying ways when the Chinese government began to incarcerate large numbers of Uyghurs in detention facilities built in the middle of the desert, far from the eyes of both the international community and the local population. With the level of secrecy surrounding these camps, it's impossible to know how many people have been disappeared into these facilities. But according to the best available information obtained through leaked official documents and eyewitness accounts, somewhere between one million and three million people have been forced into these camps, where they're subjected to dehumanizing treatment, such as torture, rape, forced labor, and routine humiliation. A Uyghur person can be arrested and put into these camps for any expression of our unique culture. Hundreds of thousands of people have been held for years without any due process or explanation.

Things are bad outside the camps as well. When I was a child in the 1970s and 1980s, televisions were still rare in the Uyghur homeland. Today, however, a vast system of surveillance has been installed throughout the region. In the cities, like Ürümchi, high-tech cameras hang on every telephone pole and can identify Uyghur individuals using sophisticated facial recognition software developed specifically for the purpose of keeping the population intimidated and in line. On corners where watermelon vendors used to park their donkey carts or trucks, military police now stand with machine guns at the ready. Policemen march in formation everywhere, and even going to buy vegetables at a bazaar requires an invasive search. A Uyghur needs an ID even to buy gas at a gas station. Of course, the Han living in the region are not subject to these same oppressive measures; they have separate lines to get into the marketplaces and train stations without any checks at all.

Much of this surveillance and intimidation is done under the pretense of fighting so-called terrorism, but the real purpose is to methodically destroy the Uyghur community. Offered the fig leaf of the Global War on Terror after the terrible events of September 11, 2001, the Chinese government took the opportunity to label regular Uyghur citizens "terrorists" for engaging in behaviors as ordinary as praying in a mosque, growing a beard, or wearing a hijab. Innocent Uyghurs have even found themselves in Guantanamo Bay. Any sign of resistance from the Uyghur community against these oppressive measures is met with overwhelming brutality and an increase in "preventative measures" such as invasive surveillance, intimidation, and incarceration. The noose of total control has been slipped around the region and tightens with every passing day.

Some scholars view the actions of the Chinese government in East Turkestan as straightforward colonialism: East Turkestan is rich in minerals, gas, coal, and other natural resources, and it covers a huge geographical area, offering potential relief for China's enormous population density. The Chinese have simply come and taken what they want, and they have suppressed any resistance to their presence or their greed. Many scholars emphasize China's tenuous historical claims on the area and the government's desire not to seem weak by ceding stolen lands back to their rightful inhabitants. Others see evidence of the state's fear that the people in other non-Han areas like Tibet and Inner Mongolia might also rebel and seek independence again, while Hong Kong and Taiwan resist being absorbed into greater China. In the end, there are no definitive answers for why genocide in any form happens. Nevertheless, that is exactly what is happening now in my homeland.

All of this explains how my family ended up behind bars on that horrible night in 2018. But it's not the full story. The hard truth I had to face that night, feeling completely helpless from thousands of miles away, is that the Chinese government took my family away for one reason: me.

PART I

GROWING UP IN THE UYGHUR HOMELAND

All the present horror in my homeland is like night and day compared to the happy childhood I had growing up with my extended family in Ürümchi.

As a young child, I was fascinated by the arts and performing. My grandfather, Zikri al-Pattar, was a famous musician, and a composer of muqam, a traditional Uyghur musical form involving complex melodies, literary texts set into verse, and intricate choreography. The tradition of muqam connects each generation to the next and is a vivid reminder of our place within our long lineage. The role it plays in our culture is so important that it has been proclaimed an Intangible Cultural Heritage of Humanity by UNESCO.

In the 1950s, my grandfather established the first Muqam Ensemble in East Turkestan under the auspices of the Uyghur Song, Dance, and Theater Troupe, where muqam and other traditional art forms were taught and performed. When I was a child, every weekend was like a festival at his house. Musicians would come from across the region to perform, show off their newest skills, play together, and learn from each other. Even as a young girl, I was outgoing, so I would sing and dance alongside the professionals without trepidation. They were tolerant and kind to me, and I learned many traditional songs and melodies at their knees. As a starry-eyed girl, I had no idea that my desire to perform would take me across the world, or that it would eventually lead to my separation from my family and the homeland I love.

When we were little, my younger brother Kaisar and I spent a lot of time at our grandparents' house, along with our cousin, the son of one of my favorite aunts. My cousin was three years older, and I looked up to him like a beloved bigger brother. He was often bossy, but I forgave him because he also protected me and kept me from getting into trouble. As for my brother, we were completely inseparable. If one of us was in a room, the other was sure to be no farther than around the corner. We were so close in age that we could have been mistaken for twins.

Before we were old enough for school, my grandfather took care of us during the day. That was the normal cycle of life in Uyghur society: when a person grows older, they take care of the grandchildren while their kids go to work; and then the kids grow up to take care of their parents. As children, we would often eat at my grandparents' house, and once we started school, we spent each weekend there. If a member of the family was missing at a meal, it was noticed and lamented. Families back then in the Uyghur region were very close-knit and loving. Ours certainly was.

That sense of community extended beyond the family to the entire neighborhood, or *mahalla*. My grandmother was an expert cook and would make huge feasts of *chuchure* or wontons in a thick broth, steamed buns filled with a savory squash filling called *kawa manta*, and *goshnan*, which was flatbread stuffed with meat and baked to crisp perfection. Whatever she made, she would share with our closest neighbors in our mahalla.

"Take this to the neighbors," she would tell me, handing me a steaming plate wrapped in a towel. "And don't let it spill on the way!"

I was only too happy to go, usually with my brother trailing after me, since the neighbors would give us sweets as a thanks for our grandmother's generosity.

My grandmother also looked out for the poorer families in the mahalla. At that time, almost no one had running water inside their houses, and we all used a communal pump outside. Somehow the neighborhood children who didn't get quite enough to eat at home all knew that they could bring a bucket of water to my grandmother in return for *leghman*, freshly made noodles cooked with meat and tomatoes, in a portion big enough to take some back to share with their families.

My grandparents' house was located near the Uyghur Arts Center, where my grandfather worked. The building had once housed the American consulate in Ürümchi, which was closed in 1949 when the American officials bolted from the region. Mao Zedong had just declared the establishment of the People's Republic of China (the communist regime that lasts to this day), which meant the end of the Republic of China and the beginning of an entirely new era in Chinese history. My grandfather was given use of the former consulate house by Saifuddin Azizi, who became one of the most important figures in the regional government as the chairman of the Xinjiang Uyghur Autonomous Region, a position that made him a link between the local government and the centralized Communist Party that ruled from Beijing. Azizi thought my grandfather played a fundamental role in the cultural life of the region, so he gave permission for him and his family to live there.

The former consulate was an enormous place, filled with furniture that had been abandoned when the Americans fled the political chaos. A huge rectangular table big enough for thirty people sat on the first floor. It had probably been used for important consular meetings, but we employed it for the massive meals my grandmother would prepare when guests came. The building was constructed in the Russian style—not atypical for the city, given the Uyghur region's location—with brick walls, shiny wooden floors, and tall glass windows. The walls were so thick that I could play on the windowsills or even curl up and take a nap on one. There were luxury chairs made of leather and wood, and fine wooden cabinets. Left to our own devices, we children used to play a Uyghur game called "Blackbird" in which one of us pretended to be a mother blackbird protecting her young from a marauding eagle. Kaisar always insisted on playing the eagle that would swoop down with claws extended as we hid behind the plump chairs, shrieking with laughter and frissons of fear.

The American officials had also left behind a small black-and-white TV. At that time, few people in the region had TV, so all our neighbors at some point would show up to watch TV with us. The reception wasn't perfect, but we got performances of Uyghur music and dance, as well as the regional news read in Uyghur. Communist Chinese films, like *Lei Feng*, about a communist revolutionary hero, were subtitled in Uyghur. Those were our least favorite and when they came on, people tended to wander away. The Chinese language and culture weren't entirely alien, because they increasingly made inroads into Ürümchi and surrounded our mahalla. But the Chinese stories and songs on the TV were so distant from our daily experience that they tended not to interest people very much. Everyone would rather watch a famous dutar player perform a muqam while dancers in luxurious red and gold dresses swirled around each other in the complex patterns of traditional dances.

We also had a gramophone that my grandfather would use to listen to music. Sometimes people would come to ask if they could borrow it for a wedding, but my grandfather would generally say no. "This is from the government, it's for my work," he'd tell them somberly. He loved to share but took his responsibilities seriously. But I also remember my aunts playing records on it for the frequent parties they held at the house.

With its red brick exterior and tall windows, the house stood out from the others in Ürümchi. At that time, many of the buildings in the residential areas of the capital city were made of mud bricks and built around courtyards that typically opened to the west. Because of the insulation the mud bricks provided, those houses were easy to keep warm in the winter and deliciously cool in the hot summers. The mahallas were all dotted with minarets, where the muezzins would call people to prayer five times a day. The streets, narrow and winding and dusty with sand that blew in from the desert, were always bustling with vendors selling freshly baked nan, dried fruits, or pots and pans, often carried in carts pulled by donkeys that wound their way down the twisting alleys. It seemed that every road led to a bazaar, where you could buy anything your heart desired, from fragrant spices to brightly colored cloth to a whole roasted goat.

Our house was beautiful, but I didn't fully understand just how special it was, a relic of old Soviet influences that had been driven out, along with a once sizable population of Russians, when the CCP asserted control in the region. I just knew my grandparents loved living there. But in 1982, when I was in second grade, the government tore it down. My grandparents moved into one of the new modern apartment buildings that were popping up all around Ürümchi. All throughout the Uyghur region, older cities were being "modernized," which meant razing entire mahallas full of the old mud-brick houses that had lasted for a thousand years and throwing up cheap Chinese-style apartment buildings. As the capital city, Ürümchi saw a burgeoning Han section built in the center of the city, with the old architecture replaced with red lanterns, gaudy signs in Chinese characters, and red banners proclaiming political slogans. In the meantime, the Uyghur residents got squeezed out of the center toward the less desirable edges.

Many of these changes had to do with the huge influx of Han Chinese to the region, especially to Ürümchi. They came for the job opportunities as well as for ideological reasons, as the government encouraged Han residents to move west to "settle and develop" the region. It was a trend that would only accelerate over the decades. In the region as a whole, the Han population increased from around 200,000 people in 1947 to more than 7.5 million within a mere five decades. In Ürümchi, Uyghurs were rapidly becoming a minority in their own city. In the northern part of the Uyghur region, the situation was even more extreme because the CCP encouraged the growth of the *bingtuan*, the Han production and construction corps, turning desert and wild lands into cultivated fields with environmentally catastrophic methods. By 2012, the Han *bingtuan* controlled more than 30 percent of the arable land in the Uyghur homeland, along with much of its water resources, leaving very little for Uyghur farmers and herders.

When they tore down the old consulate, my grandfather was as upset about the changes being wrought upon the city as about being forced out of his home. "So they'll even destroy a place like this!" he cried, shaking his head. "Today, it's just out with the old, in with the new."

At first I was excited to visit my grandparents in their tall apartment building, but after the move everything changed. Whereas in the mahalla we used to leave our doors open to our neighbors all the time—especially around the holidays when people would wander in to sample my grandmother's fluffy honey cakes called *bal piranik*—the doors were always locked in the high-rise. I had to carry a key around my neck in case my grandparents weren't home when I went over after school.

As more Han Chinese moved in, the neighborhoods were flooded with strangers, and the sense of community that held the mahallas together vanished. People didn't know each other anymore; metal bars were added to the windows and iron security doors were installed. With the high-rises, street life shrank down to a ghost of what it had once been, and the old men who used to drink tea together at tables on the street corners near the bazaars moved inside. New Chinese restaurants sprouted up on every street, but because they served pork and food that wasn't halal, prepared according to the Islamic concept of purity, you never saw Uyghurs eating there. The city increasingly felt like it was divided into two separate worlds.

With our move to the high-rise, the enormous parties my grandparents used to have, full of people and endless singing, dancing, eating, and drinking, also ended. No longer did my grandmother add one more dish to the table, and another, and another, as she used to do, especially around such holidays as Eid al-Fitr at the end of Ramadan, when people would come over to celebrate and get a taste of her delicious baking.

Despite the changes, my parents were especially happy together around the holidays. Everyone could see how close they were, even though my mother was mostly in the kitchen and my father in the living room welcoming the perpetual guests and family visitors. Today, they've been married for most of their lives, but even now I don't know the whole story of their marriage. It was always considered too private to discuss. When I was young, if I asked my mother questions about how they first kissed or how my father proposed to her, she would just blush. But she did tell me that when they got married, she was nineteen and my father was twenty-four. She had just started working at a pharmacy, and my father worked at the Xinjiang Regional Museum, which holds many treasures of the Uyghur ancestral past.

My parents were both born in the city of Ghulja in the northwestern part of East Turkestan, an area mainly populated at that time by a flourishing community of Uyghurs and Kazakhs. Today Ghulja has a population of over half a million people, but at that time, it was a much smaller city. My father, Abdulqeyyum Hoja, grew up beside a small orchard. His father made a living selling the fruit that he grew with his own hands. It was a simple life, and although they didn't have much money, the family was happy. But my father's mother died when he was fifteen, and my father was sent to Ürümchi to go to school. It took two days on the long-distance bus to get across the mountainous terrain to the capital. A few years later, my father attended Xinjiang University in the first official archaeology training course ever taught in the Uyghur region.

Although they didn't know it at the time, my parents were neighbors growing up. They lived in the same area of Ghulja, but because my mother, named Qimangul after a desert flower, was younger than my father by six years, he didn't even notice her. But in 1958, my mother's father became the head of the Uyghur Arts Center in Ürümchi and moved the family to the capital. My mother went on to study pharmacy and medicine at the Xinjiang Medical University there.

Back in those days, people tended to gather with other people from their hometown who had also ended up in the capital city. All of the students from Ghulja would get together to eat and play music and reminisce. My father says that the first time he saw my mother, he fell in love with her. She had long black hair that cascaded down to her knees like a thick, beautiful shawl. My mother was used to attention from the young men, but she told me that my father stared at her so much the first time they met that she started to feel nervous. But my father was a very skilled player of the dutar, a traditional long-necked two-stringed instrument with more than a thousand years of history. He was well known among the students from Ghulja for his musical gifts, and he slowly won her trust. After meeting several times, they decided they wanted to be together.

They had been married for only a very short time when the Cultural Revolution started. Because my grandfather Zikri al-Pattar's family was highly educated, they were targeted for "reeducation." The

Cultural Revolution destroyed educational, cultural, communal, and familial ties all over China, by design. Families, especially those considered "anti-revolutionary" because they were landowning, wealthy, intellectual, or in some other way suspect, were split apart. Children were taken from parents, married couples were separated, and ordinary life came to a halt. Uyghurs felt that the upheaval had to do with the Han and their culture, and that it shouldn't involve the Uyghurs at all. But the political forces were too strong to avoid, and none of the more than fifty ethnic groups officially designated by the CCP—from the Tibetans on the Himalayan plateau to the Hmong people of southwest China—escaped the chaos.

Big-character posters plastered with political slogans were mounted on public bulletin boards to try to indoctrinate people, and violent mass movements designed to destroy the traditional culture began. Across China, as well as in the Uyghur homeland, the "Four Olds" came under attack: old ideas, old culture, old habits, and old customs. One of the edicts that came down was that all women had to cut their hair short. When my mother heard the news, she started sobbing. It was a personal invasion, and Uyghurs particularly prized long, luxuriant hair. But there was no escape from the order, no exceptions to the new, arbitrary rule.

Finally, my mother asked my father to cut her hair. She couldn't stand the idea of a stranger doing it. She sat in a chair in their kitchen and my father wielded the scissors. She told me years later that it had taken him hours to do it. As he clipped her silky dark hair, it was the first time my mother had ever seen him cry.

Then they were separated. This happened so soon after marrying that they'd hardly gotten used to living together. My father and my grandfather were sent to the coal mines in the north, where they worked long, backbreaking days at hard labor. My mother was sent in the opposite direction to Turpan, a little town two hours from Ürümchi located in the Tarim Basin, at one of the lowest elevations in the world. Although it's in the middle of the Taklamakan Desert, the area is also an oasis, famous for producing delicious grapes that are dried and turned into a home-brewed wine called *museles*. My mother worked there for eight long years, even after my father returned to Ürümchi.

Like many families who had been ripped apart, they worried about whether they would be able to start a family. But later that first year, after having the chance to visit my father briefly in Ürümchi, my mother discovered that she was pregnant. Far from her family and everyone she knew, she worked long days and often into the night as a doctor in the village. She had just finished her schooling in pharmacology, but because the village didn't have a doctor, she provided a wide range of medical care, which included delivering babies. In the ideology of the Cultural Revolution, only those without formal education were trustworthy. Although she was more educated than the standard "barefoot doctor" whom the CCP sent out into the countryside to provide basic medical care, she was compelled to learn a lot on her feet.

In 1970, my older brother was born two months premature in Turpan. My mother named him Khedirdin. He was tiny and fragile, with frighteningly pale skin. Back then, in the villages, there weren't any incubators or sophisticated medical equipment that could keep premature babies alive. My mother stayed with him, holding him and desperately trying to keep him warm. She tried to feed him breast milk, but he lacked even the strength to latch properly. She could feel him slipping away hour by hour, and after a few despairing days, he died in her arms. He was buried there in Turpan.

After that, my mother was careful not to risk pregnancy again on any rare visit from my father until she was finally allowed to go back to Ürümchi.

Years later, my mother took me to the village where she'd worked during the Cultural Revolution. I was ten or eleven and had never visited Turpan before. It was very dry and very hot, and the sun seemed especially high in the sky.

When we arrived, all the villagers flooded out of their houses and brought their children to see her. She had delivered many of the babies herself when she'd lived there.

My mother greeted everyone as though they were long-lost family members. "And what's your name?" she asked one girl, who had presented her with a small bouquet of desert flowers.

"Qimangul," she replied, her cheeks reddening.

"That's my name too," another girl offered.

My mother beamed at them.

I was confused. "Mom, why do they all have your name?"

One of the women took my hand. "We were so grateful for the work your mother did here that we wanted to thank her. So we named our girls after her!"

That was the first time I realized how much respect my mother had garnered for her hard work and kindness. She never told us stories about all she had to deal with during the Cultural Revolution, so I knew nothing about her life then until I visited the village. Her friends in the village treated me like a little princess, giving me sweets to eat and complimenting me on my shiny dark hair. My mother toured me around the village and showed me the hospital where she'd worked back when it had been just a tiny clinic.

"I delivered a lot of babies in there," she said. Then her eyes clouded slightly. "Even when I was pregnant with your poor older brother. I still miss him." She sighed and then ran a hand over my hair. "But you were such a gift to us, Gulchehra. We wanted you so badly."

Only at the end of the Cultural Revolution when my mother was allowed to return to Ürümchi to rejoin my father and her extended family did she finally become pregnant again. The whole family treated her like a queen. She wasn't allowed to do anything around the house for fear that she would lose the baby. The family rallied around her to make sure that this one would take.

My grandmother would often describe the story of my birth to me. My parents were at a friend's house for a birthday celebration. Suddenly, my mother's water broke, and things progressed so quickly that she had to go through labor in their house. Instead of a doctor, they called in an older midwife with more than thirty years of experience. When I finally made my appearance, the midwife cleaned me up, and cried, "She's so little, but so energetic! She looks just like a little doll!"

So my grandfather gave me the name Gulchehra. The name holds a double meaning: it means "flower" but also "something beautiful, something bearing hope." It's a very rare name, and not very easy to pronounce—*Gul*, like "pull," *che* like in "chess," and *hra* as in "rah." I wanted to have a more normal name, but my grandmother would tell me, "No, the name is perfect for you. You're our beautiful little flower." I came to like my name. All the way through school, and even after I got to college, I was the only Gulchehra I knew.

My father guarded me like a treasure when I was little. He didn't want me to sleep alone, so he would hold me while I slept until his arms eventually gave out. When I was eight months old, my mother got pregnant again with my younger brother and couldn't breastfeed anymore. At that time, they believed that goat's milk was the closest thing to mother's milk. So every morning my father would jump on his heavy black bicycle and ride for an hour to a nearby village to bring back fresh goat's milk for me to drink. He did that until I was a year and half, to make sure I had a chance to grow up healthy and strong.

I was a delicate child with a somewhat fragile constitution. My father would get terribly worried whenever I had a cough or was sick to my stomach. He would go to any lengths to make sure I was safe and comfortable.

When I was six years old, an outbreak of cholera hit our area. Many of our neighbors got sick. At the same time, hepatitis B was spreading unchecked through the region and I contracted it at day care. I lost a lot of weight and was hospitalized for months. My parents were terrified that they would lose me, just as they had my older brother. Any moment they weren't working or sleeping, they were at the hospital, comforting me and making sure I was getting the care I needed.

Every day, the nurses drew blood and did tests. I cried a lot, as much from exhaustion and fear as from pain. My veins were so small that when a nurse needed to put in an IV, she had to insert it into the big vein at my hairline. If I moved around too much, the IV would pull out and they would have to stick the needle in again in a different place. Some nights my father held my head in his large hands all night long to make sure the IV stayed where it was supposed to stay.

That was the way I was raised, knowing how much my parents loved and valued me. And that I had a strong community all around me.

Sometimes I would cry when I saw the nurses coming because I knew they were going to do something to me that I wouldn't like. Once when I was sobbing especially hard, my father told me, "Little Flower, listen to me. If you smile, really smile, it won't hurt as much. Believe me."

I always believed what my father told me. So after that, every time a nurse appeared with a needle, I would smile and tell myself, *It doesn't hurt. It's okay, it doesn't hurt.*

Even today, I often find myself smiling when I'm upset. My father called it a sun shower, the way sunshine can somehow appear between rain clouds or rare bouts of rain can appear in a desert. I always smile through the pain. And every time I see sunshine through a rain shower, I think of my father.

From my grandfather, I inherited our people's culture; from my father, I learned our history. My father was a highly regarded archaeologist, and the museum where he worked was like a second home for me. At his knee, I learned about the culture and history of the Uyghur homeland. The museum held items of great significance, including the Loulan Mummy, an ancient woman who had been preserved by the dry desert conditions near the salt lake where she had been buried. The mummy's features and DNA indicate she was Indo-European, not Chinese, which points to the unique ethnic background of the people of East Turkestan. In 1980, when my father first studied the mummy, he came home and told me, his eyes shining, "Today I saw our great-great-great-great-great-great-great-grandmother! And she's beautiful, just like you."

One of my aunts worked as a guide to the exhibits at the museum, and as a little girl, I would often follow her around, mimicking her gestures and hoping one day I could hold people's attention in the same way. I learned every object in the museum by heart.

At that time, the Uyghur region was still open to outsiders, and there were visitors to the museum from Japan, Hong Kong, and across China. The CCP promoted tourism as a way to bring in money and interest, always emphasizing the Han claim over the area. For a while, the Uyghur region was a popular tourist destination: remote and beautiful, full of ancient history and ruins, and romanticized because of the role it played on the Silk Road. Sometimes tourists wanted to take pictures with me, perhaps because I looked like the consummate little Uyghur girl with my dark hair done up in braids, bright eyes, and round rosy cheeks. I would trail after my aunt, chatting freely with strangers without a hint of shyness.

By the time I got to school, I was an outgoing, vivacious girl and I made friends quickly. The elementary schools in Ürümchi in the 1970s and 1980s were divided by language, with different schools for Chinese-, Uyghur-, and Kazakh-speaking students. In some areas, the schools were combined: Han students would have classes on one side of the building, where they were taught in Chinese, and Uyghur students on the other side, where they were taught in Uyghur, except in the compulsory Chinese-language classes. Each child was put into a class, and that same cohort of students had one teacher who taught all of the subjects from first grade through fifth grade, and another from sixth grade through eighth grade. The students in each cohort became close, almost like second family.

I did well in elementary school, so I was selected from my neighborhood to attend one of the most academically rigorous middle schools in the city. It was an honor to be selected, as my parents emphasized, but it meant spending an hour on the bus every morning to get to school. To get ready, I had to get up before anyone in the family and then ride the eleven stops from the museum to Yan'an Lu where the school was. To a young child, the ride seemed interminable.

The experimental school drew the best students from around Ürümchi, and as I soon discovered, I wasn't the only one who could study. After the first Chinese-language test, the results were posted on the board—at that time, all that mattered were scores—and my name appeared way down the list at number twenty-seven.

I didn't enjoy learning Chinese. It's in a completely different language family from Uyghur, which is closely related to Turkish and uses an Arabic-derived script instead of Chinese characters. While Han children in Ürümchi could spend their entire school careers without learning any of the local language, Uyghur children were required to learn Chinese. Some parents pressed their children to master Chinese, since many workplaces required fluency in the language. Official business on a neighborhood level could be conducted in Uyghur, and of course we all spoke Uyghur at home and in the bazaars and shops, but more serious matters often took place in Chinese.

That night at dinner, I shamefacedly told my parents about my score on the test. Kaisar gave a little snort and I kicked him under the table.

My father showed his disappointment with a small shake of his head. Then he smiled slightly and said, "I see. At your old school, no one could compete with you. You didn't have to work very hard, did you, daughter? Well, at your new school, you'll see how far that gets you."

"You'll do better on your next test," my mother said, running her hand reassuringly down my hair.

"But Chinese is boring!" I blurted out.

My parents looked at each other.

"That may well be, Gul, and nobody's going to ask you or your brother to speak it at home," my father said firmly. "But we're surrounded by Chinese now. You have to know it to succeed."

By the end of that year, I was consistently among the top ten students in my class, though never first. That honor belonged to a girl named Mukerem. Her father was a prominent businessman and she always came to school dressed in pristine clothing, everything about her pale and precise: she was tall and thin, with skin the color of cream. She kept her clothing immaculate, and I used to marvel at how she never even seemed to get her socks dirty. Mine were always tumbling down and getting muddy as I danced in the schoolyard during recess.

I didn't care so much about being first in our class because I was busy with so many other activities. I participated in singing groups and dance competitions, and started to win little awards for my performances. I gritted my teeth and did well in Chinese, but the one class in which I really encountered trouble was algebra. Somehow I just couldn't wrap my brain around the equations, and my thoughts would drift away to something more interesting—choreography I was learning or a new song one of my friends had taught me.

One afternoon doing my math homework at my grandmother's house, I threw my pencil across the room in frustration.

"Gul, my sweet, what's the matter?" my grandmother asked me.

"I hate algebra!" I announced.

"But algebra is a wonderful subject! If you understand algebra, you'll understand a great many other things about the world as well." She sat down next to me. "Show me the problems and we'll do them together."

The next day as school was ending, my math teacher called me over to his desk. He was known as one of the strictest and least sympathetic teachers in the school. He had my math homework in front of him, and he pointed down at my figures. "Gulchehra, who did your homework for you this time?"

I lowered my eyes.

"It's your handwriting, but I know it isn't your work. These are old German techniques!"

"It is my work," I protested.

He raised an eyebrow.

"But I did have help," I admitted. "From my grandmother."

He stood up from his desk. "Take me to see her."

I was miserable as we walked the few blocks from the school to my grandparents' apartment. When we got to there, I knocked on the door instead of just going in as usual.

My grandmother answered the door wearing her usual simple dress that came down to her ankles and a plain cotton hijab. At the sight of a man, she tucked a few stray hairs back under the edge of her headscarf. She looked at my face and glanced up at my teacher from her diminutive height. Then she laughed. "Oh dear, are you in trouble?"

My math teacher introduced himself to my grandmother, and she invited him in for some tea and dried fruit. To my surprise, they sat in the living room and talked like old friends. After a while, I got bored and wandered away, just grateful that it no longer looked like there would be some sort of punishment in store for me.

The next day, my teacher called me to his desk again and said, "Gulchehra, do you know who you're descended from?"

I knew the names of all of my grandparents, but I wasn't sure that was what he meant, so I shook my head.

"You are the granddaughter of the first algebra teacher in the Uyghur region! Were you paying attention yesterday to what your grandmother told me?"

I had to confess that I hadn't really listened. As far as I knew, my grandmother cooked and cleaned for my grandfather, and took care of us grandkids, and spent her whole day in the kitchen. She just seemed like an ordinary housewife to me.

He sighed. "You children have no sense of your own history. Your great-grandfather built the first school in Ghulja. He was a great man. At the end of the nineteenth century, he traveled to Istanbul to study education, and brought back as many German and Turkish books as he could so that the children here could be exposed to the new learning. He taught his own five children from those books, and your grandmother excelled at algebra and geography. When her father was able to open his school, she started to teach algebra to the younger students. That makes her a mother to all the math teachers who came after her, including me." He shook his head. "And you say you don't like math! You just listen to your grandmother and do it the way she tells you to."

It took a few days, but finally I got up the nerve to ask my grandmother about her days as a teacher. Since she never talked about her past or her life before my grandfather, I didn't know how she would react to the question.

She slowly put down the cloth she was using to wipe down the table. "Yes, it's true. I taught for years when I was younger, at the school your great-grandfather started. Your cousin was named after the school. Do you know what the name means? It means 'salvation.' Because our culture is our salvation. Do you understand?" She looked at me seriously.

I nodded.

There was much about my family I didn't know. Years later, I learned that my great-grandfather had also bought a thousand acres of land to do archaeological digs to try to find one of the grandsons of Genghis Khan. His research was part of the archaeological evidence that led to the discovery of a gravesite thought to be of one of the Khan's descendants, that of Tughluq Tömür Khan. It was on our family's land, but after that land was occupied by communist troops, it later turned into a tourist site. Like many places of historical and cultural significant to the Uyghur people, it has been appropriated by the Chinese authorities as a money-making and propaganda-generating site, minimizing the vast Turkic legacy it represents.

My great-grandfather was executed by the Chinese government because he was a proponent of Uyghur independence and free education. At his school, they taught classes like Arabic, the General History of Islam, Uyghur Language, the Qur'an, Mathematics, Science, and Handcrafts. In the 1920s and again in 1938, he was arrested by the Chinese authorities for educating Uyghurs in their own culture and for serving as an advisor for Ehmetjan Qasimi, then president of the Second East Turkestan Republic established in 1944. At the time, the Uyghur homeland was fighting for its independence from China, with uprisings and military action. As the Chinese were occupied fighting with each other, Uyghurs, Kazakhs, and other groups founded the First East Turkestan Republic in 1933, complete with its own constitution and army. But over the next two decades, the Han managed to gain control over the region by force, killing hundreds of thousands of people along the way. My great-grandfather left my grandmother many books and letters from the time, which she'd kept hidden in a big wooden case. But it couldn't be saved during the Cultural Revolution, when the communists searched every house and destroyed anything of cultural significance they could find.

Learning about my family's long commitment to education—not just their own but the education of all Uyghurs—made me want to do my very best at everything I put my hand to. But despite my efforts to buckle down at my books, what I really loved was dance.

Dance is everywhere in Uyghur life. We can't be without music; it's central to our communal and emotional lives. Every Uyghur has at least one instrument at home, most often the dutar, which often hangs on the wall, although it rarely gathers dust. My grandfather was a dutar master, and my parents both played quite well. If they were feeling joyful or depressed or simply wanted a bit of after-dinner entertainment, one of them would take it down from the wall and play and sing.

Dance is a natural accompaniment to the music that fills our lives. A traditional Uyghur saying is that by the time children can speak, they can sing, and by the time they can walk, they can dance. That was certainly true for me.

At the end of middle school, I tested into the high school in Ürümchi that specialized in the arts. When I heard I was admitted to the dance department at the arts school, I was desperate to attend. I told my parents that what I wanted most in the world was to be a professional dancer. My parents told me they would consider it.

When my grandfather learned of my ambition, he told my father, "Don't let her be a dancer. She needs to go to a good school, study hard, and become a professional."

When my father relayed the decision to me, I immediately burst into tears.

"Don't cry, daughter," he said gently. "I know it hurts now, but your grandfather is right. Your studies are the most important thing."

So instead of being allowed to go to the fine arts school in Ürümchi, I was sent to the most academically rigorous high school in the city. A year later, when a well-known dance school in Shanghai invited me to study there, my father refused to let me go. My parents let me participate in some local dance groups, but only if it didn't interfere with my studies. Most of the time, I was stuck at home with my homework.

I couldn't understand it at the time. Dance and music have always been profoundly important to Uyghur life, and artists are highly respected—my grandpa was living proof of that. Given any excuse at all, Uyghur people will dance. They dance at weddings and during festivals and at any happy occasion. The choreography can be very set or could involve variations on a theme, with intricate step patterns and rhythms and graceful arm movements. Many dances represent daily activities, like bowl-carrying, or imitate the movements of animals, and often take a circular formation. Groups of men or women often stage more formal dance recitals and performances or solo performances. I would watch those performances utterly transfixed by a dancer's sparkling gold and red gown and the precise fluid motion of her hands and arms undulating over her head.

I don't know how I managed to keep up my grades because I spent a good portion of each class daydreaming about being a famous dancer. When I did listen, I sometimes heard things I couldn't understand, especially in history class. I liked our teacher—a heavy-set Uyghur man with kind eyes—but often what he said directly conflicted with the lessons my father had taught me. One day in my freshman year, he was lecturing from the book about how people had first come to the Uyghur region from Mongolia, along with the Han and other ethnicities.

I raised my hand. "Are you saying that Uyghurs are descended from Mongolians?"

"We're on page 147. Follow along, Gulchehra." My teacher patiently went on with his lesson.

"But that's not true!" I blurted out. "We're not the same ethnicity as the Mongolians. My father says the Uyghurs have always been here, for thousands of years. We belong to this land, and the land belongs to us."

My teacher's expression darkened. "See me after class, Gulchehra. And stop interrupting."

My face was burning. But I knew I was right. My father had drilled it into me from the time I was young. Uyghurs had their origins in an ancient Uyghur empire, whose well-documented relics and artifacts go back to the eighth or ninth century, and our earlier ancestors go back well beyond that. But that's not what our CCP-controlled textbooks said, and I dreaded what my teacher would have to say to me.

When class ended, I stayed at my desk in the darkened room until all of the other students had left to go home. Then I dragged my feet down the hallway to the deserted teachers' lounge.

When he saw me standing in the doorway, he sighed, gestured me inside, and closed the door behind me.

"Gulchehra, we all know your father is Professor Abdulqeyyum Hoja." He rubbed his tired eyes. "He knows more about the history of our region than anyone. But what is in the textbooks is what is in the textbooks. If you want to do well in school and pass the exams and go on to have a future, you have to learn what's in the textbooks. If you keep speaking out like that in class, you'll only cause trouble for yourself. And you'll bring trouble home to your family as well. Do you understand?"

I nodded. I understood what he was saying.

He dismissed me with a slow wave of his hand. As I was leaving the room, I heard him say behind me, "But you must never forget the precious lessons of your father. Remember that."

I went through all of my schooling with my history teacher's words echoing in my head. There were always two lessons to be learned: what was in the CCP-issued schoolbooks, and then the real history, literature, and culture, which could only be learned from people like my father, in private settings and in low voices. I even began to feel sorry for my teachers, who were caught up in a system they had no control over.

Soon my classmates and I were in the midst of studying for the *gaokao*, the university entrance examination. It is still the most important test any student in the Chinese educational system will take. Even back in the 1980s when I was in school, it determined which university you'd go to, and with that, what kind of life you were likely to have. The pressure was intense, and every little advantage could have a huge effect on the end result.

Not long before we were to take the test, we heard about a scholarship being offered at the school. One student who demonstrated excellence and was destined for greater things would be awarded an extra twenty points on the *gaokao*. That was a large margin, and could mean the difference between getting into a dream university or getting stuck with a second or third choice. The winner would be determined by a vote of all the students.

The vote was held in secret, but it was quickly apparent by all of the smiles and nudges of congratulations that I had been chosen by my classmates to receive the extra points. By all rights, our classmate Mukerem was the best student with the highest grades. But she always seemed to care only about her own success, and that meant that my classmates chose me instead.

Buoyed by the certainty of those twenty extra points, I went into the *gaokao* confident that I would do well. The test lasted a grueling nine hours over the course of two days, and by the end of it, I was so exhausted I didn't want to get out of bed for a week. But on the basis of some local performances, I'd been chosen by the Xinjiang Education Bureau to go to Beijing as part of an "ethnic students" exhibition that would travel to five different cities to dance and sing. I was to head up the student group from the Uyghur region and perform in front of Chinese citizens, many of whom had never before even seen a Uyghur in person, let alone been exposed to our culture. I thought that by performing and showing ordinary Han citizens the beauty and power of our music and dance, it might help them understand the value of our own ancient culture. My parents reluctantly agreed to let me go, despite their obvious misgivings.

I was too young then to understand that the performance of "ethnic dance" and the cultural hierarchy inherent in that framing had a long history in China. As early as the 1940s, dance troupes from the Uyghur homeland were being sent into China to entertain Han audiences. This only played into the sense of the Uyghur as being a "simple" and "backward" people, able to sing and dance, but unable to rule themselves. But as a high schooler, all I wanted to do was perform.

When I arrived in Beijing, I couldn't believe how enormous and bustling the city was. It was the first time I'd traveled outside of the Uyghur region, and there were just so many cars and buses and high-rises and people. And many of those people seemed to be staring at me. I felt my own difference keenly for the first time. My face was shaped differently from theirs, and my thick, wavy hair was different too. Even the way I moved set me apart. It wasn't hard to pick me out of a crowd. I also worried about finding halal food, which wasn't an issue back in the Uyghur region, where it was taken for granted that food would be properly prepared. With the exception of my grandmother, my family wasn't especially religious, but we took our Muslim identity for granted; it was woven into the fabric of our community. We always observed the two big Islamic holidays each year—Ramadan and Eid ul-Adha, the Feast of the Sacrifice—but otherwise, my parents generally avoided talking about religion. Still, they were constantly reminding me and my brother that we were Muslim and had to eat halal foods.

"Allah made you halal, made you pure, and you must keep halal by only eating halal foods," my father would say.

In Beijing, I got by mostly eating rice and *mantou*, plain steamed buns made of tasteless white flour. Being in Beijing was like traveling through a foreign country, with all of the challenges of negotiating unfamiliarity. At the same time, I felt an imperative to be a "model minority" and demonstrate the best of Uyghur culture to everyone I met. I even tried to be gracious when a Chinese man leered at me from across the aisle on the bus and asked me, "Hey, girl, do you people ride camels to school?"

Yet aside from all that, it was exhilarating to be on the stage performing in front of large audiences and garnering enthusiastic applause. It was a whirlwind tour, full of performances and sightseeing and constant bus travel. The stage felt exactly like where I wanted to be.

It took three days and three nights to get back to the Uyghur region from Beijing, which receded behind me like some faraway world that I might have dreamed into existence. When I arrived at the Ürümchi train station after the tour, I was suddenly struck by all of the colorful headscarves on the women around me. Men outside the mosque across the busy street were laying out their prayer mats for one of their five daily prayers. Coming back from the completely secular environment of Beijing, I felt the contrast keenly. I took a deep breath and felt myself relax for the first time since I'd left.

That faded when I caught sight of my father. His face was grim as he welcomed me home and picked up my bags. I asked him what was wrong, but he told me that we would go home and talk about it. My heart sank; I had a terrible inkling of what might have happened.

The whole way home on the bus, my father avoided my eyes. When I got home, I saw that my mother had been crying.

"Is it the *gaokao*?" I blurted out as soon as I was through the door.

My mother pulled me into a hug. "Your scores weren't what we had hoped for."

I dropped down onto the couch, stunned.

My father was very upset. "The *gaokao* is the only avenue to a better future, Gul. You know this! If you fail at the *gaokao*, you're finished. There's no good job, no middle-class life, no comfort waiting for you as an adult. Education is the only way to succeed when the deck is stacked against you."

"We know you wanted to go to the Xinjiang University literature department," my mother said more gently. "But you're ten points short." She handed me the letter with my results.

I could feel tears gathering in my eyes. I wasn't sure what I wanted to do with my life, but I knew it was going to be something involving the arts, and the literature department had appealed to me more than anything else. Now I had no idea what I would do. "Where was I accepted?"

"You've been taken by the Chinese language department at Xinjiang Normal University."

"The Normal University! I don't want to be some ordinary teacher stuck in a middle school somewhere for my whole life."

"Gul," my father said sharply, "any university is better than no opportunity at all. Do you understand?"

I nodded miserably. I was too disappointed to speak. I looked down at the paper in my hand and saw the breakdown of points for each section of the test. Then I looked up. "But where are the extra twenty points? The scholarship!"

My father shook his head slowly. "No, Gul, you didn't get the scholarship. Your friend Mukerem did. The school announced it yesterday."

"But my classmates all told me they voted for me."

"Sometimes things don't go as we expect, daughter." My father patted me on the cheek. "It isn't the end of the world. At least the Normal University took you."

I soon found out that several of my close friends got into Xinjiang University, which was the top university in the region. I was embarrassed to tell them that I'd be going to the Normal University. It wasn't what I had been working for all those years. Still, when my friends held a gathering to celebrate, I went along. Despite my own disappointment, I could still show my happiness for them.

As we sat and ate and talked, I told them how I felt. "I thought I would do all right, but I must not have studied hard enough after all."

"Well, if it helps, Mukerem isn't any happier than you are," one my classmates told me. "She's being sent to the Ethnic Minorities University in Beijing!"

"I saw her crying in the hall the other day," one of the girls said. "Her mother's so upset about her leaving that she hasn't gotten out of bed for days."

I could understand why Mukerem didn't want to go all the way to Beijing. She would be so isolated there. "Why don't we bring a little gift to her mother?" I said. "Something that might make her feel a little better."

My friends looked at each other.

"What?" I asked.

"You don't know?" one of the girls said. She leaned toward me, and our little group huddled closer over the table. "We heard that while you were in Beijing Mukerem's father went to the school and offered money to the principal if the scholarship went to Mukerem."

"So he did it," another girl said. "He changed the name on the certificate."

I was shocked, but I shook my head and said, "And look what those twenty extra points got her. Come on, let's go pay her parents a visit and see if her mother needs anything."

As it happened, attending Xinjiang Normal University was far from a catastrophe for me. Instead, it led directly to a once-in-a-lifetime opportunity.

Just a few weeks after I started my freshman year at the Normal University, I danced in a popular intramural student arts exhibition and took the first prize. It was the first time in the history of the university that one of its students had come in at the top in the exhibition, and it made me instantly famous at the school. Suddenly everyone on campus seemed to know who I was, and I was selected by the students' association to be the student leader of the arts section. I met a lot of other students that way, including Nadire, who along with a bright-eyed girl named Mehray quickly became my closest friends. Most of the students at the university were Uyghur, with a handful of Tajiks and Kazakhs as well. The small group of Han students were tracked into their own classes, so we didn't see much of them. Only those rare Uyghurs who had graduated from Chinese-language high schools were put in with the Han students.

One day a month or so into the term, I took a quick bike ride over to Nadire's house to borrow a textbook. When I knocked on the door, a young man answered. He stood in the doorway, staring at me with intense hazel eyes.

"Is Nadire home?" Something about him made me feel strange, but I spoke as normally as I could.

"She's out," he said.

"When will she be back?"

He shrugged. "Don't know."

"My name is Gulchehra. Please tell her I stopped by."

"I'm Elzat," he said, not moving from the door. His eyes seemed to be boring straight into my soul. "I'm sure we'll see more of each other."

As I rode off, I could feel him still standing there in the doorway watching me leave.

As the term progressed, we freshmen were busy testing out our new freedom. In high school, you couldn't show affection to someone of the opposite gender. Any kind of dating was strongly frowned upon both by the school and by one's parents. In a largely Muslim culture, premarital sex was very much frowned upon. But at the university, things were more relaxed. At college, boys and girls could spend time together at parties or go to a movie or take a walk with a girl or a boy alone. Although I still spent a lot of time at home, officially I lived in a dorm with seven girls. Every night, the other girls would all be gone, out to see a movie or to have a meal with a boy. I barely saw some of the girls, they were such social butterflies.

Often I was the only one left alone in our dorm room. I couldn't understand why I was so unpopular. None of the boys would even talk to me. I spent long evenings staring into the mirror interrogating my looks, wondering why no one liked me. Was there something wrong with the way I dressed or talked? Although most of the girls on campus were friendly to me, the boys seemed to avoid me like the plague.

The only boy who seemed comfortable enough to talk with me was Abdul, a student from Hotan, a town in the southwest of the Uyghur region far from Ürümchi. In most of the Uyghur region, unlike in Ürümchi, the schools didn't have native Chinese speakers as language teachers, and so their students' skills weren't up to the university's standards. To help them catch up, each student from Ürümchi was assigned a student from the countryside to tutor, and I was assigned to Abdul.

Abdul was a shy, sweet boy who was studying to be a Uyghur-language instructor. But that didn't mean that he could avoid learning Chinese, and I was a stern teacher. We met often, and he progressed very quickly. We became good friends. I liked his gentle manner and he seemed endlessly fascinated by my stories of growing up in the city. He was even taken by my scent, a perfume I had gotten from my mother. When we would study together, he would sometimes draw in a breath and sigh, "You smell like my hometown."

"What do you mean?"

"Roses. I grew up in a village full of roses. We grow them there for perfume oil. You smell just like a summer breeze."

I just laughed and turned back to the Chinese textbook. He had a girl waiting for him back in his village, and he was the kind of man who would never forget his responsibilities.

Aside from Abdul, I occasionally ran into a few boys I had gone to high school with who had also ended up at the Normal University. One day crossing campus I saw an old friend and waved to him.

"Gul!" he called. "Come have lunch with me."

We went to the cafeteria and chatted just like the old days. Then suddenly he leaned forward and said, "Everyone's talking about the guy you're dating. How did you end up dating a teacher at another university?"

"What guy? I haven't even gotten a date since I've been here!" I was mystified and upset that there was gossip going around about me.

A few days later, when I was biking home from campus, a man pulled his bicycle right in front of me. He turned his head to call hello and slowed down so he was pedaling alongside me.

"You're not living in the dorms?" he asked me abruptly.

"Excuse me, do I know you?"

"I'm Elzat," he said. "Nadire's brother. We met before at the house."

"I remember you." A suspicion passed through my head. He was behaving so familiarly, but I'd barely recognized his face.

I started biking faster. He stayed alongside me. Panting, I decided to take a sudden turn to try to lose him, but he kept up with me effortlessly.

"Why are you turning here?" he called. "Your house is that way."

I braked hard and stopped my bike. "Why are you following me?"

He looked confused. "I'm not following you."

"How did you happen to be right at that corner when I was biking past? And how come you're just biking next to me like that?"

"I used to go to school here. I graduated last year and now I teach at the Xinjiang School of Engineering. I just came back to campus to see some friends."

I decided the best defense was a good offense. "I heard that there's a rumor going around about me, that I'm dating an older man. Do you know anything about that?"

That finally seemed to affect him. He reddened slightly and rubbed a hand over his chin. "I . . . at the beginning of the term, all the guys at soccer practice were talking about a new girl on campus. You don't know the kinds of things they say! When I discovered that you're my little sister's friend, I just wanted to protect you. It wasn't anything serious. I just told them not to touch a girl named Gulchehra, because she's already taken. I didn't mean anything by it."

"It's not your business to protect me," I protested, bristling at his nerve.

"Look, you don't know the school yet, but I do. I know how the boys think. I just heard those soccer players talking and I responded like a big brother. Forgive me?" His lopsided grin softened me a bit.

"Just quit following me around," I said, and rode off before he could say anything more.

I didn't see Elzat for a little while after that. We all went home for winter break, and by the time I came back, I had nearly forgotten about him. Besides, my life was about to take a sudden turn.

One day midway into the spring term, the dean of the Chinese Department came to the doorway of my literature class.

"Gulchehra, come with me." He beckoned impatiently with his hand.

I gathered my books and left the room, my face flushed and my mind racing to figure out what I could possibly have done to get in trouble. But when I got out into the hallway, I saw that the dean was excited, not angry.

"There's a director in my office who's come all the way from Beijing. He and his associates are here to find actors and they're interested in meeting you. Come with me."

I followed him to his office, where four Uyghurs in suits were waiting. I was surprised to see that there was also a Han man with them. When we came in, they stood up and greeted me politely.

One of the Uyghur men said, "We're here looking for people to audition for a movie about Amanisahan. We saw you dancing on TV in a student exhibition and thought you might want to audition to be an extra."

My ears perked up. I knew a little bit about Amanisahan from my father. She is a very significant figure for the Uyghur people because during the sixteenth century she collected the Twelve Muqam—the basis for all traditional Uyghur music. She had traveled around the Uyghur region, listening to different musicians perform the well-known local tunes, transcribed the music, and then compiled those different versions into twelve grand, representative pieces of music. No one before her had thought to try to distill the distinctive music of the separate regions and to preserve the different versions by writing them down. She was a figure well deserving of a film.

"Have you been in a film before? What about TV?"

I could feel them scrutinizing me as I described some of my past performances. "I've done a lot of arts programs, but I've never been in a movie. But I'm a quick learner," I added.

The Han man spoke then for the first time. Later I learned that he was the film director Xingjun Wang. At that time, he was still cutting his teeth directorially, but he'd already acted in several well-known movies and would go on to direct several more. "Come tomorrow and audition for us," he said. He waved a hand at one of the Uyghur men. "Give her the address."

On my way back to the dorm, I thought about it carefully. My father wouldn't be happy if he knew about the audition. I decided not to tell my parents. I would go on my own.

When I showed up at the hotel where the auditions were being held, I immediately spotted several stars of Uyghur cinema in the crowd. They might not have been well known elsewhere in China, but every Uyghur knew their faces. It seemed the filmmakers had pulled in all of the most beautiful people in the region, and I was keenly aware that I didn't belong. I had hurried there straight from a dance class, and I was still wearing my sneakers and sweat suit. With my hair pulled up into messy pigtails and my face without makeup, I knew I must look like a kid playing hooky from school.

Finally, I was called up to the front of the room by my number: 641. More than six hundred people had already auditioned that week!

Nervously, I turned around and faced the long table. Ten people sat there staring back at me.

My heart was pounding so loudly that I thought for sure they would be able to hear it too.

One of the men looked down at a piece of paper in front of him. "Can you sing anything for us?"

"I can sing a little bit from the Nava Muqam."

"So you know the Twelve Muqam?" one of the other men asked, clearly surprised.

"Not all of them," I admitted. "But I know some." I remembered my grandfather performing the music at his many musical parties when I was little. As I started the melody, it reminded me of my family, and childhood memories came flooding back. I sang from my heart.

There was a short silence after I finished, the last note still reverberating through the room. The acoustics had made my voice sound clear and resonant, and suddenly I felt like I might have a chance to be an extra after all.

The next day there was another round of auditions. Each actress who had been asked back was paired with a male actor and had to read lines with him. It was an exhilarating, exhausting process, and over the next few weeks, the contenders were winnowed down to just a handful. I ran from my classes to the auditions every few days, not even telling Mehray or Nadire what I was up to. It felt like the first big secret I'd ever had.

One afternoon after a grueling audition, I was called into the director's office.

Xingjun sat with a big file folder in front of him. "Gulcherha, you're one of three candidates we have in mind for the lead role in the film," he told me. "Today is the last day of auditions, and we have the whole production team here to watch. We're going to make the final decisions tonight."

The news that I was in the running for the main role was shocking. I thought I was still vying for a minor part. I couldn't believe I had made it that far. I asked to audition last so I could watch what the real actresses did. As I watched the professionals up on the makeshift stage singing and acting with such confidence, I felt completely outclassed.

When it was my turn, I climbed slowly onto the platform. "Honestly, I don't really know why I'm here," I started nervously. "But I do want you to know that I believe in what you're creating. The Twelve Muqam are the most important pieces of music for the Uyghur people, and they're the foundation of our music, and to a great extent our culture. Uyghur music runs in my blood. My grandfather himself was a performer and teacher of muqam. I'd be very proud to be part of a project like this."

Xingjun turned to one of his assistants. "Wait a minute, who is this girl?" he said, gesturing with his chin. Then he turned back to me. "What's your grandfather's name?"

"My grandfather is Zikri al-Pattar, the musician and composer."

The Uyghur men at the table exchanged glances. One of them leaned toward Xingjun and said, "Gul's grandfather recorded all of the Twelve Muqam, and his versions are the muqam we know today."

Xingjun waved his hand. "You others can go. Gulcherha, you stay."

I stood in front of them as they asked me more questions. Then they tested my speaking voice, how far and how clearly I could project, and had me sing again. They asked me about my musical education.

"Young people don't listen to the traditional music anymore," one of the Uyghur producers said. "How do you know so much about it?"

"I like pop music too. But in my family, we value our traditional culture above everything else. The culture can't live on unless people still care about it. The muqam, the old musical styles, the traditional dances—I grew up with all of that. It's part of me."

Xingjun had been leaning back in his chair, but suddenly he straightened up. He stared at me intently. "You," he pronounced, "are the present-day Amanisahan. You're the one."

My heart nearly stopped. Then I blurted out the first thing that came into my head: "I have to talk to my father!"

I hadn't even told my parents that I had been auditioning for the movie, let alone that I had a shot at the lead role. I had no idea what they would say when they learned what I'd been up to. Their reaction to my wanting to go to the arts high school played vividly in my memory. They might not even let me take a break from classes to do the film at all.

"Okay, go home and talk to your parents," Xingjun said. "Call me tomorrow morning and tell us what your decision is. But don't waste this opportunity, Gulchehra. It won't come again."

On the bus on the way home, I thought about how I could tell my parents about the movie so that they would let me do it. I spun the imagined conversation around in my head until I was dizzy. All I knew was that I wanted to be part of the film. My grandfather helped to preserve the Twelve Muqam through the tumultuous twentieth century. If I could, I wanted to be part of bringing his work into the next century.

My father was sitting in his favorite armchair reading the newspaper when I got home. At the sight of him, all of my prepared speeches flew out of my head.

"Daddy, I need to talk to you."

He casually turned the page of his newspaper. "Okay, darling. Talk."

I lowered my eyes and caught sight of a headline in the paper: AMANISAHAN MOVIE TO BEGIN FILMING THIS YEAR. "Actually, it's about that," I said, pointing.

He set his newspaper down in his lap with a heavy sigh and raised his eyebrow. "Amanisahan, eh? She preserved the Twelve Muqam, you remember? Apparently, they're going to make a movie about her." He began to read the article to me.

"Yes, I know, Daddy," I interrupted.

"The film will be based on a book by Saifuddin Azizi. Your grandfather knew him, you know. He's a *good comrade*."

I swallowed. That was an expression for a Uyghur who had sold out to the Han. I could tell my father was about to give me a long history lesson, so I rushed to say, "I think . . . I think I'm going to be Amanisahan!"

He looked at me more closely. "Gul, what have you gotten involved in now?"

"A few months ago some people came to the school and asked me to audition. I didn't think for a minute that I even had a chance. But . . . but in the end they picked me."

He was silent for a moment. "Daughter, you're a student, first and last. You seem to be forgetting that. No, I can't allow it. You shouldn't have auditioned in the first place." His eyebrows were drawn and his mouth was a tight line.

"Almost a thousand people auditioned," I said to one of his shirt buttons. "Out of all of them, they picked me."

"I know the idea of this movie is exciting for you. But think about it, Gulchehra. It says right here that the director is a Han Chinese. What does he know about Uyghur culture? Do you think this film is going to be respectful to our heritage? I don't want you involved."

I wanted to scream or cry or argue, but I could tell when my father had made a decision. I went to bed without eating dinner, and in the morning I called the director and told him my parents' decision.

"What?" Xingjun caught his breath. "Don't they understand? I'm going to make you famous!"

"My father says I'm a student. First and last."

Xingjun paused. Then he said, "Tell your parents we're coming to see them."

That afternoon he turned up on our doorstep with three Uyghur coproducers. When my mother answered the door, he introduced himself and asked her politely if he might speak with her and my father.

They sat awkwardly in our living room as my mother made some tea. I didn't have much hope that they would be able to convince my father.

"Mr. Hoja, we've searched more than three months to find your daughter," one of the producers said. His name was Ilham and he was well known in the Uyghur movie business. "If her grandfather were alive, he would be very proud to have his granddaughter be part of this project."

"Please give her a chance to do this," one of the other producers said. "It will change her life."

Xingjun leaned toward my father. "Of course, we don't want to interrupt Gulchehra's schooling. We'll start filming over the summer, and we'll shoot all of her scenes first. She can go back to class in the fall like nothing happened. I can promise you, nothing will interfere with her regular life."

My father said very little as he listened to the men try to convince him. One by one, they ran out of arguments and turned silent. Finally, he held up a hand.

"None of what you have said convinces me."

I felt tears forming in my eyes.

"But," he sighed, "my daughter clearly wants to be in your film. As her father, it is my responsibility to guide her and protect her. But I cannot keep her under my wing forever. If she wants to do this, it is her decision." He paused. "On one condition. My daughter knows nothing about Amanisahan and the history. My daughter loves the Twelve Muqam and the traditional dances, but what does she know about the sixteenth century? Nothing. Amanisahan, as of course you know, is a pivotal figure in Uyghur cultural history. How can my daughter re-create her without knowing anything about her life or the historical period?" He looked at me. "First Gulchehra must study the history and learn it well. If she can pass my test on Amanisahan's life, then she can be part of your film."

The producers all broke into smiles and shook my father's hand.

"Study hard, Gulchehra!" Xingjun told me as they left, still jubilant.

I was shaking. I couldn't believe that this was really going to happen. I was going to be in my first movie!

That evening, my father gave me two books. One was a book about Queen Amanisahan that described her life and how she became the wife of Abdurashid Khan, a great ruler of the ancient Uyghurs. Then my father pulled a book off of his personal bookshelf. The book looked well loved and a bit worn around the edges.

"I've had this history book for many years. It is about the Yarkent Khanate, which was founded in 1514 and lasted through until the early 1700s. It was a great khanate, a powerful kingdom from which all of us are cultural descendants. Take good care of this book. And don't show it to anyone. This isn't the history you learned in school."

He handed it to me and I held it carefully.

"Now. Starting today, you will learn how to cook, how to clean, how to take care of a household. Amanisahan wasn't born a queen, you know. She was from a very poor family, and her father was a musician who was rich in spirit but humble in origins. The khan fell in love with her because of her singing, but she wasn't of royal blood. You, my daughter, have been raised like a princess yourself. What do you do around the house, hmm? Your mother takes care of everything."

I lowered my head. He was right. I'd never needed to learn to do much around the house, and I hadn't even really paid attention to everything my mother did every day to keep our lives running smoothly.

"How can you create a character who is a regular village girl without knowing what it feels like to work your hands to the bone?"

For the next two weeks, I studied the history books my father had given me, and in every other spare moment, I followed my mother around the house, learning about the tasks she did. I scrubbed vegetables and learned to cook a few basic dishes. I swept every corner of the house twice, and even washed our clothes by hand. My father was right: at the end of those two weeks, I did have a better sense of how difficult Amanisahan's life must have been before she married the most powerful man in the empire.

Finally, my father tested me on the books I had studied, and he didn't take it easy on me. After two hours of questioning, he leaned back in his chair. "Okay, Gul. You've studied hard. But before you go off to your movie, you need to understand some more recent history. Who wrote the book this movie will be based on?"

"Saiffudin Azizi," I said obediently.

"Yes, and I do not reject his books." My father leaned forward and lowered his voice slightly. "But never forget who this man really is. He's a good comrade, a traitor to the Uyghur people. He was once a leader of the Uyghur people, but he gave up on his homeland to move to Beijing and enjoy the spoils of our oppressors. You can respect his work, but do not respect the man. And don't forget that the director of this film is Han. The Chinese government is always in control of the narrative. Don't let down your guard for an instant."

A couple days later, I had packed a few bags and moved to the hotel the filmmakers had booked out to house the movie cast and crew. More than three hundred people were involved in the making of the film, from the producers to the cameramen to the various crew and cast members. The film had a huge budget and would be seen by large Chinese audiences. The exoticism of the Uyghur culture, one of China's officially designated "fifty-six ethnic minorities," was a draw, and the film was going to make full use of the desert scenery and traditional Uyghur dress.

Most of the other people on the set were friendly. The man who played the khan was a famous Uyghur actor, and he became like a temporary big brother to me. I called him Khan, and he called me Queen Amani. During the filming, we all called each other by our characters' names. There was a lot of pressure. I had a lot of lines to learn, in addition to all of the music. I learned how to play the dutar and the sutar parts and to sing parts of the different muqam. The costumes were elaborate and very heavy, but I didn't even take them off during the day, because I wanted to look natural wearing them.

Early on in the filming, I had to act in a scene in which Amanisahan kisses the khan. I was only nineteen years old when the shooting began, and very innocent. Khan told me not to worry, that we wouldn't even brush mouths in the scene. It was all done with camera angles.

The first time through the scene, Xingjun looked grumpy. He called for another take. And another, and another. Finally, he threw down his clipboard and marched over to me.

"How can you have gotten this far without knowing how to kiss?" Xingjun cried in exasperation. "Be natural!"

"Don't worry," Khan told me reassuringly. "You'll get it."

But by then I was crying and they had to stop filming so my makeup could be fixed. By the time we'd finished the scene, I thought I'd never want to kiss a man for as long as I lived.

The filming went by faster than I imagined. Although it was hard work and no one was getting enough sleep, I loved being in front of the cameras. The feeling of making something that other people would watch and learn from was thrilling. But I often found myself in conflict with Xingjun over scenes that didn't ring true to me. My father had made me read those books for a reason. One scene that seemed wrong to me was one in which Amanisahan asks permission from the khan to travel from city to city to gather the Twelve Muqam. In the script, Amanisahan was supposed to get down on her knees and bow at the feet of the khan. But the only time Uyghurs get down on our knees and bow is when we are praying.

That day before shooting, I told Xingjun that the scene had to be changed.

"Are you the director or am I?" he shouted.

"You're the director, of course," I said. "But any Uyghur viewer will know this isn't accurate."

Ilham finally spoke up. "Xingjun, Gulchehra has a point. This is a Uyghur movie, after all."

It was one very small victory among a lot of compromises.

Every few weeks, the filmmakers sent some of the scenes to Beijing to be cleared by Saifuddin Azizi, who seemed content with what he saw. We shot over a hundred short scenes in two months. The finish line was in sight when one evening after a long day of filming I heard a knock on my door.

Xingjun bounded into my room like a teenager. "Gulchehra, you're going to be famous! We're going to work together again in the future, I'm sure of it."

I had no idea what he was talking about. But anytime our director was happy, I was happy.

"Ilham, you give her the details. I'm proud of you, Gulchehra!" he called over his shoulder as he left the room.

I looked at Ilham. "What's going on?"

"Gul, you know we took a chance on you. Here you are, just nineteen years old and so naive. But look at how much you've learned! Saifuddin Azizi and his wife think you're wonderful in the film. And their son is infatuated."

I didn't understand what he was driving at.

"You are going to be famous, just like Xingjun said. We're planning to make three more movies after this one, all based on Azizi's books. They're already in the works. And you're going to star in all of them. You're going to play the mother of Genghis Khan!"

Something was off, and my heart started thumping. I nodded tentatively.

"And how would you like to go to the Beijing Film Academy?"

"I'm already studying literature here, and I like it." I thought of Mukerem and how devastated she and her parents had been when she'd had to leave for Beijing. The idea made me feel queasy in the pit of my stomach. "I'm very happy here in Ürümchi."

Ilham's eyes gleamed. "No, no, you're going to live in Beijing. Azizi and his wife have officially invited you to Beijing. Go to Beijing and meet their son. I'm sure you'll be very satisfied."

"Satisfied?" I felt my confusion begin to coalesce into anger.

"Are you really that innocent, Gul? You're from a good family, you're beautiful, you've shown you have talent and a future. They want to see if you're right for their son, what else?"

By this time I was trembling with rage. "How dare you! You think you can sell me to the highest bidder?"

Ilham's unctuous smile started to fade.

"I wanted to be part of this movie because it showcases our great culture. I felt I could continue my grandfather's musical legacy. I was so proud to be part of it all. But I won't marry some man I don't even know just so I can be in a film." Let alone the son of a good comrade, I thought furiously.

"Think carefully before you make any decisions, Gul."

My head was spinning, but I spoke deliberately. "I'm a person, Ilham, not a commodity. When I marry, it will be for love."

For the next week or so, we went on with filming as usual. But the luster had gone out of it for me. I felt ashamed at the thought of being bartered away to the son of a traitor. My father would be apoplectic if he found out.

One night in my room after a long day, one of the crew knocked on my door and brought in a telegram. It was very short, just three sentences: *My wife and I have decided that the actress playing Amanisahan is too immature. This film is too important for a main role to be miscast. The part must be recast.*

All my efforts, all my studying, all the tears and sweat I had given to the production—it was all for nothing. My whole nascent film career was over before it had had a chance to begin. I dropped the telegram on the bed. I was so stricken that I couldn't even cry.

I heard a faint knock on the door. I didn't move, but the door cracked open and Ilham poked his head in. When he saw me there, he came in quietly.

"I guess you've learned what happens when you don't know what's good for you."

I looked at him in disbelief. Then I got hold of myself and wiped the tears from my face. "So this is what 'art' is here? This is how Uyghur women are treated?" I lifted my chin. I wouldn't let him see just how crushed I felt. "Yes, I've learned a lot."

I decided to leave that very day. They owed me my entire salary, but I refused to accept it. I felt so humiliated, and the last thing I wanted was their money. I took only my things and my father's dutar, which I had used in the film.

One Uyghur coproducer caught me as I was leaving the hotel. His look told me that he knew what had happened. He had a big envelope in his hand and he held it out to me. "These are photos of you from the filming. As a memento."

"I don't want them," I said, my voice barely audible.

"Keep your chin up, Gul," he told me. "You're leaving with your dignity intact."

As soon as I got into the taxi, I started crying huge painful sobs. Before all this, I'd thought that art was the highest pursuit. It was pure. I'd also been taught by my parents that history was something to be respected, and the truth was to be maintained. But I had learned that not everyone felt that way. Now all I wanted to do was erase the entire painful episode from my mind.

"Miss? Are you all right? Where should I take you?"

I told him my parents' address. I knew they would be surprised to see me. During filming, we were allowed only a single two-hour break on the weekends to go home and say hello to our families. This being a Tuesday, they wouldn't be expecting me.

When I got there, I went in quietly through the front door. My father was sitting in his study as usual, and he caught sight of me in the hallway.

"Oh, Gul, you're back for a visit?" Then he noticed I was carrying my suitcase and the dutar, and he lowered his book.

"I'm done with the movie. They said I'm too young for the role." I rubbed a hand down my face. I knew my cheeks were tear-streaked and my eyes were swollen from crying.

He didn't ask me anything, and I went straight up to my room, where I took a long, dreamless nap. I got up feeling disoriented and despondent. I splashed some water on my face and went downstairs, where my father had clearly been waiting.

"Now tell me, daughter, what happened."

Haltingly, I told him the whole story and got through nearly all of it before I broke down in tears. All of my hard work had been for nothing, just because I wouldn't allow myself to be sold like some piece of meat.

My father breathed a long sigh. Then he said, "I'm proud of you, Gulchehra. I've raised a good girl, a strong girl. Today I feel successful as a father." He stood up restlessly. "I didn't stand in your way because you wanted so badly to be part of the film. But I was so worried that you'd regret being part of it, all the distortions. Things that aren't even in Azizi's book. That Han director is just making it up as he goes along." Then his tone changed. "Go upstairs and get ready for dinner. Your mother is making *güle-qag polo*."

Güle-qag polo was one of my favorite dishes, a fragrant saffron rice dish cooked with dill, fava beans, dried fruits, and nuts. I could smell the delicious aromas from the kitchen, and I suddenly felt very glad to be home.

It was already the end of August and classes were about to start again. I hadn't even told my closest friends that I was acting in a film that summer, and now I was relieved because I wouldn't have to explain anything to them. I felt humiliated, not only for myself but for the Uyghur people. I'd had a firsthand taste of how our people's story was distorted and manipulated.

When I got back to campus, I tried to stop brooding over what had happened and refocus my attention on my studies. I joined a dance troupe and each day after class, I attended several hours of dance practice. The busyness kept me from thinking too much about my disappointment and the humiliation that had come along with it.

As soon as the semester began, I started seeing Elzat everywhere I went. I hadn't seen him all summer, but suddenly his bicycle route seemed to take him down all the same roads as mine. He somehow seemed to know my schedule, and most afternoons, when I came out of dance practice, he was there outside the building, casually leaning on his bicycle. Sometimes he just waved, other times he tried to chat for a few minutes before I went on my way. I wasn't rude to him, but I didn't welcome the attention. He was tall and good-looking, with broad shoulders and muscular legs from playing soccer, but something made me feel that parts of him were hidden and unknowable.

In the meantime, I started going to parties again, and it felt good to spend time with my fellow students, laughing and listening to music and dancing. Part of me was happy to be a normal college student. I was often asked to dance, but one night two young men seemed particularly keen. I didn't recognize them from campus, but I danced with both of them one after another. I barely had a chance to take a breath in between songs.

When I left the party and was heading back to my dorm, the two men followed me out. Both were tall and muscular, and had a bit of an edge about them.

"Are you headed north or south?" one of them asked me.

"Neither," I said tartly. I wasn't looking for an escort home.

"She's coming with me in any case," the other man said.

"The hell you say!"

In the blink of an eye, they were scuffling right in front of me, shouting at each other. I was terrified and started backing away.

"Hey! Neither of you are going anywhere, not with her!"

Elzat appeared out of nowhere. He stalked over to the two men and pulled them apart roughly. Next to him, the other two men looked diminished, like little boys.

"What's the matter with you two! You're just embarrassing yourselves, thinking you're good enough to even walk this girl home. Now get lost!" He gave each of them a good shove, and they meekly withdrew.

The whole interaction had happened so quickly that I could barely believe it had happened at all. Still, I was shaky from adrenalin and fear. I'd never seen two people fight so up close before.

"Are you all right?" Elzat asked tenderly. "They didn't hurt you, did they?"

"No," I said. "I'm all right."

"Can I walk you back to your dorm?" He raised his hands. "Just to make sure you get there safely. Promise."

I briefly wondered how Elzat had happened to be there on that street corner. I hadn't seen him at the party. But the thought slipped from my mind into the cool evening air. He looked strong and handsome standing there in the faint light from the buildings, and for the first time, I agreed to let him walk with me.

Life slowly returned to normal, but I still felt bitter about the film. I missed the excitement of the production and the cameras, but I couldn't seem to let go of my anger and sadness at how it all turned out.

In the meantime, Abdul was a bright spot. I looked forward to our tutoring sessions, and his kindness always cheered me up. I wanted to return the favor somehow, so when it snowed for the first time that fall, I decided to play a traditional Ürümchi game with him, which involved hiding notes in the snow.

He went bounding through the snow like a puppy. "I've never seen anything like this! We only get a sprinkling of snow in Hotan."

"Well, if you find my note, I'll buy you a bar of chocolate. And if you don't find it, you have to buy me one!"

He paused for a moment, his forehead wrinkled. "Chocolate?"

"Chocolate, you know, the candy. You used to only be able to get it in Beijing. But now you can buy it right here in Ürümchi."

The perplexed look didn't leave his face, and I realized that he had probably never seen chocolate before. It wasn't the kind of thing you could find in a rural part of the Uyghur homeland in the late 1980s.

"Come on," I said. I led him straight to one of the big stores near campus and bought a bar of dark chocolate, one of milk chocolate, and one studded with pistachios. I opened the wrapper of the dark chocolate bar and held it out to him. "Try it. It'll be the best thing you've ever tasted."

He eyed it suspiciously. "But, Gul . . . it looks like . . . cat poop!"

We both broke into giggles. "Okay, okay, but it tastes like heaven. Try it!"

He took a cautious bite, then a bigger bite. A look of pleasure came over his face, and he clutched the bar with both hands. "I'll never forget this day, Gul. First real snow, and now a taste of heaven!"

The next day after dance practice, I went to see my grandmother. My resentment about the film felt like a burden that weighed me down more each day, and she'd always been the one I'd gone to as a child for comfort. She read my face easily and asked me what was wrong. I sat on her couch and told her everything that had happened with the film. By the end I was crying, more out of rage than sadness.

When I was done, she sighed and said a few prayers for me, asking for Allah's protection. Her voice was so rich and strong, it made me feel instantly better.

"You've had a sheltered childhood, Gul, but there are bad people in the world. Being a beautiful woman will bring you opportunities, but it brings a lot of danger too. You have to be smart, smarter than the people who want to take advantage of you."

I wiped my face with her handkerchief and nodded.

"Now you finally see why your grandfather didn't want you to be a dancer, don't you? You have natural talent, because of course it's in your blood. But you have to channel it toward something else. There's no freedom in art here."

And just like that, I was released from my anger. Throughout my childhood, I hadn't understood the reason my family discouraged me from pursuing dance as a career. I'd been in exhibitions and performances from the time I was a young girl, but now I was done. I had finally learned the lesson myself. If I was going to be any kind of performer, it had to be for my own people, on my own terms. I wasn't going to be a marionette parroting lies.

But my ambitions were caught up in the much larger political changes that were happening all around us. The line between any kind of public performance and propaganda was quickly being erased, and I would be drawn further into a system I didn't believe in.

PART II

A FALL TO EARTH

For most Uyghurs in our homeland, the late 1980s and 1990s brought both an economic boom to the region and catastrophic unemployment. This might seem conflicting, but underlying that growth were Han-run companies and Han-run government projects, and very little of the wealth that was generated trickled out into the Uyghur community. Instead of hiring Uyghurs, bosses would bring in Han workers from China to work on construction crews, energy industry projects, and road building. There were communication problems, because almost none of the Han migrants to East Turkestan spoke Uyghur, and also outright discrimination, because many Han viewed Uyghurs as lazy or unwilling to take orders from a Han boss. As a result, even Uyghur college graduates—some of our best and brightest—had trouble finding work in Ürümchi. In the meantime, the Han population exploded. By the year 2000, the Han constituted more than 40 percent of the nearly 18.5 million people in East Turkestan. Uyghurs found themselves increasingly marginalized in their own land, especially in the northern and northeastern regions, where Ürümchi is located, and where the Han population was concentrated.

On the pleasant, tree-lined campus of Xinjiang Normal University, I felt relatively insulated from the outside world. Because my family was educated and relatively well-off, and highly respected within the community, I proceeded along under the assumption that my generation would grow up to be successful, independent adults, as our parents had before us. My cousin had already made something of himself and was working in the government as the deputy chief of staff for the district head of the Saybagh District of the city of Ürümchi. He had a fair amount of power and influence locally, and he always had time to help us with any little bureaucratic issues that came up, such as getting the proper documentation to do anything, from changing an address to enrolling in a new school. But none of his connections nor those of anyone else in our family protected us from the larger political and social forces operating within China. When I was in my third year of college, something happened that shattered my relative innocence, something that remains a deep scar in my life and that heralded worse things to come.

It was New Year's 1993. My younger brother was nineteen and a student at the prestigious Xinjiang Medical College, studying to become a doctor. I was in my third year at Xinjiang Normal University. That night, we were both planning to go out for New Year's Eve, and the house was filled with activity and pleasant anticipation. I was meeting Mehray to go to a party on campus with her. She was so lovely and vivacious that before long I knew we'd have every boy in the room hoping to dance near us.

Kaisar stuck his head into my room just before dinner. He riffled my hair teasingly and asked me if I would iron his clothes. "Come on, Gul," he pleaded. "I need these for the party tonight, but there's something I have to take care of first. You want your brother to look his best, don't you?"

I laughed and agreed to iron his clothes yet again. He was right—I was proud of my handsome little brother, and if he did the ironing the creases would just get worse. He'd grown up to be tall and fit, with a head of thick black hair and eyes that danced when he smiled. But he still liked to pinch my cheek and muss my carefully combed hairdo just as he used to do when we were kids.

"Where are you off to?" our mom called from the kitchen. "I'm cooking. Stay and have a good meal before you go off carousing."

"I'll be back soon. Don't let them eat everything before I get back!" He gave her a loving pat on the cheek and was gone.

I spent the afternoon ironing our outfits, putting on my makeup, choosing and re-choosing my dress, making sure I looked perfect. My brother hadn't come back, so I took a quick catnap. Our parties always started late in the evening and didn't end until the next morning, with people singing and dancing to music that went all night.

I had just finished dressing when there was a pounding on the front door. My heart leapt into my throat. No one ever knocked on the door like that. My father was in his study and my mother was still in the kitchen cooking a big meal to celebrate the new year, so I went to the door.

When I opened it, three policemen were standing there: two Han and one Uyghur. The Uyghur officer was familiar from around the neighborhood, but I'd never seen the two Han policemen before. Instantly, my hands started to sweat. We tried to avoid Han policemen as much as possible because they were generally known for their ruthlessness when dealing with Uyghurs. Something serious had to have happened for them to show up at our house.

"Does a Kaisar Keyum live here?" one of the Han officers said, his tone sharp. He tried to push me aside, but I held my ground.

My father rushed out of his study. "What's going on?"

The policeman showed him a piece of paper. "We have a warrant to search Kaisar's room. Show me where it is."

I was confused. My brother had left just a few hours before; he should be back any minute. My mind was racing with possibilities—he must be hurt, a car accident, a fire. . . .

"He's in big trouble," the officer said. "You have to let us in."

"What's happened?" my father said. "Tell me what's going on, and then I'll show you his room."

One of the Han policeman stuck his face close to my father's. "You have no idea how much trouble your boy has caused. Your whole family is under suspicion. Do you understand me? Just show me his room."

Shaking, but not willing to back down, I put my hand up and demanded, "Let me see the warrant. And where are your police badges? How do we know you are who you say you are?" I was terrified, but I was determined not to simply capitulate through fear.

The Uyghur policeman stepped forward. He was a young man with a gentler expression than the others. He said, "Miss, please. Just be cooperative. This is a very serious situation. You're going to have to let us in."

Suddenly, one of the other policemen grabbed the hand that I had held up. "That ring," he said roughly, pulling at my finger. "Did your brother give it to you?"

"Of course not! It's my grandmother's ring. An heirloom." I was beginning to grasp that something was terribly wrong. I moved out of the doorway and the police pushed their way inside.

They searched the house, collecting things from my brother's room and shoving them into plastic bags. My father followed them around protesting, while my mother and I huddled together against the wall. Then one of the policemen pulled out a small stack of money from a drawer. Another policeman was at the closet, throwing brand new clothes that we'd never seen before on the floor. My mother and I looked at each other, stunned. What was this stuff doing in our house? The policemen took it all, along with Kaisar's photo albums and even a few books.

As they were leaving, one of the policemen ordered us brusquely, "Come to the station tomorrow."

My mother caught the Uyghur policeman at the door and begged him, "Please, tell me what's happening. At least tell me where my boy is."

He shook his head. "I can't say anything yet. He's still being questioned. But your son was involved in a burglary. They think it has to do with drugs."

My mother leaned against the door as it closed, her face pale. "This is all a mistake! They've gotten our Kaisar mixed up with someone else. He's the best student in his class, how can he be involved in anything like that?"

That evening was a nightmare. Of course, no one went to any parties, and the food my mother had so lovingly prepared turned cold on the table. Despite the late hour, my father started calling all his friends with connections, but nobody had any information. We went to bed silently well before midnight, having no idea what had happened.

The next day my father, mother, and I went to the police station. They wouldn't let us see Kaisar or even tell us if he was there. But we did learn that he'd been arrested along with four other students at the Medical College. They were accused of breaking into the Ürümchi police chief's house, a prominent Uyghur in the community, and stealing thirty kilograms of gold from his cupboard. No one asked what the police chief was doing with thirty kilos of gold in his kitchen.

The chief had ordered the houses of all five boys searched. At the same time, the police told us, they assumed that given the boldness of the crime, drugs were sure to be involved. If they were, the burglars would have to sell the gold in order to get cash to buy drugs. So they'd stationed Uyghur policemen in the Uyghur gold stores around town, where they'd found my brother trying to hawk some bars of gold and had arrested him.

We left the station completely at a loss. Nothing the police told us fit with what we knew of my brother, or his friends. None of it made sense. Why would five medical students from well-to-do families break into the house of the Ürümchi police chief? It would have been farcical had it not been so frightening.

My brother was tortured for three days in the police station. He was hung by his arms from chains and beaten. When he refused to confess or name any accomplices, they just beat him harder. Suspects aren't treated well anywhere in China—if you're arrested, you're considered guilty unless proven innocent—but the fact that Kaisar was Uyghur meant that he was subject to the worst treatment. The police had no fear of any repercussions for brutality or neglect; they had the full force of the CCP behind them. They knew it, and we knew it too. We didn't learn the details of his detainment until later, but we had our fears.

When we got home, we ransacked the house, looking for every bit of cash we had. We called our relatives to see what we could borrow from them too. We collected 10,000 yuan, a sizable sum of money, within a day or two. We thought it might serve as some kind of restitution.

My mother wrapped the cash up in a scarf and put it in her purse. She went to the police chief's house and knocked on the door. When he came to the door, she held the money out to him with both hands. "I'm Kaisar Keyum's mother. Please, he's my only son," she begged. "He's done something wrong, but please be lenient with him. Just give him a chance to finish school. I can swear we'll never let anything like this happen again."

The police chief was a large Uyghur man with a pronounced belly and a thick gold watch on his wrist, the very image of a good comrade. He towered over my mother. He brushed away the stack of money contemptuously. "You're lucky I didn't shoot your son when I had the chance. He's a fast runner, but he's not going to get out of this one."

On her way home from the police chief's house, my mother had a mild heart attack and collapsed on the street. She ended up spending the night in the hospital. My father and I anxiously sat by her bedside all night. I think that was the day her heart broke.

All we could do was wait. My brother had gotten caught up in a system we barely understood and had no control over. I started to skip classes to stay home with my parents. During the six months he was in jail, the whole house was cold and silent. It felt like a mausoleum. We dragged ourselves around, never laughing, barely speaking more than a few sentences to one another, our eyes red and sore from crying. Each day at dinner, my mom would set out a plate for my brother and fill it with food. She moved more gingerly after her heart attack, as though there was something lodged inside of her body that never stopped causing her pain.

"He'll come back," she'd say. "I know he will."

I wanted to be strong for the family, but normal life became more and more difficult. I had been a popular, outgoing student, invited to all the parties. But I dropped everything. It was as though I'd gone blank. I started wearing all black clothing and lost fifteen pounds from not eating. It got to the point that one of my teachers called me into her office to tell me she was concerned about me.

"Gulchehra, have you . . . have you gotten into drugs? You're not the girl you used to be."

"Of course I haven't!" I was shaken.

"A lot of good kids do," she said sadly. "It's like a plague that came out of nowhere."

Two or three years before, I had never even heard of heroin. Now it seemed to be everywhere. Drugs, heroin in particular, had infiltrated the Uyghur community seemingly overnight, coming in via recently loosened borders with neighboring countries like Afghanistan. The CCP was encouraging trade, but along with legitimate goods came opiates. No one really knew what these drugs were, and no one had any idea how much damage they could cause to individuals and entire communities. Because of the endemic unemployment in the Uyghur community, a lot of young people, men in particular, were sucked into a cycle of addiction. Alcohol abuse was also on the rise, despite the Islamic prohibitions against it. But at least that was a known evil. As addiction spread through the community, some Han began to view Uyghurs as likely drug dealers, a stereotype that spread through China and fed fuel to the idea that Uyghurs were criminals and a dangerous element.

It was during that period of severe depression that Elzat began to court me in earnest. He came to visit, sitting politely in the dismal silence that had overtaken our whole house. He never expected me to talk, let alone for any of us to entertain him. He was just there. If we needed anything from the shops, he would bring it that same day. He ran errands for us and kept an ear out in the neighborhood for any news about my brother, though people were mostly too afraid to gossip about the incident. All five students came from prominent families, and the case had shocked the whole community. No one knew quite what to think. As my parents withdrew further and further into their own misery, I began to feel like Elzat's calm eyes and quiet breathing next to me were the only thing keeping me from falling apart.

As we became closer and more comfortable around each other, I even told him a secret that I hadn't revealed to anyone else. When my brother and I were teenagers, my mother had undergone an operation, which I later understood to be a partial hysterectomy. Because of the family-planning rules that the CCP enforced punitively in the Uyghur region, my mother had been forced to undergo several abortions. Each time, she wept bitterly over the lost child and whispered things that only my father could hear. It also took a terrible toll on her body, and eventually she had to have an operation. The one-child policy was enforced, though very unevenly, throughout China. In the Uyghur area, where families were traditionally large and each child was seen as a gift from Allah, the psychological burden of this policy imposed by the Chinese government was terrible. Along with the physical ramifications, my mother suffered hormonal and psychological side effects. Suddenly, she began fighting with my father in a way my brother and I had never heard before. Her voice was harsh and frightening, and she said terrible things to my father. At first my brother and I would beg them to stop fighting. Later, when it happened I would hide in my room and furiously bury my thoughts in my journal, while my brother left the house.

"When I asked my dad why he stayed, he said that now that she was sick, she needed him more than ever," I told Elzat.

"Your father is good man, and a good husband," Elzat said. "I hope I can make as good a husband to a virtuous woman one day."

"My brother couldn't take the fighting," I said. "He just started leaving the house, staying out until all hours. That's how all of this happened."

Elzat patted my hand lightly.

"Why didn't we save him?" I whispered, my sore eyes stinging from yet more tears. "How could we have let this happen?"

After months of agonizing waiting, the police finally came and informed us that we could go to the prison to visit Kaisar. My mother reacted like a drowning person being thrown a buoy.

For two nights before our trip to the prison, I spent hours peeling roasted sunflower seeds, one of my brother's favorite foods. I peeled until my fingers hurt. I just wanted him to have a little taste of home.

When the day came, the pain of seeing him in prison, so pale and thin, a shadow of the person he was, nearly took my breath away. We cried and hugged him tightly, just happy to have any contact after so many months of not even knowing where he was.

They gave us only half an hour together. There wasn't enough to time to say much of anything or to ask him why he had done what he had.

My mother sobbed the whole time. "Why didn't you just take my jewelry, Kaisar? If you needed money, why didn't you ask us? We would have given you anything!"

He just shook his head and didn't answer.

"Are they feeding you, my son?" she asked. "You've gotten too thin."

"Don't worry about me, I'm just sorry for everything that's happened." He turned to my father, tears springing into his eyes. "This is the biggest mistake of my life. I know that. I . . . I didn't know how to get out before it was too late. Please forgive me."

The guard who had been standing along one wall watching us gestured impatiently. It was time for him to go back to his cell.

"Sister," Kaisar said. "I'm so sorry." He pulled me into a hug and held me tightly. I didn't want to ever let him go. As he released me, I felt him slip something down one of my sleeves. He caught my eye. "Take good care of our parents while I'm away."

And then he was gone again.

I could feel the edge of what felt like paper scratching against my arm, but I didn't say anything, not even on the bus ride home. When we were finally in the safety of our own house, I pulled the note out of my sleeve and handed it to my father. We were shocked at the words Kaisar had written:

Dad, I helped steal the gold and I want to atone for what I did. But they're forcing me to admit to crimes that I didn't commit. More than three hundred cases! But I didn't do any of it. I've listed everything I can remember from what they made me sign—dates, case numbers. Look at the years. For some of them, I was barely eight or nine years old. Please do something before the court date.

My father turned to my mother. "We need the best lawyer we can find. One who can't be intimidated."

That same day, they started calling everyone they could think of. It turned out we had a distant relative who worked in the Ürümchi municipal court. The very next day, we went to him to plead for his help.

He agreed to take the case, but he warned us that we would be fighting an uphill battle. "Unfortunately, it's a fairly common practice. The police will bring someone in for one crime, and then torture him until he confesses to a whole litany of other unsolved crimes. They just want to close the old cases. I know of several other examples of this happening to good Uyghur families. The Han authorities know they can act with impunity. Who's going to stand up to them?" He sighed and put his glasses back on to look down at the note my brother had written. "But it's good that you know about it. Kaisar was very smart to give you the dates of the crimes. We're going to have to tackle the individual cases one by one."

We nodded. We would do anything.

"You must know this too," the attorney said to my father gravely. "If Kaisar is convicted of all of these charges, the penalty will be death."

Every single day for two months straight, we worked our way through the list of crimes my brother had supposedly committed. My father went tirelessly to five houses a day, my mother and I went to another two or three. We brought a few photos of Kaisar at different ages and showed them to the people involved in the cases. We asked each of them if they recognized my brother, if he was the perpetrator. Over and over again, they said no, they'd never seen my brother before.

At one house, a middle-aged woman answered the door in an apron and green flowered headscarf. I knew that her house had been burgled seven years before.

"Excuse me," I said, "I wonder if I can ask you about the burglary that happened here."

She rubbed a hand down her apron. She had obviously been cooking. "That was years ago," she said, a hint of suspicion in her voice.

"I know. My brother's been accused of the crime and we're sure he didn't do it." I saw her stiffen and I hurried to explain. "Will you please look at a photograph and tell me if he looks like the man who did it?"

"Well, I never saw him," she said. "We were sleeping, and he was out through the window with our things before we got to him. All I saw was his van pulling away."

"Please, just look." I held up a photo of my brother at twelve years old. "This was my brother at the time of the crime."

She leaned in to take a look, and then broke into broad laughter. "This is a joke, isn't it? How's that little kid going to steal my husband's antique trunk, hoist it up through the window, and then drive off in a van like an angry goat was after him?"

I slipped the precious photograph back into my pocket and held out a piece of paper. "My brother could be executed for the crimes he's been accused of. Will you sign this affidavit testifying that you don't believe he was involved in the crime against you?"

The woman wiped her hands on her apron again and took the piece of paper. "It just isn't right the way things are these days," she muttered. "Locking innocent people away."

At house after burgled house, we explained what was happening and asked the person to sign an affidavit. It felt like rolling a boulder up a hillside, and at any point it could just come barreling back down on top of us. We were so tired by the evening that we could barely drag ourselves to the dinner table. But in the end, we collected more than three hundred signatures in those two months. We handed the stack of affidavits to the attorney, and he in turn brought them to the court. One by one, the charges were taken off my brother's list of offenses. We wept together in the lawyer's office, as much from exhaustion as relief.

But the original charge of burglarizing the police chief's house still stood.

The trial was held six months after they first arrested Kaisar. Just that year, the Chinese central government had come out with a new drugs policy, which it called the "People's War on Drugs." Harsh new punishments were set out, including an obligatory death sentence for the possession of fifty grams of heroin. Fortunately, neither my brother nor his classmates had been caught with any drugs on them. But we learned that my brother's case, along with those of the four other students, had been chosen as a model case for the new law. Our lawyer told us that meant the government intended to make an example of them, and the court would be obligated to mete out stringent punishments if they were found guilty.

This was in keeping with the way the CCP had begun to deal with the Uyghur region. Young Uyghur men in particular were explicitly viewed as criminals or criminals in the making, and crimes were punished as harshly as possible. Seemingly every chance to intimidate the Uyghur population was viewed as a victory; fear had begun to be employed as a potent weapon to prevent people from organizing, speaking freely, or trying to promote Uyghur culture.

At Kaisar's trial, I sat with my parents near the front of the courtroom. Behind us were rows and rows of college students, friends who had come to support the accused. A few of their teachers at the Medical College had even shown up.

When my brother and his friends came in, a hush fell over the courtroom. They were all handsome and tall, and dressed in their best clothes for court. It seemed unimaginable that they could commit any crime at all, let alone be involved with drugs. I was crying, but I kept my eyes fixed on Kaisar, to let him know that we supported him. We would never abandon him.

The government lawyers made their case. They claimed that the boys had been using heroin for more than five months. They'd been introduced to it at a party and had quickly become addicted. At New Year's, they had run out of cash to buy more drugs, and so they picked a house to rob in a wealthy Uyghur neighborhood.

None of it made sense to me, and because everything Kaisar said was monitored, we didn't know the real story. But although our lawyer argued his case persuasively, that the students had not been involved in drugs at all, but simply made a terrible error in judgment, my brother and the others were all convicted. We had not dared to hope that the verdict would be otherwise.

Still, when the sentence was given, everyone in the courtroom gasped.

Ten years!

Under ordinary circumstances, a nonviolent burglary would carry a one- or two-year sentence. For a university student like my brother, sometimes the court would show leniency and order restitution instead of a jail sentence. But now my kind, talented brother would spend the entirety of his twenties in the confines of a jail cell.

They let us hug once, quickly, before they led him away. They would have a police van waiting outside to take him to prison. Frantic,

I sprinted to the back of the courthouse. I couldn't just let him go. It didn't take very long for the guards to bring him out in handcuffs, his nice suit already mussed and wrinkled. I called his name and tried to hug him one last time. The police shoved me aside and hustled him into the back of the van. It pulled away, and I ran after it, trying to keep Kaisar in view for as long as I possibly could. He was sitting in the rear of the van, one hand chained to the side, and through the window his desperate were eyes staring back at me.

I had been just barely keeping it together, but after the verdict, I couldn't eat, I couldn't sleep, everything seemed meaningless. I felt like everything in my life had changed in that one moment. Before Kaisar was arrested, I was headed for great things. I would practice my dance moves or recite poetry in front of the mirror, dreaming of performing for enormous crowds. But after the trial, I just stopped caring about anything. Sometimes I went to class, and sometimes I couldn't force myself to get out of bed. I didn't sing or dance or even hum to myself. I stayed with my parents most of the time instead of in the dorm, and withdrew more and more from my friends and classmates. I didn't even want to talk with Mehray, although she never said a single judgmental word. I just wanted to be left alone.

Still, Elzat came around often, whether or not I was up to talking. Gradually, I opened up to him about my depression. I told him how different my parents seemed, older and more fragile. I couldn't go to them for help or to talk about my feelings. They could barely handle their own pain. Even my father's gait was different; suddenly, he moved with the hesitant steps of an old man.

At every meal, my mother still set out a plate for my brother and arranged it with the choicest tidbits. Our meals were mostly silent, with none of the joking and laughter that had filled our family home before all of this had happened. Any happiness felt like a betrayal of my brother. Even living a normal life was a betrayal.

A few months after Kaisar's trial, the authorities let us visit him. It was a frightening, shameful experience. When we arrived at the jail, we were treated like criminals ourselves. My mother and I had dressed very carefully in crisp long dresses with our hair pulled back modestly, and my father was wearing one of his best suits. Nevertheless, the guards looked at us with contempt. They threw forms at us to sign and then made us wait on a narrow bench in a dirty waiting room. They seemed to think that if we were there to visit someone inside, we must belong in there too.

Still, I didn't care about the rudeness and the way the guards seemed to look right through me. I missed my brother so much, and we were allowed to see him only once a month at most. After how close he and I had been for so long, our separation was like a thorn in my heart, sometimes waking me in the middle of the night with sharp pain. Not a day went by when I didn't think about him or worry about his welfare. I knew my parents felt the same way.

One month, about nine months into Kaisar's sentence, I asked my parents if I could visit my brother alone. The visits were a terrible strain on them, seeing my brother caged like an animal and being unable to help him. It was also obvious to me that my brother wouldn't talk openly in front of them about what was happening to him. We could both tell that the ordeal had weakened our parents.

My parents agreed to let me see Kaisar alone, so I put on a plain, tidy outfit and gathered in a basket a few things he had asked for, like clean pairs of socks and some fresh nan.

The guard coldly took the forms I'd filled out—the same ones I filled out anew every single time—and let me through to the inner room. Inside were two long rows of chairs, separated from each other by glass barriers. The inmates were behind a glass wall, transparent but seemingly utterly impenetrable. I took a seat on the hard wooden chair the guard gestured to.

My brother was brought in and shoved into the chair on the other side of the glass wall. I immediately put my hand up to the glass and he put his fingers against mine on the other side. It was as close to contact as we could have. He had new lines on his face and his eyes looked strained, but he was still the boy I'd grown up with, the one I'd protected and coddled and scolded the way older sisters do. I had to choke back tears.

He picked up the phone on his side of the glass, and I picked up the one on mine. We knew the guards would be listening, so we spoke carefully.

"Where are Mom and Dad?"

"I asked them if I could come alone," I told him. "I wanted us to be able to talk."

His eyes shifted away from mine. "Don't worry about me. I'm doing fine here."

"That's what you always say. Tell me the truth."

He smiled wanly. "Sister, the truth is I've made a terrible mistake and this is the price. I've accepted that. I've done a lot of growing up. This is how it has to be." Then he shook his head as though freeing himself from something. "Besides, I really am fine." He flashed a grin. "They have me tutoring the other prisoners in Chinese, can you believe that?"

I could smile a bit at that—my brother's grades in Chinese class had never matched mine.

Someone had come in and sat in the glass cubicle next to mine. A faint reek of cigarettes, beer, and sweat floated over to me. A man was brought in to the chair across the glass from him.

"They're treating me all right, I promise," Kaisar said. "The food is terrible, though. I can't wait to dig into that nan."

I noticed that the two men who had just come in weren't talking to each other. I felt their eyes slithering up and down my body, and I pulled my coat closed over my chest.

My brother's eyes narrowed and he leaned forward suddenly toward the man in the cubicle next to mine. "Hey, that's my sister. Sure you want to look at her like that?"

I was afraid to turn my head. Out of the corner of my eye, I caught a glimpse of a thin, hard face above an open-necked shirt. He seemed to be in his late twenties, with a long neck and an unusual tattoo that spread across his forehead just above his eyebrows.

The man smiled and his eyes narrowed down to unpleasant slits. "Come out here and make me stop."

My brother's body tensed and he half rose from his chair.

"You!" A guard was heading our way. "Forget where you are?" He put a restraining hand on my brother's shoulder.

The other prisoner sat back in his chair, crossing his arms contemptuously. There was something tattooed in Chinese on the back of his hand in blue ink, likely gang related. He couldn't be much older than Kaisar, but he looked like he'd seen a lot more of the inside of prison than my brother had.

I didn't know why the two men wanted to rile Kaisar up, but I knew that I had to leave before things escalated. I wrapped my coat around myself tightly as though it were armor and stood. The stench of alcohol and sweat made me want to retch.

"Gul, tell our parents that I'm fine." Kaisar got up before the guard could yank him to his feet. "And don't ever come here alone again." Then he dropped the phone receiver and was gone.

Three days later, we got a phone call from a guard at the prison. My father took the call, and as he listened his face turned a frightening gray. He put the receiver down and silently went into his office for the rest of the afternoon. I could hear him making more phone calls from there, but I couldn't hear what he was saying.

At dinner, my father was very quiet. Then he said, "Kaisar is in solitary confinement."

My mother gasped. I felt a cold hand grip the back of my neck. I had a terrible feeling that it had something to do with my visit.

"What happened?" I forced myself to ask.

My father wouldn't look at us. "I spoke to a few guards and they all say that he attacked a man unprovoked, some other prisoner. I couldn't get any more information out of them." He let out a deep sigh. "I'll go see the lawyer in the morning."

It took a month or two before the lawyer came back to us with the story of what had happened. It turned out that it did involve the prisoner who had been eyeing me in the visitor's room. He was a lifer, in for gang activities and murder. He and my brother had been at odds for some time, for what reason we never knew. Perhaps he was jealous of my brother, or perhaps he was just bored and had nothing left to lose. After my visit, the lifer had told Kaisar that he had a beautiful sister and then gave him some filthy details about exactly what he'd like to do to me.

My brother had only been able to take it for so long before he'd given him a good punch in the mouth. If Kaisar let it go on, he'd have lost the respect of the other inmates and would be vulnerable to anyone and everyone. The lifer had smiled through his bloodied teeth, met my brother's eye, and then deliberately slammed his own head into the sharp corner of a door. Blood gushed out of the side of his head as the guards rushed into the room.

The lawyer got one of the witnesses to recount the true story to the guards, and they let my brother out of solitary. But by that time he'd spent three months locked up in a tiny dirty room alone, and I knew that I had put him there. Pain was my new reality.

The burden of my brother's incarceration completely stopped me from dancing. Before I had danced because I had joy in my heart, and because I wanted to express the beauty of the world in a directly physical way. Afterward, I felt such heaviness that I thought I'd never again be able to lift my chin, let alone move my arms and legs in dance. With everything going on, I didn't even miss it.

But one afternoon, a student caught me as I was leaving math class. "The president wants to see you," she said breathlessly. "Now!"

I straightened my clothes and tucked a few stray hairs back into my braid before I headed to his office. I no longer cared much about how I looked, but I wanted to be presentable.

I stood before the president's desk with my hands politely folded, waiting for him to speak.

"When you came to our school, Gulchehra, we were all so proud to have a student like you among our midst," he began. "Academics, singing, dancing—so much talent!" He lowered his voice and looked at me thoughtfully. "I know about your brother's situation. It must be very difficult for your whole family. But you cannot let it influence your life too much. You're a young woman with a bright future ahead of you. It would be a tragedy compounding a tragedy were you to let that future fade away."

I nodded obediently, but I felt nothing. I didn't care anymore.

"I want you to know that the faculty is considering offering you a position at the university after you graduate."

That got my attention and I glanced up at him for the first time. A possible job offer was nothing to sniff at; all of my friends were worried about finding work once we graduated. I hadn't had the energy to think much about how I would find a job, but I didn't want to be a drain on my parents. I wanted to be an independent person, and a stable job in a good university would let me do just that.

The president was still talking. "There's a very important arts festival this spring, and all of the universities will be participating in the performances and competitions. We want to put our best foot forward, of course. Naturally, we'd like you to compete in the dance competition. If you do well and bring glory to our university, I can't see how anyone would think of not giving you a position here."

His voice was mild, but his meaning was clear. If I didn't perform, the job would go to someone else and who knew what kind of future would lie ahead of me. My head started spinning. I felt like I'd been shocked out of some kind of stasis. Suddenly, I had a visceral sense again that I had a future, and that future depended upon my actions.

I squared my shoulders slightly under my baggy black cardigan. "It would be my honor to compete for the school, sir. I'll do my best."

It quickly became apparent to me that the festival was a big deal. Any occasion in which Han students and Uyghur students competed against one another took on additional layers of meaning; a deep cultural pride was at stake. The university hired a famous dance teacher from the Uyghur Arts Center at significant expense to choreograph a dance for us. The basic idea was to have a dancing corps and a single soloing flower. I was to be the principal dancer, the flower in the center of forty other dancers. To my excitement, Mehray was selected to be part of the corps.

We had two months to put the show together, and I threw myself in wholeheartedly. We had practice every single day, sometimes for hours at a time, and my body was constantly sore. We traded foot massages and laughed together about the big callouses. It felt so good to be part of a team again, and to be around friends with their normal lives and concerns. Elzat wasn't happy that I was suddenly spending so much time at practice instead of with him, but I barely noticed his grumbling.

With forty-one dancers, we couldn't fit into any of the university dance studios. Instead, we had to use one of the campus cafeterias between mealtime hours. The floor was oily and sometimes dirty and it didn't make for the best atmosphere, but we had nowhere else to practice. Everyone was working as hard as they possibly could. I'd learned complicated dance moves before, but this was by far the most challenging choreography I'd been given. Much of it was based on traditional Uyghur dance, with lots of intricate hand gestures extending out from the body and graceful torso movements from side to side. But there was also a section of ballet-inspired choreography, which I was less familiar with. Especially after not dancing for months, I felt like I had to play catch-up and there wasn't much time in which to do it.

We even had a semiprofessional dancer in our corps, the wife of one of the professors at the university. Aynur had once danced with a regional dance troupe. She was in her mid-twenties, but with her heavy makeup and thin eyebrows, she appeared to be older than she was. She was slim and short enough that she always wore high heels. We all assumed she was there because she was bored.

One evening more than a month in, we were practicing in the cafeteria after they'd cleaned up from the dinner service. I was working on the ballet section, in which I had to do a high jeté and land precariously on high heels. I'd been working on it constantly since the choreographer had shown me the move, but I still hadn't perfected it.

I chose a corner of the cafeteria where I wouldn't be in anyone's way and started to jump, pushing myself harder and harder. I began to feel my leaps really start to take off. My leg muscles trembled from the effort, but I felt exhilarated. I wanted to take off flying. I had just about exhausted myself when I took a last jump, and I landed on a slick patch on the floor. My heel slid out from under me, and before I knew what had happened, my knee slammed into the floor with a sickening crunch. My body crumpled to the floor with such force that my watch smashed into thousands of pieces.

"Don't move, Gul, don't move an inch," people were telling me all at once.

I was too dazed to do anything but lie there and listen to them talking as though from a far distance. Finally, two of the male dancers picked me up like an injured bird and carried me to the clinic on campus.

Practice was canceled for everyone for two days. The doctor told me that I'd been lucky. I hadn't done any lasting damage to the kneecap, but everything was stiff and swollen. She told me I should stay off of my leg for at least three months, not even walking if I could help it.

"But I have to dance in a competition in two weeks!" I told her. "The whole team is counting on me. I can't just stay off of it."

The doctor snapped the chart shut. "You're not competing in anything but how much rest you can get in a day."

I went to see the university president again, limping in carefully on crutches. My knee was swollen and sore, and hot to the touch. But I was willing it to get better quickly. The dance competition had brought me back to myself, made me nearly whole again, and I couldn't bear the idea of having it taken away from me.

When I got into the president's office, I saw to my surprise that Aynur was already there, sitting delicately in a chair to one side of the desk. I cautiously sat down in the other chair.

The door to the office opened again and in came Mr. Wang, the CCP representative at the school. All the students knew him from afar. He was in a very powerful position, as all of the consequential decisions at the university had to be vetted by him.

Mr. Wang lost no time. "Gulchehra, I've spoken with the doctor. She says that you have a significant injury and need to rest. Your health and safety are our priority, naturally. Now, as we know, there are forty other dancers involved. Forty other dancers who have worked tirelessly to bring honor to our school. Our goal is to win. It isn't an easy task, but our students are sacrificing their time and energy to make it happen. We appreciate all of your efforts, of course. But it's time to step aside."

The president sighed heavily. "We've decided to let Aynur dance the principal part."

"No!" I cried without thinking. "No, there are still ten days to the competition. I've practiced day and night for this!"

"The doctor says there's no chance you'll recover quickly enough to dance safely."

"Gulchehra," Aynur said softly. "I know the moves. I've already been practicing your choreography. I'll do the team proud, I promise."

I was desperate. "Trust me, I'll be ready to dance when the day comes. I'll come to the practices and learn any changes in the choreography."

"We can't risk losing the competition because of you," Aynur said, her voice as soft as a snake in grass.

"Please don't take this away from me," I said, fighting back tears.

Mr. Wang and the president glanced at each other.

Finally the president said, "We'll give it a week. Aynur, you dance at the practices, and Gulchehra, you let your knee rest. After a week, you can both dance for us and we'll decide who will perform."

When I showed up at practice the next day, Mehray caught me by the arm and hugged me tightly. She looked down at my knee, which even underneath a compression wrap was obviously swollen. "Are you going to be okay in time for the competition?"

"Yes." I didn't let any doubt at all creep into my voice.

The choreographer clapped his hands to call all of the dancers together, and they rushed to take formation.

Mehray drew in her breath. "What's Aynur doing in the center? She's in your spot!"

I shrugged as best I could with the crutches under my arms. "She thinks she's going to dance my part."

Mehray raised an eyebrow. "Oh? She'd better think again."

I squeezed Mehray's arm, and let her run to join the group.

After a week, my knee was much better, but still quite painful. I'd concentrated completely on getting better, resting it and massaging it, using ice and warm compresses. I'd tried everything I could think of to hurry along the healing process. The night before I had to dance for the president, I begged my mother to give me a numbing shot for the pain.

"Gul, I can't do that," she said, pinching the bridge of her nose. Her hair had begun to go gray and she squinted now when she wrote out prescriptions. "You're likely to make it worse."

I went over to her chair and sat down beside her legs, like I used to do when I was a child. "Please, Mom. I need this. After everything . . ."

She stroked a hand over my hair, and then lifted my chin to look into my eyes. "Poor girl. I'll see what I can do."

The next morning when I arrived at the campus theater, several rows in the auditorium were already filled with high-level officials from the university, including the president and Mr. Wang. Dancers were warming up along the edges, and they smiled at me as I came in.

Mehray waved me over. "How's your knee?"

"It's okay," I said. "I'll be able to dance." My knee felt tender and stiff, despite the shot my mother had given me that morning.

"This will help with the pain for a few hours," she'd told me. "Don't overdo it. You don't want to turn this into an even more serious injury."

Finally everyone took their place on the stage. Aynur was called up to dance first. I watched her spin around the stage. Her footwork was light and accurate, but there was no passion to it. She looked like she was dancing from memory rather than from feeling. And the corps dancers around her looked like they were just going through the motions.

Everyone clapped politely as Aynur left the stage. I tugged at my dance costume nervously. I had to nail this. The other dancers whispered encouragement as I took my place among them. Mehray flashed me a big smile. She believed in me, and it gave me courage.

When the music started and we began to dance, the room suddenly sparked with energy. Everyone could feel it. Our jumps were higher and our spins were faster. I pushed my extensions as far as I safely could, touching that same joy I'd always felt when dancing. I wanted to prove to myself more than anyone else that I could do it. I would never give up trying.

When we finished, the dancers let out hoots and cheers. Several of the other girls hugged me. We knew we had a winning routine.

The school officials in the audience were glancing at each other. The president stood up and asked us to clear the room for ten minutes while they discussed. When we came back in, we stood there expectantly, ready for the announcement.

"We've decided," Mr. Wang said, "that Aynur will dance at the competition."

There was a shocked silence in the room.

I couldn't believe what was happening. But there was nothing that could be said against a decision made by the representative of the CCP, and we all knew it. I didn't even glance at Aynur, I just slipped out of my dance costume and let it fall to the floor. I stood there in my practice sweats, ready to leave. My knee was starting to throb, and suddenly I felt as if I was back in that hotel room on the movie set when Ilham told me I had lost the part. I started to limp toward the door.

"Wait. If Gul isn't dancing with us, I'm not going to dance either."

I turned around slowly. It was Mehray. She also had taken off her costume and stood there disheveled, her eyes furious.

"Don't you walk away, young lady!" Mr. Wang yelled at her. "Your behavior will not go unpunished!"

"Aynur isn't even a student here," the lead male dancer said quietly. "We don't want to go into the competition with a ringer. What if someone finds out and we're disqualified? That's all of our hard work down the drain."

There was silence in the room for a breathless moment. Then all thirty-nine dancers began to shed their costumes until the cafeteria floor was littered with brightly colored cloth.

Mehray turned to Mr. Wang. "Perhaps Aynur would like to stand in for us all."

Then she took my arm and we left the room one united group, just as we were on the dance stage.

The next day, one of the deans at the university called our house and told me to come to her office. She was a Uyghur woman with a kind, broad face and piles of books covering the whole surface of her desk.

She cleared her throat. "Well, Gulchehra, you've certainly shown your natural leadership abilities. I've just come from a meeting, and we've decided to allow you to dance."

I covered my mouth with my hands in delight. I was going to get my chance after all!

The next week passed like a dream, with rehearsals seemingly day and night. My knee hurt, but I could dance, and dance I did.

We went to the competition and danced our hearts out. Every move I made, every hand gesture, every jump and every lift, all of it was for my brother. My feet felt lifted by little propellers and every step I took seemed like a little leap. In the end, our routine wowed the judges, and we ended up taking first place. I had never seen Mr. Wang smile before, but that day he was grinning.

It was only a dance competition, and yet it shaped my future in ways I could only begin to understand. First, I received an official offer of a job at the university for when I graduated. My future seemed certain at last. Second, just as importantly, Mehray became a lifelong friend. She'd risked so much to stand up to the university authorities, and I learned from her bravery and selflessness. Sometimes you have to take tremendous risks to do what you feel is right. I had been taught by my father that the word *Uyghur* originally meant "togetherness" or "unity." I vowed never to forget how vitally important that loyalty was.

As my senior year continued, I felt my life had finally gotten back on track. But my brother was still dealing with daily life in the Chinese penal system. Weeks would go by without incident, and then something would happen to disrupt the fragile equilibrium, like when we got word that my brother had risked his life to save another inmate.

On an otherwise ordinary day, an inmate in Kaisar's ward had managed to steal a sharp paring knife from the kitchen. He brandished it and threatened to kill himself unless the guards let him walk out of the jail. Everyone knew that would never happen, but they didn't want the man to kill himself on their watch. One of the guards tried to grab him, but the man slashed at him with the knife. Then he made a long cut down his own arm as a warning, sending bright red ribbons of blood onto his clothing and down onto the floor. After that, no one would get near him.

Kaisar had chatted with the man before and knew that he was a Hui Muslim. The Hui are ethnically indistinguishable from the Han, but they have practiced Islam for centuries. After the CCP takeover of the Uyghur region, hundreds of thousands of Hui from western parts of China like Gansu moved into the area along with the Han to benefit from the same economic opportunities. They had the reputation of being very pious Muslims, and my brother used that to his advantage.

He approached the man very cautiously, stopping several feet away. "Friend, it's okay if you die. You're just a drug dealer, no one's going to care if you die in here. But you can't kill yourself without taking the Shahadah."

Even though my brother and I hadn't been raised in a devout family, we still knew the essentials of our religion, and Kaisar knew that would get the man's attention. The Shahadah is a declaration of belief in Allah. It is the first of the Five Pillars of Islam, dictating how a good Muslim should live their life, and it is often spoken aloud to affirm one's faith.

The man stopped waving the knife around for a moment.

"If you take your own life," Kaisar persisted, "you'll go to the deepest hell. You might as well say the Shahadah and help yourself a little before you go by affirming your devotion. I'll say it with you. *I bear witness that there is no god but Allah*," my brother started to recite. "*I bear witness that Muhammad is the messenger of God*."

The man began to pray too, and he closed his eyes and bowed his head, blood flowing freely down his arm to the floor. Quickly, two of the guards closed in and got hold of him. They forced the knife from his hand and he began to sob.

"Let me wrap his wound!" Kaisar said urgently as he pulled off his own shirt to stanch the blood. "He's going to bleed to death."

After that, even the guards began to respect him a little. For his actions, the court reduced his sentence by three years and stationed him in the infirmary, where he worked as a nurse or orderly or cleaner, whatever was necessary.

"It's not exactly freedom," my brother told us, "but at least I have something to do all day."

Thinking of Kaisar trapped behind bars, I often felt guilty about the freedom that I had out in the real world. It made me all the more determined to do my absolute best at whatever I set out to do. I was working on my senior project, collecting local dialects of the Uyghur language from outside of Ürümchi. As part of that project, I went to the city of Kashgar, a more than thirty-hour train journey from Ürümchi, to do research.

Outside Kashgar is a beautiful village called Opal. It's set in a harsh desert landscape, but the village encompasses an oasis with fountains and tall, narrow poplar trees. Opal was the home of Mahmud al-Kashgari, an eleventh-century lexicographer of Turkic languages and one of the most famous figures in Uyghur history. From my father, I'd learned all about his books on linguistics and the foundations of the Uyghur language.

It wasn't often that a college student from the capital came that far south, so some officials from the Kashgar Educational Center offered to take me to Mahmud al-Kashgari's elaborate tomb and the mountainous countryside around it. In fact, that was the reason I'd wanted to do research so far from home. From the time I was a small child, my father had told me about Mahmud al-Kashgari and the huge influence he'd had on Uyghur culture. His influence could be seen everywhere in our present-day language and literature. Many call him the father of the Uyghur language, and he was a teacher to us all. I wanted to make a pilgrimage to where he had lived and studied and written his famous *Dīwān Lughāt al-Turk*, or *Compendium of the Language of the Turkic People*.

Mahmud al-Kashgari's tomb is adjacent to the famous Forty Springs of Opal Village, set in a protected park of about a hundred acres surrounded by barren, dry mountains. The springs feed the surrounding greenery, and the close hillsides are covered with cedar and pomegranate trees. Anywhere touched by sunshine is covered by wildflowers of every color, along with wild strawberries and low evergreen shrubs. With the wild rabbits, nightingales, and cuckoo birds flitting serenely through the woods, it was like stepping into an oil painting. As we walked among the flowers humming with bees, I thought about whether Mahmud al-Kashgari himself had drunk from the sweet spring water, all those many centuries ago.

After our tour around the park, as the officials and cadres from the center sat eating kebabs and drinking beer, I started to get bored. I politely asked if I might look around a little on my own.

The head cadre gestured with his kebab and a wide smile. "Of course! Walk, enjoy our beautiful scenery, take plenty of photos to show all your friends at home how wonderful it is here!"

I took a bottle of Pepsi with me in case I got thirsty, found a nice view, and began to write in my research journal about what we had done that day. It was early spring, and the weather was beautiful, with a gentle breeze that mitigated the intense sun. In the desert, the sun can seem enormous, like a pulsating, oppressive orb. That day, the sunshine was more like a gentle caress as I sat there enjoying my moment of quiet and solitude.

As I was writing in my journal, I caught sight of a small girl coming toward me from quite a way off. She came closer and closer, and then stopped about fifty meters away. She looked at me shyly, quietly, without saying anything. She was very thin, and her face was smudged with sweat and dirt. She was holding a piece of cloth that she had gathered into a bag.

I called to her, "Come here. Sit with me for a while."

She dipped her chin shyly. "Are you finished with your drink?"

I had to lean toward her to hear her. "Would you like to drink some of this? I haven't even opened it yet."

She shook her head no.

I could tell she wasn't going to come closer if I kept talking to her, so I pretended to ignore her and went back to my writing.

As soon as I looked occupied, she began to creep toward me again, before stopping several feet away. I glanced up at her very casually. "Are you thirsty? Here, have a drink."

"I'm not thirsty. I need your bottle."

"My bottle." I was surprised. "Why?"

"So I can trade it in." She gestured at her makeshift bag. "I've already collected eleven bottles. If you give me yours, I'll have enough to go to the village and sell them."

"You can have my bottle when I'm done, I promise." I patted the ground next to me. "Sit for a while."

She twisted her arms together reluctantly and stayed standing.

"Do you live here?"

"Down there." She pointed toward the crest of the hill where a handful of houses dotted the valley. A few goats were clambering around the rocky hillside as though weightless, seeking out anything green to eat.

"What's your name?"

"Anargul," she said shyly.

"We both have flowers in our name!" I told her, laughing. "Do you know what your name means?"

"Pomegranate flower," she said, smiling for the first time. "We grow pomegranate trees, like our neighbors."

"Why are you collecting these bottles?" I asked her as she finally sat down next to me, her slight frame barely casting a shadow beneath the sun.

"Each bottle is worth eight cents," she told me seriously. "When tourists come here, they just throw their bottles away. I collect them so that my brother can go to school. He tested into high school in Kashgar, but the school fees are expensive. If I can find enough bottles, he can stay there. He wants to be a teacher. After he graduates, he'll support me so I can go to school in the city."

"How old are you?" I asked.

"Seven. My brother's fourteen and he's very smart."

"Why isn't there a school here in the village for your brother?" I took a small packet of dried figs from my purse and put them between us. When I took one, she did too.

"The closest high school is fifty kilometers away. Even the elementary school is half an hour's walk from here." Anargul happily nibbled on the figs as she talked.

It was hard to see such a small child carrying such a heavy burden. But she seemed cheerful rather than resigned. I suddenly vividly saw all of the good fortune I'd had throughout my life. Everything had been laid out in front of me like a feast—schools, new clothes, good food, clean places to sleep and bathe. Our parents hadn't spoiled us, but we had never gone wanting. Why shouldn't this other little flower have everything she needed as well?

But I was from the capital, where there were at least some opportunities for Uyghurs, like the job I had been promised at the university, and Anargul and her family lived in a rural, largely Uyghur region, and none of the wealth that the Han were extracting all around her—from oil, gas, coal, minerals, water, and other natural resources—ended up in the hands of ordinary local people. The per capita GDP in the southern part of the Uyghur region, where the population was 95 percent Uyghur, Kazakh, Tajik, and so on, averaged half of that of the whole region. Across the board, wealth was concentrated where the Han were.

I handed her the packet of figs and the full bottle of Pepsi. "Take these home with you and tell your parents they have my admiration."

She took the gifts tentatively.

"The next time I come back to Opal, I'll look for you," I promised. "And keep going to school!"

She nodded and skipped away down the hill with her prize in her hand.

I quickly wrote down our whole conversation for my research project before I went back to the group. I could feel the wheels in my brain spinning. As soon as I got back, I said to the group, "You're the ones responsible for education in the Kashgar region, right?"

"That's right," one of the cadres said, his voice amused.

"This is the birthplace of Mahmud al-Kashgari, the greatest educator this region has ever seen. But I just learned from a local child that there isn't even a middle school in this village!" I was full of indignation, but I knew that the real issues couldn't be addressed, not in public, and not with these men. "Isn't it your duty to make sure there are schools for every child?"

The men were quiet for a moment. Then one of the senior cadres said, "Yes it is, and we pay for as many children as we can to go off to Ürümchi to study. After they go to the city, they don't want to come back. That's the problem. The village doesn't have good schools, that's true. But there isn't enough money to provide good salaries for teachers. Do you want to come here and build up an educational program?"

I had no answer for him. My home wasn't in Kashgar. But Anargul had touched me. I wanted to find a way to help her and all the other children like her, both to teach them about their own rich culture and to help them get ahead in a society that was completely rigged against them. There had to be some way.

When I got home from my trip, I told my father all about Opal and Anargul.

"The wealthy get wealthier, and the poor only get poorer," my father said. "Well, what are you going to do about it? You're going to graduate from the Normal University. You're being trained as a teacher. What's your solution?"

"I don't have one," I said. I didn't admit that I wanted to do something bigger than being in one little classroom all day. "But it doesn't seem right that all of the students in Ürümchi just end up staying in the city and teaching other city kids."

"Won't you be doing just that if you end up staying at your university and teaching there?"

I nodded. "But if I go to Opal, or some other little village, I'll just be stuck there, teaching a handful of kids at a time. I know that can make a difference, but . . ."

"You want to have a broader impact," my father finished for me. "My daughter, be careful what you ask for."

My first clue of what might have been in store for me came a few months before my graduation, when the Public Security Bureau came to the university to find student guides for an upcoming exhibition. The so-called People's War on Drugs had been ramping up—the same policy initiative that Kaisar had been caught up in—and the PSB was putting on an informational exhibition about the influx of drugs into the region and all of the severe punishments that awaited those who broke the law. The bureau wanted fifteen or twenty good-looking young men and women who could speak both fluent Uyghur and Mandarin. The same dean who had helped me keep my place in the dance competition thought that I fit the bill, so she asked me if I wanted to be nominated as a candidate. From her face, I could tell that she thought I might refuse because of my brother, but quite the contrary, I wanted to help other people avoid falling into the trap of drugs and violence. I auditioned and was chosen to be one of the guides.

Each morning, bright and early, I took the bus to the Xinjiang Sports Stadium and joined the other guides. The exhibition filled the entire arena with zigzagging booths and posters. We practiced for days, learning what the People's War on Drugs was, what the different illegal drugs were, and what their terrible effects could be. We heard all about what was happening in the Uyghur region, teenagers and promising young adults getting sucked into a vortex of crime and desperation. That was very familiar territory to me, and it was painful to listen to. During all of the lessons, I kept thinking, *This is the thing that destroyed my family*.

For the others, the exhibition was an opportunity to advance their budding careers as officials or PSB officers. But for me, being there was like a kind of revenge.

The last morning of training, as we stood in a neat line dressed in our smart matching uniforms, the head trainer pointed at me. "I hope you all know your lines as well as Gulchehra does. She's so professional, she could be on TV!" he joked.

The other guides laughed, and I laughed it off too. But it was as though the idea were a little hook that caught in my brain and wouldn't let go.

When the idea of being a professional personality was presented to me so explicitly, it was like a switch flipped. That was my big platform; that was where I could speak to a lot of people, and make a real difference. I started to dream day and night about becoming a TV star.

When the exhibition opened, every school was required to send their students and every work unit had to come through the exhibition hall. Company by company, workers were let off for an afternoon so they could attend the exhibition. I became known as one of the more popular guides and people would jostle to get into my group. When it was all over, the chief of the PSB in Ürümchi came to congratulate us on a job well done. Afterward, he pulled me aside.

"Gulchehra," he eyed me seriously, "we're going to offer you a job as a junior member of the International Drug Crimes Unit. First, we'll need to train you for two years in Shanghai."

I was completely taken aback and blurted out the first thing that came to mind. "I'll have to talk to my father."

On the bus home, I felt torn. I never wanted to be a good comrade, benefiting from a system that relied on the oppression of so many others. On the other hand, this could be a chance to help my brother.

If I were on the inside of the system, I would have the connections I needed to try to get him out of jail. I went home that night and told my parents that I'd been offered a job with the PSB.

My father's expression darkened. "Gul, I kept you from doing so many things that you wanted to do, always pushed you to do better, study hard, be successful. And for what?"

"But, Daddy, you don't understand. I'll be able to help Kaisar."

I saw out of the corner of my eye that my mother had begun to cry silently.

"No!" My father sat up even straighter in his chair. For a few moments, he looked the way he had before my brother had been arrested—full of vitality and confidence, unbowed by the world. "Kaisar is my responsibility, not yours. He's already lost his dreams, and I cannot allow that to happen to you too. Is that what you've been dreaming of, becoming a policewoman?"

"Of course not," I blurted out. "I want to be on TV!"

He sat back in his chair.

"What on earth are you talking about?" my mother said.

"I've been thinking about it. If I want to reach the largest number of people, or teach the largest number of children, what better way than television?"

My mother sighed the way she had when I was a child and told her I wanted to be a professional dancer someday.

"Gulchehra. My daughter." My father's eyes looked tired again. "If I've learned anything, it's that a parent's greatest joy is to watch his children bloom, and his greatest despair to see their potential crushed. If you want to pursue a career in television, I won't stand in your way."

I looked to my mother. Slowly, she nodded, her face still wet from tears.

"In that case, how am I going to turn down the chief of the PSB?" My stomach clenched at the thought. "How can I say no to them?"

"Just tell them it's your dream to be a teacher," my mother said quietly.

"That's right," my father said. "Tell them you have a job waiting for you at the Normal University. They can't very well tell you not to become an educator, can they?"

And that's exactly what I did. They were grudging, but as my father predicted, they couldn't discourage me from teaching. Then I went to the dean who had been such a source of support. I told her about turning down the PSB offer.

"Well, thank goodness!" she cried. "We'll get to keep you after all!"

I looked down at my hands. "Dean, thank you for everything you've done for me. So much of my success is thanks to you."

She smiled warmly. "We do our best for our best students."

"But I can't spend my life in a classroom. I don't want to teach just a few hundred students at a time. I want to teach our whole nation." I glanced up quickly to meet her eyes. "Do you understand?"

The dean was quiet for quite some time. Then she said, "I'll make a few calls for you."

The dean set up a meeting with the university president and vice president for the next day. When I told them that I wanted to work for Xinjiang TV, they tried everything in their power to dissuade me. They told me I would make a great teacher, and that television wasn't a serious profession. Besides, Xinjiang TV was the biggest local TV broadcaster, and although it wasn't part of the national China Central TV network, it was still subject to a lot of Han oversight. But nothing they said deterred me. I had already made up my mind.

"You know what this will entail, don't you?" the president said. "First, the university would have to officially rescind your job offer. Then, in order to be even considered by Xinjiang TV, first you have to be vetted by the Radio, Film, and Television Bureau. That's run by the central government, you know. It's all Han over there. They control all the personnel decisions for the television station. But to even get in the door of the bureau, you have to have an official introduction from a known entity, like a university or a company that has solid political connections."

"But . . . the Normal University has those connections, don't you?" I asked tentatively.

"We do," said the dean, looking at her colleagues.

The president sighed. "You're taking a big risk, Gul. You know you're turning down guaranteed employment, right? For life!"

"Yes," I said in a small voice.

He gave a quick nod, and I was dismissed from his office for the last time.

After making the arrangements, the vice president of Xinjiang Normal University brought me himself to the interview at Xinjiang TV, in a slick black car owned by the university. I had dressed very carefully that morning, combing out my thick black hair and wearing a modest dark blue dress that set off my eyes. I was so nervous I was trembling.

The vice president brought all of my official documents—my diploma, my grades, awards that I had won, commendations from teachers—in a heavy envelope. It represented everything that I had accomplished so far in my young life.

The modest Xinjiang TV building sat in the long shadow of the Radio, Film, and Television Bureau. The bureau was an eleven-story rectangular concrete building with rows of identical windows overlooking a large parking lot. Guards flanked the entrance, and only those who had an appointment could make it past the security desk. We made our way into the bureau and found the human resources department. A secretary led us up to the office of the head of HR.

When we knocked, a tall Han woman with big moles on the side of her neck opened the door.

She waved us into her office without bothering to introduce herself. The office was large and plain, with a long, bare conference table in the middle. She walked to the head of the table, leaving us to stand at the far end.

The vice president of the university began to tell her about my accomplishments, the awards I had won, the skills I excelled at. I listened quietly, my heart beating fast. I was steeling myself to answer any questions the HR head might have. I had prepared my answers carefully.

The vice president of the university passed the huge dossier down the long table to her.

The head of human resources didn't even glance at the envelope. "We don't have plans to hire anyone this year," she said coolly. Then she flung the dossier back down the table.

As my precious papers spun on the table, my heart sank to my stomach. I had been studying hard for sixteen years by then. I had put everything I had into my studies. But in that moment, it seemed like all of my efforts had been for nothing. She hadn't even looked at my paperwork!

"Fine," I told her. "If you don't need me, I don't need you." I threw the envelope with all my documents back on the table with a loud *thwack*. I was ruining my chances of ever working at the station, but in that moment I just didn't care. I had been insulted and I wasn't going to take it meekly.

I rushed out of the room, not wanting her to see my tears. White hot humiliation filled the space where my enthusiasm had been.

"What kind of student are you?" she shouted after me. "I've never seen anyone so rude!"

I heard the vice president of the university apologizing profusely as he scooped up my dossier and followed me out. As soon as he caught up to me, he stopped me.

"Gul, what are you doing? You're destroying your whole future! Your future is gone. Poof! Up in smoke!" He looked angry, but I now know that he was also afraid.

My temper was still raging. "What did *I* do? If she doesn't want to give me a job, fine. But how can she be so rude?"

I couldn't accept it. All I had wanted was to be considered, but she hadn't even given me that.

That afternoon, a secretary from the university called and told me to come to the president's office for a meeting. I didn't want to go.

"What have you gotten yourself into now, Gulchehra?" my father asked me. "If the president of the university tells you to go, you go."

I was still furious when I reached the president's office. Several top administrators were there waiting for me, their faces grim. They told me that I had to go back to Xinjiang TV and apologize. If I didn't, future students would never be able to find work at the station again. They couldn't risk being blacklisted by the Radio, Film, and Television Bureau.

"It doesn't just have to do with you," the president told me. "Your actions will affect all of the students who come after you."

I protested fiercely. I didn't want to apologize. But eventually they wore me down and I promised to go back to the station and apologize.

I returned to the station the next day, just wanting to get it over with. But instead of taking me in to see the same woman, I was shown into the office of the bureau chief. He was sitting behind his desk when I knocked on his door.

"So, you're the student who threw her dossier at the head of human resources." He didn't look up from his desk.

"No," I said hotly. "She threw the papers at me. I was just returning them. If she doesn't need them, then I don't need them either."

He glanced up at me over his big, thick glasses. "How can such a small person have such a large voice?" He leaned back in his chair, the hint of a smile beginning to form on his face. "Tell me, if you were to come work at Xinjiang TV, what would you want to do?"

I took a deep breath and said, "I want to do a show that showcases our Uyghur culture."

His face was impassive.

"A children's show." I had talked it over with my father carefully before applying for the job. Children's shows wouldn't be controlled at strictly as shows intended for adults. And it was essential that children learn about their own heritage—the future of our whole tradition depended on it. I wanted other children to learn what my grandfather and my father had taught me. "More and more of the programming now is Chinese and just dubbed into Uyghur. I want to do a program in Uyghur, with Uyghur stories."

The bureau chief frowned, and my heart sank. I was frightened that I had gone too far. My father had always warned me not to trust Uyghurs who were in positions of power. They had only risen that far by getting along with their Han bosses. Many of them were good comrades; but some of them had maintained a degree of independence. It was impossible to tell at first glance. The bureau chief had spoken to me in the Ürümchi accent familiar from my childhood; I could imagine him having grown up in the same mahalla as I did, eating the same nan and enjoying the same tart yogurt. But perhaps he actually believed that the Chinese programming was better, or he felt no particular loyalty to his own culture. Perhaps he was in an especially precarious situation in his own job and couldn't afford to take any risks. Just because he had a Uyghur face didn't mean we were on the same side. I swallowed hard. I might have just made a very dangerous mistake.

After a long moment, he picked up a pen from his desk. "Okay, Gulchehra Hoja. I'm willing to give you a chance. Come and see if you can make your children's program a reality. Of course, you're going to have to prove yourself first. But I'll sign your work papers."

By graduation, everyone knew I had gotten the job at Xinjiang TV. Mehray was delighted for me and insisted on hosting a congratulatory dinner with a group of our friends the night before graduation. Even Abdul came, although I had completely neglected his Chinese lessons after my brother's incarceration. He was preparing to go back to his village to marry his childhood sweetheart and take the job as a Uyghur-language teacher that was waiting for him.

When I told him I was sorry I hadn't had time for our lessons, he laughed and waved it off. "Chinese won't really come in handy back in my village," he said. "I'll be the only one who speaks it there anyway!"

"You know you're taking a very important job," I told him.

He frowned slightly at my solemn tone. Then he nodded without saying anything.

Even in the time we'd been in college, those things we were willing to say aloud had been steadily whittled down.

After the graduation ceremony the next day, the graduating seniors milled around on the campus green, reluctant to separate. I was meeting Elzat for a fancy meal later. We were still seeing each other, and in a few months he was going to go to Shanghai for a year of intensive language study at Jiaotong University. He'd decided that he might want to go abroad to study physics in a Western country. Because education in Germany was relatively inexpensive, he had been working hard to learn German.

Everyone was going off on their own adventures, scattering in all directions like sand blowing across the desert. Things would never be the same.

Abdul found me near the steps of the library talking to Mehray. He looked handsome and very young in his suit, which was at least one size too big for him.

"Gulchehra," he said shyly. "Will you take a photo with me? I want to always remember you."

Mehray grabbed the camera. "You won't need a photo," she said crisply. "Soon you can just turn your TV on and you'll see Gul right there in your own living room!"

He laughed. "We don't have a TV yet. But once I've started working, I'm going to buy one for my new wife."

"You'll make a very good husband," I told him. "Now pose!"

We took a photo together and Mehray went to find a few of our other friends for a group photo.

Abdul pulled some folded papers out of his pocket. He handed them to me, as though he were giving me a precious ancient scroll.

"What's this?"

He looked away, abashed.

I unfolded the paper. It was thick and decorative. A faint scent drifted up. "Chocolate?"

He smiled. "From the first time I ever tasted chocolate, or even knew it existed. Keep them, okay? Now maybe you'll always remember me."

I watched him walk slowly away. I probably wouldn't see him again, and I felt a little pinch in my stomach. Graduation marked a new phase in all of our lives. Abdul would go home to his faraway village to get married and start teaching. Mehray still had one year left of college, but she had already lined up an offer to work for a youth publication in Ürümchi after she graduated. And I was about to start my dream job at Xinjiang TV. We weren't children anymore, sheltered by our parents and kindly school officials, experimenting with different paths our lives could take. We were about to go out into the real world and face all the challenges that awaited.

PART III

THE SEEDS OF DISILLUSIONMENT

My initial job at Xinjiang TV was as an assistant writer and coproducer. There were only three new hires that year: me, a recent graduate from the college of art who was hired as a music editor, and another woman who was a video editor. They gave us a month-long training session during which we learned the basics of how things worked around the station. But as time went on, we weren't given much responsibility and my excitement waned. We were expected to come in early and leave late, but at the office we just sat around or did menial tasks like ferrying water to the hosts and bringing in the newspapers for the senior writers. At home, whenever I saw one of my relatives, they asked me when I was going to be on TV. With frustration, I had to tell them that I wasn't hired as a presenter; I was just a producer, and a junior one at that. But secretly, I was burning to make my own content and someday host the sort of shows I'd pitched in my interview.

A few months later, slogging through yet another endless day steeped in boredom, I was chatting with my young colleagues about the lighthearted, entertaining, but educational show for kids that I imagined making. I had sketched some of it out, so I showed it to them. When they all seemed to really like the idea, I said, "Well, let's make it."

"But how?" the video editor protested. "We've got no money, no access to cameras, no skills. How are we supposed to make a program on our own?"

"We do have skills. We went to school, didn't we? And whatever we don't know, we can learn."

I was eager to prove myself, and it was going to take more than just sitting around waiting for something to be handed to me; I needed to make my own opportunities. Like so many times before in my life when I needed help or advice, I went to my father first.

"If you want to get noticed," he told me, "begin with our art and tradition. Nothing anyone could come up with on their own could be as rich. And if you want to do a show for children, music is a perfect teacher. You should start there."

I mulled over the idea. Despite the creeping censorship in public life that all of us felt, we could still promote Uyghur culture in subtle and nonthreatening ways. Music and stories for children might just fit the bill.

I decided to go back to my high school, where I spoke with the vice principal, who had also been one of my teachers. I asked if I could film some of the students playing instruments and learning. After a little consideration, he agreed to the idea. Then came the harder part. Taking a chance, I told him that I didn't have money to buy film or pay for transportation. I needed help. The vice principal was a kind man, and whether he thought the program would be successful or just because he wanted to support me, he agreed to give me 2,000 yuan—around $350—from the school budget.

It was more than I could have hoped for from him, but still it wouldn't be enough. At the station, we filmed with professional videotape that cost 250 yuan per sixty-five-minute tape. To film a half-hour program, I would need at least four tapes. That alone would eat up nearly half of what the vice principal had given me. I also needed to hire a cameraman and other support staff, who generally charged 150 yuan per day. We'd be shooting for several days at least. It all added up quickly. I figured I would need to raise a total budget of around 5,000 yuan for the show.

I wasn't about to give up. I decided to pay a visit to the Ürümchi Musical Instrument Factory. The owner of the company was a friend of my father, and I figured he would see me. Fortunately I was right.

"I'm making a program to introduce children to our traditional instruments like the dutar, where they come from, how they're made, how they can be played. If you're interested, we could film some segments in your showroom. It'd be great publicity for you." I could tell he was interested because despite the fact that he was a very busy man, he was still listening. "Parents will think of you first if they decide to buy an instrument for their children."

He nodded thoughtfully.

"But to make the show, we need an initial investment. I have two thousand yuan, but we're three thousand yuan short." I gave him my most winning smile. "I guarantee it will bring you business!"

"My biggest fear," he said, "is that our children won't learn our own instruments. Have you heard what's on the radio? Half of it's Chinese and the rest is junk. I'll support your project."

And with that, we had our budget.

With some simple equipment and a basic script in hand, I went back to the school's music department. I asked if one of the teachers would be willing to give a lesson on camera. In the middle, to give the children a five-minute break, I read a children's story with a little music video. By the time we finished filming and editing, the show was around thirty minutes long.

My colleagues weren't sure we should show the video to our bosses at the television station. They were worried we might get fired for going outside our purview without even trying to get permission. But I wouldn't let all of our work go to waste. I was proud of what we'd done, and I was sure kids would like it too. I persisted until finally they agreed. We would take the risk.

I called the bureau chief who had hired me, along with the president of Xinjiang TV and the director of operations. I told each of them that we had made something and wanted their feedback and guidance. We might have been just starting out, but we had our own voices and a vision of what TV for a Uyghur audience could be.

So we arranged a viewing. My hands were shaking as I put the video on. It felt like our future careers were resting on this one moment. If they didn't like what we'd done and thought we'd been wasting the station's time, we could be fired that very day. The others had told me that if anything went wrong, it would be my head, as the ringleader, that would roll.

The video started playing. For the first five minutes or so the bosses chatted among themselves, not paying any attention. But then I came on-screen to introduce the program and to talk to my imagined audience. I had deliberately dressed young, and I kept my voice high and girlish. I wanted the kids to relate to me as an older sister.

When they heard me speaking, the bureau chief, the director of operations, and the president of the station started to watch in earnest. Then, when the show was over and the music had ended, they stayed silent. No one seemed to move for minutes.

I held my breath. This could spell the end of my brief stint in the television business.

Then the bureau chief started to clap. "You did this by yourselves?" he asked.

We nodded tentatively.

"No help from anyone?" he said skeptically. When we nodded again, he smiled. "Okay, bring me a release order to broadcast it, and we'll see what the reaction of our audience is. We'll make a decision after that."

"But . . . but it isn't ready!" I cried.

"It looks ready to me. We'll put it in the lineup this week."

A few days after it aired, we were all summarily called into a meeting.

"Gulchehra," the office director said, "the others tell me that you're the one responsible for this show. Is that true?"

I swallowed hard and nodded.

"Do you know how many phone calls we've received about the program?" He looked very solemn. "Parents, teachers, children . . ."

I dropped my eyes to the floor. Had our show really been that bad? Had we inadvertently said something that had upset the censors? We hadn't put in any political content, but at that point, in the mid-1990s, even existing as a Uyghur had begun to seem political.

"Everyone loves it!"

A sense of relief washed over me. I wasn't about to be fired!

"Gulchehra, put together a team," he said. "You can keep making the show."

My program was born that day. Until I had my real children, it was the closest thing I had to a son or daughter. And it was clear very quickly that we had hit upon something that worked. When I started my job at Xinjiang TV at the tender age of twenty-two, owning a color television was quickly becoming a status symbol in the Uyghur region. Everyone wanted to bring the world into their own living room. But most of the programming on Xinjiang TV came from elsewhere and was either dubbed into Uyghur or left in Chinese and given subtitles.

Uyghur children needed programs in their own native language that told the stories of our traditional literature. Many Uyghurs had the sense that our culture was being subsumed by the Chinese culture. Along with outright censorship—including the suppression of public protests and the summary closure of many periodicals the

Han authorities deemed to be "low quality"—there was the creeping cultural influences of Chinese TV, radio, and movies. All of the political realities in the Uyghur region reinforced that dynamic: anything Chinese was the wave of the future, while anything Uyghur was "backward."

I was determined to counteract that as much as I could, while still remaining under the radar. After all, how much trouble could a children's program cause?

As I focused on my professional goals, I was also making time to see Elzat. Dating in the Uyghur region wasn't like dating in the Western world. It was all very chaste, and the community at large served as a kind of omnipresent chaperone. I was very busy at the TV station, and he had a full teaching load, so we didn't actually spend much time together. But we knew that we were a couple; we had an understanding between us that didn't need more of a definition.

One afternoon, when it became clear that Elzat and I were seeing each other seriously, my mother took me aside and spoke to me about men directly for the first time.

"If you want to have a boyfriend," she told me, her tone serious, "choose very carefully from the beginning. Once you really pick one, that's it. He'll be your husband one day."

I felt my heart drop a little.

"Elzat is a very fine man." She smoothed my hair back. "Handsome, steadfast, from a good family. He's been there for you throughout all of our family troubles. I just want you to know that we approve of the choice."

"He is five years older," I said tentatively. "I'm not sure if we—"

My mother shook her head dismissively. "That won't matter down the line. What matters is that he'll be a good provider for you and your children."

That seemed to be the lesson that every Uyghur mother taught her daughters back then. There was no sex education—we didn't even have much of a sense of basic anatomy—but there was a strong expectation that your first boyfriend would be your last. Otherwise, you would be considered flighty, or worse, morally suspect. I couldn't tell my mother that I had already begun to doubt my feelings for Elzat.

The winter after I started working at the TV station, Elzat left for Shanghai to study German, and I stayed back in Ürümchi. At first it was hard; I missed him and his reassuring presence. I had gotten used to talking to him nearly every day, and after he left, that was reduced to a phone call once a week. Slowly, however, I started to realize that my life was still full without him. He had strong opinions about what I should wear and what colors he liked and didn't like on me. Ever since Kaisar had gone to jail, I had depended on Elzat to help me make decisions big and small. With him gone, I found that I relished the sense of rediscovered autonomy. I began to enjoy being on my own, having the freedom to decide how I could spend my time, and how I would dress.

I also valued the time and freedom to throw myself into my work. I spent twelve-hour days in the office, writing scripts, deciding on themes, finding child participants, and filming segments. My face became so recognizable from the show that parents stopped me on the street to tell me excitedly how much their children loved me. I knew a lot of that had to do with my on-screen personality, but an aspect of it was the content of our show as well. I wasn't a politician, and I wasn't a freedom fighter. But I was still trying to make a difference in some small way.

My work led me to cultivate relationships with people in the business community in the Uyghur region, which would eventually prove to be key in several ways. The TV station had given us a budget for the show, but that didn't cover anything except the bare bones: videotapes, cameraman hours, a skeleton crew, and my small salary. If we needed other props or supplies, or wanted to film on location somewhere, we often didn't have the money to do it right. Still, we did what we could with a tight budget. There was always some kind of traditional Uyghur music, and often I sang something. I read stories and acted out the different parts. I also used riddle poems from the Uyghur tradition in which an object is described and you have to guess what it is.

During one brainstorming session, I came up with an idea to make our show more interactive. I wanted to get our young viewers involved. When we taped the next show, I read one of those traditional riddles.

"Listen carefully now, my friends. What has a stone inside of food, and food inside a stone?"

I read it a second time. Then I turned to the camera. "Do you know what the answer is? If you think you know the solution, send me your answer in a letter. Everyone with the right answer will get a prize!" At the end of the program, I recited the address of the station.

The next day, there was a pile of letters on my desk. The following day, that pile more than doubled. We were inundated with mail! So many kids had sent in answers that it took several hours to sort through them. And many of them had the right answer: the apricot, which has a stone that houses a bitter almond.

It was a sign that lots of kids were watching the show and wanted to participate, and I was delighted about that. But there was one small problem: I had no prizes to give them.

In desperation, I went to the bureau chief and told him the situation. "I can't disappoint the kids! I promised them."

He laughed. "I was wondering when I'd see you in here." He pushed his glasses up on his nose. "But I'm afraid we don't have the budget for any kind of prizes. You got yourself into this mess, you'd better figure out a way to get out of it."

I thought frantically about what I could send to the kids—postcards with an interesting photo? A handwritten note from me?—but nothing

I came up with seemed like a real prize. Then I remembered going to the head of the Ürümchi Musical Instrument Factory when we were filming our very first show, and I had an idea. I took an entire day to go around to all of the toy companies and candy producers in town. I told each boss about the show and how the kids were so excited to participate.

"If you sponsor one of our riddles, we'll give a short introduction to your company and your product. *This week's prize is from the Xinjiang Date Candy Company!* We'll thank you for your support on the show, and the kids will get to know your product when they receive their prize."

It turned out that most of the businesspeople I talked to were glad to support our program. The bureau chief at the station was pleased, too, because it helped build business relationships between the station and the community. And the kids got little prizes for solving the riddles, in a win-win for everyone. It wasn't just that it was good publicity; more and more, everyone seemed to be chafing at the overwhelming presence of Chinese-language media and the attendant cultural pressure. People felt the need to support anything that would help preserve our heritage amid a clampdown by the authorities.

This was a sea change from the 1980s, when I was growing up. Those years were a period of relative permissiveness and liberalism in the Uyghur region, as the Chinese authorities in Beijing were debating among themselves how best to incorporate East Turkestan into China as a whole. Across China, there was a general loosening of the violence and oppression of the Cultural Revolution period, and even the Uyghur region was given some latitude to engage in traditional music and dance, like the big parties my grandfather used to throw, and some religious expression, at least on a small scale and in the privacy of one's home. Women like my grandmother could wear the hijab without being harassed and men could wear beards if they chose to.

It was a period during which the terrible wounds of the Cultural Revolution began to heal, and Uyghur intellectuals focused on establishing historical legacies and developing the national consciousness of Uyghurs. Historians recorded a Uyghur history that stretched back to the Huns, musicians compiled the canonical musical heritage of the Twelve Muqam, and writers produced novels and poems that helped to shape our collective national identity. There was a kind of flourishing that was as rich as it proved to be short-lived.

During that period, a number of Islamic and Uyghur-language schools opened, particularly in smaller towns and cities, and by the end of the 1980s, over ten thousand students attended such schools across the Uyghur homeland. Many people welcomed these schools as a chance to educate their children in traditional Uyghur customs and beliefs and, crucially, to have them receive instruction in our own language. Many had long viewed the incursion of Han people into the Uyghur region as an impossible combination, a mix as dangerous as fire and dry kindling.

By 1990, we all felt the ground shifting underneath us. My brother and I were still in high school and just getting hints of the political situation from the sound of low voices . . . The decade kicked off with one of the largest protests seen in the Uyghur region since the bloody repression at midcentury. In Baren, a modest and conservative southwestern town with a largely Uyghur population and a sizable Kyrgyz minority, a protest broke out against the sudden imposition of restrictions on free religious expression. More than three hundred people took to the streets, angry about the local authorities' decision to prevent them from building a new Islamic school and mosque in the town. Things escalated when armed police were called in and began to shoot at the protesters indiscriminately. The official media reported that police had quelled a violent demonstration, sacrificing their own safety and, in some cases, their lives in the process. But what we heard from other Uyghurs was that somewhere between ten and fifty peaceful protesters had been killed by police forces simply for trying to protect their right to practice their religion in peace. Facts were thin on the ground, but tensions ratcheted up, even as far away as Ürümchi.

In response to the protests, the Han authorities closed down mosques and Uyghur schools. Some mosques were razed, while others were repurposed for nonreligious use, with a total disregard for how local people felt about their religious sanctuaries and centers of community life. Officials targeted "illegal religious activities," by which they meant most public and peaceful expressions of Islamic faith. They compelled the imams to undergo ideological education and affirm their loyalty to the Chinese state, and Han Communist Party members were sent to the Uyghur region to oversee the reeducation of religious leaders and to make certain the rules were being adhered to. In the end, more than 10 percent of the imams were forced to give up their role as religious and community leaders because they refused to capitulate. The new regulations meant that even neighbors meeting together in the privacy of their own homes to practice their faith or discuss Islam was forbidden. Ostensibly, religious activity was targeted, but it felt like our whole culture was under attack. We all had grandmothers who wore a hijab or a cousin who went to the mosque.

Across the Uyghur region, murmurs of trying to reestablish East Turkestan as an independent state simmered. For the Chinese authorities, this was a major problem. They were concerned about latent hostilities between the two communities—Han and Uyghur—and what they called "splittists," or Uyghurs who thought that the Uyghur homeland should be controlled by Uyghur leaders. Since East Turkestan is home to large deposits of oil and natural gas, as well as mineral deposits and vast cotton fields that all add to the CCP's coffers, the stakes of a potential independence movement in the Uyghur region were high.

Amid this climate of increasing hostility, I saw my children's program as a small part of the effort to protect the Uyghur culture and its ancient traditions. Because it was for kids, I could still fly somewhat under the radar. And since I myself was so young at the time, barely out of my early twenties, I didn't have a full grasp of the dangers I was courting.

I also had other things on my mind, like trying to maintain my relationship with Elzat despite the distance. We struggled to find things to talk about during our weekly phone call, and I began to even dread the conversations, which made me feel terribly guilty. I was watching my friends getting married and seeing how thrilled they were to begin the next stage of their adult lives. Each seemed so in love with her husband, so eager to share a home with him, make decisions together, have children and a future together. And though I was so happy for them, all I could think of was how much my feelings for Elzat had faded while he was away. We never fought, but that was because I deferred to him. At work, I was outgoing and opinionated; with him, I felt like I was constantly cramming my real thoughts and feelings further and further down inside. With the children's program, I was involved more deeply than ever with Uyghur music and Uyghur literature, but Elzat wasn't particularly interested in artistic endeavors. He found listening to stories about my work boring, and when he talked about physics, I could feel my eyes glaze over.

The year passed quickly, and when Elzat came back from Shanghai, I couldn't go to meet him at the airport because I was filming for the show. But when I did see him a few days later, I could feel immediately that something had changed. It wasn't just the year apart and the inevitable estrangement that comes with that; it was something deeper that went unspoken. He seemed distracted and even more distant emotionally. Still, we tried to go back to the way we had been before. I kept expecting him to want to have a serious talk with me, and then, a few weeks after he'd gotten back, he did.

We sat on a bench in one of Ürümchi's poplar-lined parks with a pleasant fall breeze riffling our hair and the sunshine glinting off of the paved paths. He picked up my hand and held it in his.

"Gulchehra, it's time."

"It's time for what?" I felt a small pinch of alarm. Could this be the moment that he told me everything was over? I both wanted him to say it and dreaded hearing it.

"We've been together for six years. We know each other so well, and there are expectations for us and our future. I want you to know that I won't neglect my responsibility to you."

I lowered my head. Now I knew what he was building up to.

"I think it's time that we plan our wedding."

My heart sank with the flatness of his voice. There was no excitement, no eagerness, nothing like love in his voice. It was the sound of a man who'd steeled himself to follow through on a longstanding agreement he no longer remembered why he'd entered into. It wasn't what I had ever planned for myself, a marriage with little real affection, only a heavy sense of responsibility.

I said nothing. I was afraid that if I spoke I would blurt out everything I really felt. I had been a TV host for a year and had talked to hundreds of people from behind the camera. But now I couldn't find a single word to say in front of this one man.

Elzat took my silence as assent. "I'll bring my parents to your house tomorrow. Our mothers will work everything out." He patted my hand before letting it drop gently back into my lap. "Everything will be fine, don't worry."

The next evening, his parents came over, and our families talked happily together. My mother was delighted that finally something good was happening in the family. For many years after my brother's

Above: My bowa Zikri Elpattar (center, at mic) was a famous Uyghur musician. Here he is recording muqam in the 1970s, the traditional melodic music of the Uyghur. He was a composer of a type of muqam called *ruhsari muqam*, and his music was widely used in many popular Uyghur operas and as the melody to many songs. Bowa began to show his talent in the late 1930s as a leading member Sanayi Nafesi, a group of Uyghur-based artists in East Turkestan. In later life he was the head of the Uyghur Theater and Muqam Ensemble. It was a house full of artists and musicians, and the house I grew up in.

Left: Bowa on the right, aged around seventeen, with his best friend, Qeyyumbeg Hoja (no relation), who would later become a general in the East Turkestan National Army during the East Turkestan National Independence Revolution.
Right: Sanayi Nafesi, 1941.

My brother Kayser and I were always close growing up. He was only a year and a half younger than me. He never called me Gul, only ever *hhede*, or "sister." He is my soulmate. Every time I think about the fact that I'll never see him again, I weep.

At the Urumqi city high school dance festival, we won first place for our dance: "The Flower and the Butterflies." I am the flower in the middle, the lead dancer!

I visited Beijing during high school as representative of Uyghur High Schools and one of the best students in the region.

LANDSCAPE OF EAST TURKESTAN

Above: I'm posing here, but what I truly love is the landscape behind me. There is nowhere in the world quite like my home.

Below: The landscape here in Kashgar Toqquzaq is beautiful too. But it was six-year-old Anargu, seated next to me, who would be one of the most important people in my life. Meeting her inspired me to do something that would inspire Uyghur children to have a dream. The next year I would have my chance.

At Xinjiang Normal University, I studied to become a teacher. **Above:** I'm teaching a class of sixth graders as part of my practical learning. I taught them Uyghur language and literature. On the blackboard behind the class is written "Must learn Chinese. Know Chinese. Use Chinese." A sign of things to come.

Left: In my second year at university, I visited Japan for the seventh World Student Dance festival, representing the whole of China. I won a gold medal.

Aged twenty-three, I became the first children's TV presenter in the Uyghur language in East Turkestan. I'm wearing a traditional *etles* dress and the *doppa* hat. It became something of a trend to wear them in schools after I started presenting!

Shooting a program at Kashgar Maralbeshi County Elementary and Middle School. I had become really quite famous!

On the front cover of the only children's magazine in East Turkestan, *The Young Flowers of Tarim*. "Tarim" is the main river that flows through the South of East Turkestan. We refer to it as our Mother River.

Dressed as a butterfly for one of the programs.

My family are the most important people in the world. Me and my momma, my grandmother, who helped raise me. She taught me how to love and appreciate the world.

My brother, my cousin, and me on my twentieth birthday.

My dad on his sixtieth birthday. He sent it to me here in America with the message "Salam Aleikum, my dear daughter. 60 Years! I miss you so much."

My mom, looking beautiful on *her* sixtieth birthday.

Mom, Dad, and Kayser three years after I left. They had changed so much in that time.

Kayser, my brother, texted this photo of my mom and dad in the garden of their house in Ghulga Turpanyuz to me. "They are waiting for you," he wrote.

I arranged my father's sixty-fifth birthday from America in 2006. All his friends came to celebrate his amazing life with him. At least four of the people in this photo have subsequently been placed into concentration camps.

When I got my visa to the USA, I spent all my savings on my dream trip to Paris. I sent this photo to my dad with the message "I am feeding love to freedom and peace." In East Turkestan, pigeons symbolize these things—and I was free.

Mom and Dad in Urumqi hospital where Dad was having physiotherapy in December 2017, just days before they were arrested and disappeared. For two years, this was the last photo I had of them.

The last photo taken with my family, a few days before I left for Europe. I never imagined that I wouldn't return to East Turkestan. My dream is to take a photo like this one more time

incarceration, there didn't seem to be any good news at all. It was just desolation and sadness.

Watching the two sets of parents chatting companionably about the timing of the wedding and where we should live and what we would need for our first apartment, I just felt numb. My parents were clearly thrilled by the news of our engagement, and I couldn't go against their wishes. And there would be ugly rumors if Elzat and I didn't do what was expected after having been together for so long. There was already enough talk about Kaisar and his situation, which never seemed to go away. My parents just wanted one of their children to settle down and follow the path of an ordinary, quiet life. And that wasn't an unreasonable wish for a parent to have for a child.

When I had tea with Mehray a few days later and told her about the wedding, a wide smile blossomed on her face. Then she looked at me and it faded.

"But, Gul, aren't you excited about it?" Her velvety dark eyes looked into mine with concern. "You're about to marry a good man, a man who'll take care of you for the rest of your life. Why do you look so sad?"

I swallowed hard so I wouldn't start crying. "I'm not sad."

She shook her head. "How long have I known you, hmm? Don't I always read you like a sister?" She gave one of my sleeves a sharp tug. "But you and Elzat are both successful, you both have bright futures. And you look good together. You're such a perfect match!"

Our fragrant tea was steaming on the table in front of us, untouched. The waitress had brought little dishes of roasted sunflower seeds and dates as well, but I felt like I'd never be able to eat again. My stomach was tied into little fiery knots.

"I watched all of our friends getting married this year," I told her, "and they all can't seem to bear to be separated from each other for more than a few hours. But Elzat and I just spent a year apart and, by the end, I felt more content being on my own than I ever was with him."

Mehray looked shocked. "You're really not happy, are you?"

"I don't think I'm in love with him," I whispered. I felt ashamed at the words, and ashamed about how I was feeling. How could I not love him, after six years of being together? I wasn't at all sure what love was at that point, but it couldn't feel like this, a burden as heavy as an anchor weighing down my heart. I was still dependent on Elzat for emotional support, and that had been true since Kaisar had gone to jail. But that wasn't the basis for a lifelong marriage. "I feel like the whole thing's a lie," I blurted out. "And I don't want to have to lie for the rest of my life."

"If that's really the way you feel, Gul, you have to talk to Elzat." Mehray stared at me very seriously. "And you have to talk to your parents before this goes any further."

I knew she was right. But I couldn't go to my father. Despite everything I could and did share with him, this was too personal. And my mother had enough on her plate already. I decided to go to my grandmother, who had given me good advice from the time I'd been small enough to climb up into her warm, aproned lap.

I sat down on the old familiar couch in her apartment and came straight to the point. "Grandma, I don't want to get married."

"What do you mean?" Her gentle face creased into deep wrinkles around her mouth. "Aren't you happy with Elzat? He's a nice boy."

"He is nice, but . . . I don't feel anything for him. Mom and Dad want me to get married, have a family, have a normal life. I understand that. But how can I marry him if I don't love him?"

"Oh, Gul." She patted my cheek like she used to when I was a girl. "You've been with him for so long, I assumed you really loved him. But if you don't love him in the deepest part of your heart, then no one can force you to marry. We're Muslims. In Islam, if you don't want to be with someone, you can't be forced to be with them."

"But Dad and Kaisar only go to the mosque on holidays," I said. "And Mom doesn't even pray."

My grandmother looked shocked. "In her heart, your mother is a good Muslim woman. Doesn't she abide by the rules of Islam? She may not express her faith openly, but there are many reasons for that. You're an adult now, you know how things are here now. I'm an old woman, no one's going to care what I do in the privacy of my own home. That isn't true of your parents. Your father is already under a lot of pressure because he won't join the CCP. Everyone has to be careful these days."

I nodded, chastised.

"Go talk to your mom," she said, her voice softening.

"She's going to be so disappointed."

"Better a few days of disappointment than a lifetime of unhappiness," my grandmother told me.

She was right. I went straight home and found my mother in the kitchen. I had to talk to her immediately or I would lose my nerve.

"Oh, Gul, I'm glad you're here! I've been thinking about wedding invitations. Cream or pale blue paper, what do you think? You can think about it, but make a decision as soon as you can. We'll have to get them printed soon so we can send them out in time."

"Mom, I'm not ready for this wedding."

She stopped stirring the wide pan of *polo*, fragrant with carrots and lamb. "What?"

"I don't love him."

She was silent for a long moment. Then she snapped, "What do you mean, you don't love him? Why did you stay with him for six years then? If you felt this way, why didn't you end it years ago?"

My heart felt like a trapped bird frantically flapping its wings inside my chest. I looked at the floor. "I don't know why. But we were just apart for a year, and I had time to think. I just feel we aren't right together. I didn't even miss him while he was gone, and I don't think he missed me either."

"Shame!" Out of nowhere, my mother was crying and shouting, shaking her head so hard that her salt-and-pepper hair began to come loose from her bun. "This is so shameful! How can I bear more shame in my life? Your brother brought shame to our family, and now you're going to do something like this? How can I tell your father about this? What have you become? What sort of rumors are going to spread about you and our family? Can't we just have some peace in this family?"

I had never seen my mother so completely out of control, not even in the worst months after my brother's conviction when she couldn't sit down at the table for a meal without crying.

"If I get married, will there be peace in the family?"

The question only seemed to make her angrier, and her eyes narrowed. "Your father and I have been waiting for this moment for six years," she hissed. "You've been holding onto this man for that long, what will people think when you toss him aside? How can you make us lose face like this!"

Then she lifted her arm and hit me across the cheek, one sharp, stinging slap.

I sank down into a chair at the kitchen table. The side of my face burned like I had been branded with a scarlet letter. I had never been hit before in my life, and I felt stunned. Would everyone think I had been playing Elzat for a fool? That I was some kind of loose woman? That all our family members were criminal and sordid? I couldn't bear the thought. I felt a part of me turning very hard, like ice forming over what once had been a warm pool of water.

"I won't dishonor our family, Mom. I'll do my duty." I stood up from the table and looked her straight in the eye. "And I think cream. For the announcements. Everything else you and Elzat's mother can decide."

By any measure, our wedding day seemed like a very happy occasion. Most of our family friends from our old mahalla came, along with my father's colleagues, people from the TV station, and all of Elzat's family and friends as well. We had a huge cake and a banquet with more food than could be eaten in a month. There was live music played by musicians I'd known since I was a girl, and constant dancing and laughter. I looked the part of the blushing bride. My black hair was pulled back in a chignon studded with white flowers, with fine ringlets framing my face. I wore a long white wedding dress with a beaded bodice and a filmy veil with hand-stitched lace. My father had given me a delicate string of pearls as a present, and my mother helped me with my makeup so that my eyes were dark and radiant. Elzat was dressed in a well-tailored tuxedo, his hair carefully coifed. He looked as handsome as a movie star. Even the weather was sunny and the perfect temperature, with clear air that smelled like it had blown in from the mountains to our venue at a pretty spot on the outskirts of the city. On the surface, everything was perfect.

But inside, as I took my wedding vows I felt like I was telling the first real lie I'd ever told. And it was one I would have to live with for the rest of my life.

That night, lying in bed next to Elzat for the first time, officially as husband and wife, I felt my heart harden with resolve. If I had to be in a loveless marriage, I was going to avoid having children for as long as I possibly could. In the meantime, I would focus on my career completely. I was going to see just how far I could make it.

It was a good time to throw myself into my work. Our show went from brand-new to popular to almost universally known across the Uyghur region over the course of a year. I started to get so much fan mail that I could no longer answer it all, not even just with a postcard with my signature on it. I felt a responsibility to my young fans, so I asked the station to hire an assistant to separate the letters into categories: those with messages that I absolutely had to personally answer, those for whom a postcard would suffice, and those that my assistant could answer on my behalf.

I received a lot of letters from kids in the countryside. They would watch our shows, filmed in different interesting parts of Ürümchi, and dream about city life. The tone of their letters was usually wistful. It was as though even at a very young age, they already felt limits imposed on their dreaming. I wanted to show them that kids outside of the city mattered, too, but because of our lack of equipment and small budget, we couldn't go very far outside of Ürümchi. There was no way we could bring the show to a child in a village eight hundred miles away. The Uyghur region was much too big for our one video transmitter to cover.

Then one little boy wrote me a letter that I couldn't ignore. *I love your program and every night I close my eyes and wish I could be on it. I want to play with the city kids, but I know they wouldn't want to play with me. I wish we didn't have to be so poor.*

Everything about his letter touched me. I didn't want the kids from the countryside to feel any less special than kids who grew up in the cities. The economic divide was palpable everywhere, but it was especially obvious in the countryside, where Han company bosses enriched themselves and Uyghur workers in cotton fields and in coal mines barely made ends meet. Part of my mission with the show was to bring all Uyghur children together with their common heritage. Enjoying our Uyghur stories didn't require any money or advantages; they were for everyone.

I took the letter and marched into the bureau chief's office. I was still grateful to him for giving me a chance to make my own dream a reality. I wondered if he'd also listen to the dreams of our viewers.

"Thank you for hiring me," I said without any preamble. "It's been more than a year now and I hope you feel it was worth it."

He smiled. "I see every day what a good decision it was. You've reinvigorated this station. You've done everything you said you wanted to do."

"Not quite everything. Do you remember promising me we'd try to reach as many kids as possible?"

He nodded warily.

I handed the boy's letter across his desk and waited while he read it. Then I pointed to the map of the Uyghur region that hung on his wall. "As you know, here we are in Ürümchi." I dragged my finger all the way to the edge of the poster. "And here is that little boy's village. How are we going to bring the show to him?"

"If he has a TV, he can watch it," the bureau chief said.

"But look at his letter. He doesn't want to watch the show, he wants to be part of the show!" I paced a bit in front of his desk, my body thrumming with energy. "Right now, we're only filming in the city. All these privileged city kids and tall fancy buildings and wide paved roads. We never show what's going on in the villages. We never film using kids from outside of Ürümchi. It makes them feel overlooked, or even worse, like they're not as deserving as the city kids. That's not what our show is about."

The bureau chief sat back against his chair and was rubbing his chin thoughtfully. "Well, what do you propose to do about it?"

"I want to go into the villages and film there. But I can't do it with the equipment we have now. The range is too limited, and we don't have the vehicles. I just want to show the village kids that we value them too. Shouldn't that be one of our goals?"

He shook his head ruefully. "Gulchehra, you could talk a horse into wearing a hat."

I smiled at that. I knew I sounded impassioned, maybe even a little crazy, but that was the way I felt.

"Okay, okay," he sighed, "I'll take another look at your budget. Write me up a proposal and we'll see what we can do."

I practically ran back to my cubicle to write up a new budget. A week later, we had a new camera, a new van, and a new budget line for travel. From that moment on, I was committed to filming at least half of our shows outside of the city.

My team and I began to travel throughout the whole Uyghur region. I wanted to teach these kids in person, read them stories, and have them tell me their own village stories. At the same time, filming our children's show in these areas meant that our viewers in the cities would also learn about what it was like to grow up with a communal well instead of running water in your building. Above all, though, I was learning more than anyone. I'd grown up in a privileged family in the capital city, and there was a lot I myself had never seen before. I began to feel that I'd spent my life being selfish and narrow-minded. Just as Anargul had unexpectedly set me on my path of pursuing a career in television, every one of those village kids had something to teach me.

In many of the villages, the poverty was so severe that children were sent to school without breakfast. The children would be lethargic at their morning lessons, not because they didn't want to learn, but because an empty stomach is more distracting than anything else. I had a chance to talk to the rural teachers about the challenges they faced, the lack of books, hungry children, parents who pulled their kids from classes to pick cotton during the harvest season. Then I'd go back to Ürümchi and phone up someone I knew from the Education Bureau, if only to report what I'd seen. By that point, I knew a lot of powerful people, and I wanted more than anything to use my connections to do some good.

And each time I saw joy on a child's face when we got out of our van carrying toys and books that they could keep after we finished the filming, it made me feel like I was doing the real work, bringing Uyghur children together with each other and with their cultural heritage. I felt like I was witnessing their minds expanding as they shyly examined the camera that the cameraman would film them with and learned about how radio waves travel across long distances. I might not have been able to talk about any of the real issues, like our Uyghur textbooks being replaced by Chinese ones, or how "atheism education" was now the rule in the schools, but I could share Uyghur stories with the children and speak to them in their mother tongue on camera. I was toeing a line, but I kept everything light. I thought as long as my show was seen as just kids' entertainment, I could avoid trouble.

In the meantime, it was an added bonus that I was spending a lot of my time on the road instead of coming home to the cold, quiet apartment I shared with Elzat. Things between us were cool, but stable. I had resigned myself to living the rest of my life with someone I didn't fully love. It was a sacrifice I could make for the sake of my family.

One day I returned from a trip half a day early, and Elzat was still teaching. I was feeling restless, so after I finished unpacking and putting away my things, I started to tidy up our apartment. Usually, Elzat did most of the cleaning. He was neater than I was, and always wanted everything in its proper place. I couldn't keep track of all of his rules for where things go, so we just tacitly agreed that he would take care of it and I would try my best not to mess it all up. But I noticed the bookshelves hadn't been dusted for quite some time, so I picked up the duster and went to work. I left the smaller books in place, and the bigger ones I picked up and dusted individually. Last on the shelf was a big German dictionary that Elzat had brought back from Shanghai. I picked it up to dust it and a piece of paper and two photos dropped out from the pages.

I picked the pictures up and almost without looking I knew they were photos of Elzat with another woman. She was Han, fairly tall, with long, straight black hair. He looked happy and relaxed, their shoulders touching familiarly. On the back side of both photographs was the word *Shanghai* and the year when he studied there before our marriage.

My blood slowed in my veins and I could feel it pulsing through my scalp. My face felt hot, then cold, and an odd combination of rage and disbelief raced through me. I looked at the letter, but it was written in German with a few Chinese characters here and there. I could tell from the date that it had been written in the last few months. At the bottom was a full Chinese phrase: *I love you.*

I dropped the duster on the floor. In that moment, nothing mattered to me aside from understanding exactly what was in that letter. I picked up Elzat's heavy German dictionary and painstakingly translated the letter word by word. It took me the whole afternoon, and certain sections I couldn't really understand even with my rough translation. But by the time I was done, I had learned that the woman had been in the same language program as Elzat in Shanghai, and they had become involved with each other there. She was very unhappy that he and I had gotten married. She had written: *I know you're a good man and you feel responsible for her. But you're not happy and neither am I. I know this isn't just a fling between us. It's love.*

I sat in the chilly room as though I were a stranger in my own house. All of the objects around me—the crystal vase that had been a wedding present, Elzat's tidy work desk, the framed photo of the two of us on his bookshelf—all of it seemed alien to me. In that instant, the old Gulchehra, the one who had been alive since my birth, was gone. My heart was dead. I didn't feel any pain. I only felt a sense of shame. It was the shame of having been betrayed. That he had cheated on me meant that my life was a joke. I had sacrificed my happiness to marry him, and now it turned out that he had done the same for me. He wasn't any happier in the marriage than I was. The humiliation cut so deeply it felt like I'd been stabbed. I had met him at eighteen years old and married him at twenty-four. And now, not even two years into our marriage, I had learned that he'd had an affair. In one instant, everything was destroyed.

I didn't know what I should or could do, but I knew I couldn't stay there for one moment longer. I grabbed my purse and started to walk toward my parents' house. All I wanted was to talk to my mom and feel her comforting hand on my hair. I was so shocked and humiliated that I didn't even given a thought to what her reaction might be.

When I arrived, I found my parents huddled together on the couch. It looked like they'd both been crying.

"What happened?" I asked, confused. It seemed as though they'd heard the news already.

"It's Kaisar."

I thought that I was too numb to feel anything but humiliation, but my heart dropped at the sound of his name. "Is he okay?"

My father stood up unsteadily. "He was in a fight with another inmate. His sentence has been extended by three years."

"How can that be? He's been risking his own safety to prevent fights, and all of a sudden he's in one? There must be something else going on."

"We'll get to the bottom of it," my father said. His voice was exhausted.

My mother hadn't even looked up at me. They both seemed so fragile, as if every year that passed aged them as much as five.

All of a sudden, I felt I couldn't tell them. I couldn't add to their mountain of sadness. I sat down on the couch and put an arm around my mother and let her cry against my shoulder.

It was dark by the time I left their house, but I still wasn't ready to go back to my apartment. I couldn't face Elzat, and it was too late to stop in at one of my friends' houses without causing alarm. Then I thought of my cousin. All throughout our childhood, my cousin was the one I went to if I had problems with the other kids in the neighborhood. He always looked out for me and was as close to me as a big brother would have been. I trusted him with my entire being.

I started toward his house, which was on the other side of town. By the time I knocked on the door, it was past ten o'clock. I must have looked disheveled and wild-eyed, because as soon as my cousin's wife saw me, she gave her husband a glance and stood up from the couch.

"You two can sit and have a good chat. I'm going to bed." She quietly shut the door and we had our privacy.

I didn't mince words or try to make things sound better than they were. I told him everything about the letter and the photos I'd found, and I asked him what I should do. My eyes were completely dry, though my voice shook as I spoke.

He thought for a long time. Then he sighed. "Gul, you're a married woman now, and you've traveled more than any of us! You've seen a lot. But on the inside, you're still very naive. You've always had a pure heart. But you don't know a man's world. None of us talk about it with women, not our mothers, not our wives, not even our sisters. When I got married . . ." he hesitated. "I'd had a few girlfriends before. I never talked about it with my wife, and it has no influence on my marriage now. Men have their needs." He looked embarrassed. "Look, maybe when this happened Elzat was feeling very alone in Shanghai. He doesn't know anyone there, right? He must have been missing you very much. It's hard to leave a beautiful young woman behind. Maybe this whole thing was just a terrible mistake and he regrets it all now."

"If it was a mistake, why did he keep the letter and the pictures?" I tried to keep my voice calm, but I could feel my anger growing. At least I was feeling something again. "Why couldn't he talk to me about it when it happened? Or when he got back here? How could he have kept everything secret from me? His own wife!"

"Gul," he said gently, "it's late. You're exhausted and not thinking straight. You should go home. Talk to Elzat. Tell him you know, and be honest about how you feel. But don't make any decisions right now. You don't want to do anything rash."

I shook my head and was about to speak, but he suddenly grabbed my arm. He hadn't touched me like that since we were children.

"Listen to me very carefully, Gul. If you divorce, it will make your whole life worse. You're beautiful, and you're successful, but a divorce would ruin all of that. What would your bosses at the TV station think? You're supposed to be a role model! If a woman divorces, everyone blames the woman, not the man. No matter what had gone on, and no matter who's at fault. And how can you explain that your man had an affair with a Han Chinese woman?"

I dropped my head. I'd heard people say that putting Han and Uyghurs together was like making sheep and pigs live in the same pen; you could try to force them to get along, but they wouldn't comingle. I didn't know a single mixed Han-Uyghur couple, and intermarriage was essentially unknown. In addition to the social and political pressures keeping us apart, the differences between our cultures were hard to overcome. And yet here my own husband had had an affair with a Han woman.

"It's so shameful to everybody involved," my cousin continued, "that he would get involved with someone who doesn't share our values. I never took him for a good comrade! If you absolutely can't stand living with him, just move out quietly and don't tell a soul if you don't have to. But you should know before you do anything that every man has his dirty laundry. Don't blame him too much."

I pulled my arm away and left my cousin's house without another word. I walked aimlessly down the street, not even paying attention to the direction I was headed. I felt betrayed for a second time. My cousin had defended Elzat, had taken his side! He might have thought that he was helping me or protecting me by just telling me the reality of the situation, but it didn't help.

I was already a long way from home, but I just kept walking and walking like I could somehow walk straight out of Ürümchi and into a different life. It was dark, and men were out in front of restaurants drinking. It wasn't very safe for a woman alone after dark. But a small part of me wanted to be attacked. I wanted some kind of revenge, I wanted Elzat to feel some echo of the pain I was now feeling. I wanted to hurt him, and I didn't care if I got hurt in the process.

When I got back to our apartment building, Elzat was waiting for me outside the main gates. He knew I'd found the letter because I'd left it with the photos on his desk where he would see them.

He took a step toward me. "Thank God you're home, Gul! I was so worried about you."

I pushed past him without looking at him. "Worried about me? Really?"

He followed me silently up the stairs to our apartment.

When we were inside, I finally turned to look at him. "Why didn't you tell me you're so unhappy?"

"I'm not unhappy! I'm very happy with you."

"How can you be happy with me and at the same time be having a love affair with another girl? It makes no sense. If you kept those pictures, she must mean a lot to you."

He was shaking his head. "No, you don't understand. The letter came in the mail and I panicked. I didn't know how to get rid of it without you noticing. I know it was incredibly dumb, but I just hid it in the book so I could deal with it later. I was going to rip it up and throw it out. I don't have any feelings for that girl."

My rage was giving way rapidly to hurt, and tears started to gather in my eyes for the first time that day. "You've destroyed me," I whispered. "Do you know that? You've already killed me. I'm not the same Gulchehra I was when we got married, and if I ever really loved you, I certainly don't anymore. Before we married, I knew we weren't right for each other, but even the plain affection I felt for you before is gone. I had respect for you before. But now I feel nothing at all for you." It was like looking at someone I had known long ago but who was now a virtual stranger.

"I'm so sorry. It was a terrible mistake! I didn't—"

"What are we going to do?" I interrupted. "I can't just pretend to be man and wife anymore. It's all a lie!"

He followed me into the kitchen. "Don't say that! It's not a lie. It's all real."

"This will kill my parents. But I can't stay here."

His eyes were getting wild. "Don't say that, Gulchehra. I'll die if you leave!"

I looked at him bleakly. "I'll die if I stay."

He reached over to the cutting board and suddenly there was a kitchen knife glinting in his hand.

I took an involuntary step backward. "Stop, Elzat. Just stop it."

He had started to cry, his handsome face mottled and twisted. "You can't leave me, Gul, I can't allow it."

"What are you doing with that knife?" My panic was growing. The whole scene was unbelievable, like out of a movie, and I felt detached from my body.

He looked down at it as though he hadn't noticed he was holding it. "You don't think . . . I'd never hurt you! How can you think that? How can you even think that." His voice broke. "I'd never hurt you," he whispered.

"Then put that down." I tried to sound sensible, but the situation was spinning out of control.

"If you leave me, I'll kill myself." His grip on the knife tightened. "I mean it, Gul, I'll kill myself. I don't want to live if you're not my wife."

"Stop all of this!" I shouted. We had been keeping our voices down for the sake of the neighbors, knowing that nearly everything could be heard through the thin walls of the apartment building. But I couldn't stand it anymore. "Put that knife down, Elzat. You're acting like a child!"

He started sobbing and lifted the knife to his throat.

I lunged forward and grabbed for it. I managed to get hold of the handle where it met the blade, and the thin sharp edge tore through my skin as though it were air. Blood streamed down the front of Elzat's shirt.

He looked down at it, perhaps thinking at first that it was his own blood. But it was coming from the side of my hand, where the knife had made a deep, nasty cut. Staring at my hand, he dropped the knife to the floor, where it clattered and slid into a corner. He sank down against the cabinets, holding his head and crying.

I wrapped my hand in a kitchen towel and raised it above my head. It didn't hurt yet, but it would leave a scar. I looked down at the crouched figure of the man who had once been my husband and felt my heart contract with a new emotion: pity.

After that night, I went to stay with my parents for a few days. I didn't tell them what had happened; I couldn't bear to bring them more unhappiness. But I did ask my mother to cut my long, thick hair. She was shocked at the request, but finally complied. It was like she knew something had happened and I wasn't the same person anymore. Maybe she thought I was finally accepting my role as a wife and fully adult woman. I supposed in a way I was. When she was done, I had a sleek shoulder-length cut. I turned my head this way and that way, admiring the way my hair fell against my cheeks. A modern woman, I told myself. A brand-new, modern woman.

I had taken a few days off sick from work so I could stay at my parents' house and try to put myself back together. But I couldn't avoid work and other people forever. If I hoped work might be a refuge from the chaos of my private life, I was sadly mistaken.

All the signs were that the political environment was continuing to tighten and that eventually it was going to affect my show. For a start, the Chinese authorities had begun cracking down on *mashraps*, the informally run community social clubs for boys and men. As my family had so painfully learned through Kaisar's experience, drugs were running rampant through the community, even intravenous drug use, which also spread diseases like HIV. To try to prevent this scourge that was decimating the young male population, community elders turned to traditional gatherings like the mashrap, where teenaged boys and men could joke around, eat, play games, sing, dance, talk about Islam, and generally blow off some steam in a healthy way. Younger boys were organized into soccer teams, which trained and competed fiercely among each other. By 1995, more than ten thousand boys were taking part in the mashraps. It gave them structure and a source of support and had only positive effects on the overall community. But the Chinese authorities saw only an alternative power structure to their own and a potential source of trouble.

The crackdown on the mashraps was precipitated by a movement among some mashrap members to boycott alcohol. Like drugs, alcohol had a negative social impact on Uyghur communities, and some mashraps encouraged their members not to drink, inspired also by the Islamic prohibition against alcohol. But most of the liquor stores throughout the Uyghur region were run by Han businessmen, and drinking is an important part of male Han culture. The decision to discourage alcohol usage was seen by the authorities as divisive and possibly a sign of latent "splittism." The authorities moved quickly to ban all mashraps and any associated gatherings, even including the soccer games that many boys loved and relied upon to give their after-school lives structure. Boys just like my brother had been. I could only imagine how different Kaisar's life might have been if he'd had access to a mashrap—he likely never would have gotten involved with drugs at all. He'd probably have been a doctor by now, perhaps even a father, and certainly a productive member of society instead of being locked away to rot in a jail cell.

After the ban, many of the mashraps simply went underground, but a few groups persisted openly. That year in Ghulja, the city west of Ürümchi where both of my parents were born, the mashraps organized a soccer tournament, and when the authorities refused to give permission for it to occur, more than a thousand people gathered to protest. They were met by heavily armed Han soldiers and military vehicles.

Although by some miracle no one died that day, the message was clear. No part of Uyghur life was safe; anything could be taken away from us at any time, even something like our children's soccer clubs.

Or our children's TV program.

Not long after I got back from my sick leave, I was called into a meeting. The bureau chief was there, along with several Communist Party representatives. It wasn't an extended meeting, but it changed everything about the way we worked.

The CCP officials were there to present us with "suggestions" for new programming. We were asked to present more bilingual programming and to use a lot less Uyghur-oriented content. It was clear to everyone that these suggestions were very much obligatory. As part of the new initiative, we were urged to produce "friendship programs" with Han students that showed both Uyghur and Han children playing and learning together.

It didn't necessarily look onerous on paper, but at the TV station, we all knew how different Han culture was from Uyghur culture: we have different languages, different religious beliefs, different music, a different history, different stories, different holidays and festivals, even different ways of interacting with each other. Han and Uyghur children didn't often spend time together, even when they attended the same schools. Parents discouraged it too. Han parents tended to teach their children that Uyghurs weren't safe, and Uyghur parents were afraid of their children being dragged into something they didn't understand, possibly putting themselves and their family members in danger.

By this point, in the run-up to the early 2000s, things were already looking dark, and then an official policy of so-called bilingual education was implemented across the Uyghur region. According to the official propaganda, it was a simple initiative to increase the Uyghur population's knowledge of Chinese. But in fact, it was a new major step toward the annihilation of Uyghur culture and the inculcation of Uyghurs with Han traditions, atheist attitudes and morals, and Chinese social mores. Educators, from elementary school teachers to university professors, had to change their language of instruction to Chinese. Even courses in Uyghur literature and the history of the Uyghur region, limited and biased as they were, had to be taught in Chinese. Uyghur textbooks were systematically destroyed and replaced by Chinese textbooks, and teachers were required to undergo a rigorous reeducation. When the legislation was enacted, it felt like the sudden blow of an axe. But the axe had been hanging over us for a decade.

It immediately proved difficult to produce these friendship programs. No matter what we did to make it convincing, everything seemed fake and staged. The Han children looked uncomfortable around the Uyghur children, and the Uyghur children looked frightened, as though their every gesture or expression would be interrogated, as it very well might be. No one could behave naturally on camera, and that of course affected my performance as well. I had a sinking feeling at the end of each taping, knowing that we'd have to rip it all apart and try to salvage whatever we could from the raw footage. Salvaging anything was getting harder and harder.

One day, I was called into the local CCP office and told that I had taught a confusing story on my program that would lead children to the wrong conclusions.

Surprised, I asked the officials what they meant. I couldn't think of anything I'd put on the show that would be confusing to children.

"You told a story about a sheep and a wolf, do you remember it?"

Of course I remembered the story. It's an ancient folktale that nearly every Uyghur knows. The story is fairly simple, and it was one my father had told me as a child.

A sheep and his three lambs live together in a cozy little house. One cold winter's day, the sheep goes out to find food, and on his way back home, he sees a wolf curled up outside in the freezing weather. As he approaches, he sees that the wolf has two small pups snuggled up against her belly. The sheep feels sorry for the wolf and her babies, and asks them why they're out in the cold. The wolf responds politely and says they're on their way to the city and have nowhere to stay on the road. The sheep invites them back to his house to get out of the cold. The wolf and her puppies trot along behind the sheep, seeming as gentle as can be. The wolf reassures the sheep that she's completely harmless—her legs are old and tired and she barely has any teeth left after her good long life. The sheep begins to trust the wolf, and eventually he has to go out again to find food, leaving his lambs alone with the wolf and her pups. When he returns, he finds that the wolf and her young are gone and there's nothing left of his beloved lambs but a few tufts of downy wool.

My father had made sure I understood the lesson: it's important to be kind and generous, but it's equally important to be wise in one's actions. One must always know one's enemy and not be deceived or too trusting in dealing with them. It was a lesson that any person could use in their everyday life. But the people at the Communist Party Office were convinced that I had aired it with a political intent.

"There are thousands of old stories. Out of all of them, why did you pick this one?"

"It's a straightforward story," I told them, trying to keep the indignation out of my voice. "I interpret it simply, and so do the children. People need to be careful in their judgments of whom to trust. Doesn't that apply in any culture or social situation?"

In the end, it didn't matter what I said in the meeting. They'd already made up their minds. I was told that in future before I could use a story in one of my productions, I had to clear it with the office. Only once they'd signed off could I use it. That was the beginning of the end of my editorial freedom at the television station. And I knew all of my Uyghur colleagues were finding themselves in the same boat.

While all of this was going on at work, Elzat and I were barely speaking. I came home each day exhausted and often went straight to bed. He was sleeping on the couch, and the apartment had taken on the chaotic look of an unhappy home.

One night I couldn't stand it, and I went out into the living room. "We have to do something about this situation, Elzat. One of us has to go away for a while."

"I won't give you a divorce," he said.

"Fine, but I won't live like this forever."

"I know," he said wearily. "I think maybe we do need some time apart, to remember what we appreciate about each other. Remember that grant I applied for to study abroad in Austria? I just heard that I got it."

"Good. I hope you'll be very successful." My voice was stiff and unnatural.

"I'll have to go to Beijing first for an intensive language class."

"Maybe you'll meet someone nice there," I said bitterly.

"Don't, Gul, please." He looked at me beseechingly. "I'm doing this for us. When I come back, things will be better between us, I promise."

"Fine," I said, not believing a word of it. "If you need help packing, let me know."

After Elzat went to Beijing, I was sent out into the field even more. Because I was a well-known figure by that time, the Communist Party officials at the station wanted to use my status in Uyghur society to promote a new social program ostensibly aimed at helping Uyghur get better schooling. The authorities in Beijing had started a program to send impoverished Uyghur kids away from their homes to get a Han education. It was a highly unpopular program among parents, of course, so I was ordered to produce stories encouraging parents to send their children to twelve different cities in China to study Chinese.

When I met these children, I saw firsthand how wrongheaded and cruel the idea was. The children were taken from the only homes they had known and the parents they loved and trusted and put into a completely unfamiliar environment. Separated from their language, people who loved them, and their own culture, they were put under appalling stress at such a young age. Some of them weren't eating; others missed their parents and friends so much that they could barely stop crying. It was unbearable to look into their eyes and see such pain there.

All while I was under orders to put together shows promoting this program, I wondered, If they really want to help us, why not build good schools in the Uyghur communities? If these children live in poverty, why not help their parents financially instead of taking their children away from them? It seemed that the point couldn't be to enrich the Uyghur communities and help the people but must be something much more insidious—to destroy Uyghur homes, families, and the passing down of culture and beliefs from one generation to the next. Removed from their parents, grandparents, and entire communities, these children were being set adrift, severed from their own heritage. All there was to grab on to was whatever their Han teachers and authorities threw to them, life rafts that could bring comfort only to the desperate.

It made me think back to Anargul and her brother in Opal Village, having to leave home just to try to get a basic education. I had tried more than once to find Anargul, but when I wrote to her village, no one returned my letters. I had hoped to send her some money to help her continue her own education, after she'd worked so hard to help her brother. But she had disappeared, perhaps into further poverty or perhaps toward something better. I had no way of knowing.

But I did know that no good would come of taking small children away from their parents. Still, on camera in show after show, I was required to say that it was an excellent policy, enacted for the good of the community. I had to talk about how much the Communist Party cares about Uyghur children and what amazing opportunities they've given them. *Look, the kids are so happy! They've never seen such big buildings and fancy cars before!*

But for kids, happiness has nothing to do with big buildings and fancy cars; it has to do with love and safety, family and friends. Those things were being taken away from them.

I was increasingly forced to lie to the kids I'd built my whole career around helping, and it was completely devastating.

Now, in interviews kids participating in the program would often cry when I asked them to describe their new lives away from home. So instead of letting them answer the questions their own way, I would have to write a script before each show. In the past, one of the main pleasures of our show for me—and for our viewers too—was the amazing and unexpected things the kids would say in front of the camera.

But for these segments, I had to coach each child carefully. One little girl looked barely older than five years old, and her tiny hands were almost too small to hold a microphone.

I led her onto the set gently. "Are you ready?" I asked her, forcing a smile.

She looked down and nodded, her small lips trembling.

"Listen, I'm going to ask you if you like studying here, and do you know what you're going to say?"

She nodded again.

"What will you say?"

"That I'm very happy studying here," she whispered.

"And then I'm going to ask you if you like the city. And what are you going to say?"

"That I like the city so much that I don't miss home anymore." Her voice was steady, but she had begun to cry silent tears.

My heart clenched like a fist. I felt like an abuser coaching a victim. I leaned down close to her ear and whispered very quietly, "I know you miss home. I know what you're feeling, and I feel awful too."

She wouldn't look me in the eye. Of course she didn't trust me—how could she?

One of our Han producers approached us, beckoning for the girl to come in front of the camera.

I straightened up and put on a fake smile. "I know this is your first time on television, and I know you're very nervous. But on camera, you have to seem happy, okay? Don't cry."

It was all an act. An insidious, oppressive sense of guilt invaded my life, staining everything I did. I loved those children. My whole career was built around them and the innocent joy they found in so many things. I remembered the eyes of those Uyghur kids. They were hoping I would help them go home, that I could bring a message to their parents to come take them back. But my hands were tied. Instead, I lied and said these were the luckiest children in Xinjiang.

My show had turned from a source of constant happiness in my life into a burden that weighed so heavily on me that I started to sleep fitfully, frequently waking up from nightmares. Sometimes I imagined what it would be like if I had children myself, knowing that the state could send them away from me anytime it wanted. How could I live with that, and how could I participate in promoting a policy I knew was deeply inhumane?

When I got back from filming those segments, I went to talk to my father. I was exhausted from the trip and could barely hold back my tears.

"I just don't think I have the strength to keep doing this anymore," I told him.

He looked at me with surprise. "What happened? You set aside lots of other opportunities so you could take this job. What's changed?"

When I told him what I'd seen, and all the suffering I'd witnessed in those children, he shook his head. "It's a big responsibility to be in a position like yours. Whatever is happening in the society, you have to confront it directly." He took my hand. "Daughter, all you can do is face it and not give up. You have to find the tiniest opportunity to give those kids hope. Even if there's only one minute in a thirty-minute program when you can tell them a little bit of our history or teach them to be proud of themselves for who they are, that's your victory."

But I struggled to do even that. Every second was tightly scripted. The censorship policies became more and more stringent. They controlled our topics, our scripts, our participants. They limited our budget to keep us on such a tight leash that I started to feel like I was choking.

It was more and more apparent that as an employee of Xinjiang TV, I was a cog in the enormous wheel of the official media, which is controlled tightly by the Chinese government. Then in 1997, over several days in February, Ghulja erupted into protests again. This time it turned violent. The mashraps hadn't completely dissolved in the years since they had been banned, and there was tremendous frustration that people weren't allowed to gather or speak freely, practice their own religion, or make a personal decision like not drinking. People shouted religious slogans, and some called for independence for East Turkestan. The Chinese authorities responded quickly and brutally with guns, police dogs, and tear gas. When the protesters refused to back down, and indeed, more citizens took to the streets over the coming days, the Chinese authorities bused in soldiers and security personnel from surrounding areas, even from as far as the Chinese city of Lanzhou. They locked down the city, and paramilitary police patrolled the alleys and terrorized ordinary citizens who crept out to do necessary tasks like buy groceries.

I knew about the protests, though not in detail, from friends and relatives in the area. They whispered on the phone that thousands of people had been arrested, and hundreds killed. There was talk from reputable sources that arrested protesters had been held outside in frigid temperatures after being sprayed with water cannons, leading to frostbite and even a few amputations. Everyone was living in fear, watched over by Han soldiers who clearly had no qualms about using force to keep the locals down.

That March, when I visited my parents' hometown of Ghulja with my father, as we did every year to see family, the city seemed completely different. It was as though a pall had fallen over every single household. No one spoke in the street or gave friendly greetings to neighbors, but instead people hurried on without looking anyone in the eye. You could feel the fear in the air like a miasma. Out shopping with my aunts and female cousins, we were stopped by Han policemen holding rifles. I'd never seen a gun before in my life and all of a sudden one was being pointed at my legs. The police demanded to see our IDs and when they saw I wasn't from Ghulja, they asked me questions about what I was doing there. I looked them in the eye as I spoke, not willing to show my fear to them. But when they finally let us go on to the market and we started to walk again, my legs were like jelly.

"That's how it is now," my aunt whispered, holding on to my arm tightly. "Who knows for how long. They're in control now."

My father had taught me that the Uyghurs had always ruled themselves, except for brief periods when they were dominated by another power like China. But hearing about the brutality in Ghulja, I didn't know what was possible anymore. The suppression had become blatant and violent, even though according to the Chinese themselves, the Uyghur region was supposedly an "Autonomous Region." Even in Ürümchi, it had begun to be difficult to speak openly to our neighbors and friends, so only rumors and whispers broke through the official stories broadcast on the mainstream TV and radio channels. But it was discussed elsewhere, even around the world. Years later, I learned that the Ghulja massacre led directly to the US Congress voting to expand their Radio Free Asia broadcast coverage to include a Uyghur-language service.

After what became known as the Ghulja massacre, all the employees of Xinjiang TV were required to study the Chinese language and Chinese political thought. We had constant political propaganda meetings involving indoctrination and recitation of slogans, and we had to change our programming to suit Beijing's line. Out were stories from the classical Uyghur canon, and in were stories about the Chinese emperors and their exploits.

I kept going into the office early and leaving late, working hard; at that point, it was all I knew how to do. Elzat was in Beijing, my parents and friends were busy with their own lives, and I was trying to keep up with all of the pressure at the TV station. I was an assistant producer, so I had some level of responsibility. I was also allowed into parts of the station I hadn't been allowed into before, like the tape room where raw footage was kept.

One day, I was in the tape room looking for a tape that had been marked for reuse. As I searched the shelves for something we could tape over, I caught sight of one labeled *Ghulja 1997*. My heart thumped in my ears so loudly I thought everyone in the station must have been able to hear it. Before I could reconsider, I grabbed it, shoved it into the player, and watched as protesters appeared in front of me. The camera angle was from high above, perhaps the top of a building, and the crowd below seemed so small and vulnerable. But the people were lifting their fists, shouting, standing together in solidarity. For a moment, my heart lifted. They were so brave, and it gave me a flash of hope. Then I remembered those policemen aiming their guns at me and my aunts and cousins. I remembered the streets of Ghulja seeming like a ghost town, and all of the brutality that had followed the protests. Then it hit me: some of the people I was looking at were probably dead.

I heard a sound at the door and hurried to put the tape back in its sleeve. I went out, pretending like nothing had happened. But after that, I couldn't look at a Han policeman the same way. Each one had become a potential murderer.

Soon I was sent to undergo bilingual training so that I could broadcast in both Chinese and Uyghur. Although my Chinese was excellent and I had an easier time with it than many of my colleagues, the political pressure was like a ticking time bomb. In my travels, I was also increasingly aware of the disparities between the way Han and Uyghur people were expected to live. Many of the benefits that the burgeoning economy of late-twentieth-century China had brought to Han citizens had not reached Uyghur communities. It was obvious just walking around the cities and towns: the Uyghur-populated areas were poor and tended to be pushed to the outskirts, while Han areas had better infrastructure, better waste disposal, better transportation, better access to services of all kinds. Even in areas with a high Uyghur population and some Uyghur representatives, like in the southern part of East Turkestan, everything was ultimately controlled by Han officials, party secretaries, and police. All of the Communist Party secretaries in the government bureaus, private enterprises, and state-owned enterprises were Han. Uyghurs weren't allowed within the upper echelons of the society, where our fate was decided in many decisions both large and small. That meant that economic power, political power, and increasingly social power were all concentrated in the hands of newcomers to the region who didn't understand the Uyghur language or culture, and who in fact denigrated anything Uyghur as being backward. To them, Uyghur culture was a threat to be stamped out.

I saw clearly that the programs we produced no longer represented the truth. My scripts were edited heavily to present Chinese government policies in the most positive light, while covering up the Uyghur people's suffering. I couldn't film children speaking naturally or behaving naturally. We came under stricter and stricter censorship, until nearly all of what I was told to say I no longer believed myself.

Elzat returned from Beijing after six months, and almost immediately he started preparing to go to Austria to continue his studies. I'd gotten stronger in his absence, although sometimes I'd be walking down the street or riding on the bus, minding my business, and I'd see a happy couple in front of me, holding hands or leaning against each other, and I'd feel a sharp pain go through me. I had become more independent and was making my own decisions now, but it had come at a terrible cost.

His visiting scholar visa from the State Education Commission finally came through and he left for Europe in the late fall. I didn't even see him off at the airport. I was busy filming a segment for another "friendship program." In my heart, I had already said goodbye to him a hundred times over.

I was working long hours and barely home at all at that point. All I did at the apartment was sleep and occasionally fix something to eat, and that suited me just fine. The place was too full of unhappy memories for me to be comfortable there.

The millennium was approaching, and for the big transition, my team and I were working on a special New Year's program. It was all in Chinese instead of Uyghur, as all our programs were now. We had several different segments about how to kick off the new millennium right, how to let go of the past and set out toward the future with a clean slate. We had suggestions for how viewers could better themselves—including the obligatory suggestion to work hard to learn Chinese—and how they could stop being weighed down by things that were no longer positive influences in their lives.

As I walked home on New Year's Eve, I thought to myself: Here you're telling all your viewers that they have to have a plan for the new era, a new beginning. What about you?

I spotted an internet café near my apartment that was still open despite the holiday. I didn't want to go straight home anyway. I had just learned how to use email, and I decided to send a message to Elzat:

> Happy New Year. Today is the last day of December of 1999. A new year is beginning. I told viewers today how to prepare for a new beginning, what we should do, what we should have, what we all deserve to have. For my whole life I've been thinking about the happiness of everyone around me. I've just followed along, making sure everyone else is satisfied. I think now I need to begin this year with honesty. So first, I want to be honest with you. If you're happy, if you can find a new love or a new life there in Europe, I want you to know that I'll be glad for you. I feel now that my life is better without you. I've decided I want a divorce. We don't have to hurt each other or our families. We can just do it quietly. But we have to begin to follow our hearts.

My heart was pounding and my face felt hot as I hit the send button. I hadn't even known what I would say when I'd started writing, but I found that I said what I'd really been thinking. I stood up slowly from the computer station and went home.

I'd been in bed already for a few hours when the phone woke me up.

"I'm coming home tomorrow."

"Elzat," I put a hand over my eyes, "it's the middle of the night here."

"I just want to come home to you. I don't want to study anymore. I just want to be with you. I'm only here because I wanted to make you proud. I don't want to lose you. You might feel like you can live without me, but I can't live without you. I told you that I don't love anybody else. I never will."

I listened patiently as he talked, but all I could think was that he didn't have the courage to take the next step in his own life. He didn't have the courage to get divorced and live with the embarrassment. And he wouldn't have the courage to marry a Han Chinese woman, even if he loved her. But he was in Europe, no longer under the thumb of our traditions. He could take a chance if he wanted to. And I could tell from his eyes in the pictures that he loved the thin Han woman standing next to him.

Finally he paused to take a breath. I said, "Why don't you just marry that Han woman and live in Europe?"

"You are my wife and I'm your husband. That's how it is. I'm coming home."

My patience broke. "Don't put this on me, Elzat. If you don't want to stay there and study hard, don't pretend it's all because of me. You're there because of your family, and because you want to make something of your future. And you can be sure of this—if you come back, I'll leave. I can't live with you anymore. Do you really want to give up everything that you have there just to come home to an empty apartment?"

"I'll stay here if that's what you really want." He sounded defeated. "But you have to come see me. We have to spend some time together.

Look, if you come here and it doesn't work out, I promise I'll give you a divorce. But we have to give it a real chance. Don't we still owe our families that much?"

I thought about it for a long moment. He wasn't going to give in and I was tired of fighting over the phone. Maybe if I could see him in person, I could convince him that we both needed to move on. I said, "Okay, I'll come. If I can get a passport and a visa."

At that point, it was already difficult for Uyghurs to leave the country, and very few Uyghurs were issued a passport when they applied for one. It was yet another form of control. The Chinese government, increasingly worried about dissident activities abroad, was not at all eager to have Uyghurs share their experiences with the outside world. But because of my status as a TV personality, I was able to get a passport with the backing of the station. And since I was applying for a spousal visa for visiting scholars, all we needed was for Elzat's sponsoring professor to sign off on it. In a matter of a few months, I had all of my paperwork in hand.

While the applications were grinding through the official channels, my family got some of the best news we'd had in years. One evening our lawyer called to say that my brother was being released from jail early for good behavior. He had provided medical treatment to many of the other inmates, taught Chinese, encouraged his fellow prisoners to study and better themselves, and in general had been a model prisoner. On the few occasions when he had been accused of fighting inside, our lawyer had stepped up and demonstrated with testimony from other inmates that my brother was the target, not the aggressor.

The night Kaisar came home, my mother couldn't stop touching his face, as though she couldn't believe he was really there. My father walked around with a smile that we hadn't seen for what felt like decades. My brother looked older and moved more warily, jumping at little sounds. But he settled back into the house quickly and it felt like we began a new life as a family. Suddenly, there was animation in my parents' faces that hadn't been there for the better part of a decade. My mother's laughter rang out from the dinner table again, and my father had a spring in his step that took years off of his age. Seeing my brother on the couch reading the paper with my father or eating the food my mother lovingly prepared for him—in her eyes, he had gotten much too thin—I felt a lightness in my heart that I thought had left my life for good.

My trip was still weighing on me, however. My family just thought that I was a lucky girl, heading off to Europe to spend some quality time with my man. In fact, I intended to go, talk things through with Elzat, and then come home and tell them that we were getting a divorce. I couldn't tell them now and cast a shadow over everyone's happiness so soon after my brother had finally come home.

Two nights before I was to fly to Vienna, I had my twenty-eighth birthday. My parents threw a party in a restaurant in the center of Ürümchi. They booked three tables and everyone—Mehray, my cousin and his wife, several of my friends from the TV station, Kaisar, my aunt and uncle—came in the best of spirits to wish me a happy birthday and to give me a good send-off. The restaurant served huge platters of *polo* with lamb, plates of noodles cooked with luscious chicken on the bone, big baskets of plump pillowy nan, and thin succulent skewers of roasted spiced meats. There was also entertainment: women in long dresses with gold embroidery dancing Uyghur dances to live music that I knew so well and had loved my whole life. The singers and dancers all knew me, and they took turns wishing me bon voyage and teasing me about being reunited with my handsome husband at last.

Even my beloved grandmother came to the party. My grandfather had passed years ago, and she had just turned eighty and was in a wheelchair, but she insisted on being part of the celebration. She had even worn a new silk headscarf for the occasion. She barely ate anything at the meal, but clapped along to the music like a young girl. And everything was all the sweeter for the whole family because my brother was with us, quieter than he had been and more watchful, but also gradually returning to the person we all remembered.

It was an extravagant occasion to mark a crucial turning point in my life. Of course at the time, I had no reason to think that it would be my last birthday with my extended family and the last time I would see most of my friends ever again.

At the end of the evening, I gave my mom a huge hug and thanked her for planning the evening for me. "I'm only going to be gone for three months!" I said, laughing a little. "You didn't have to do all this for me."

My mother ran a hand over my hair. It was still shorter than it had ever been before, but silky and thick as ever. "Three months can be a long time, my darling."

"Long enough to learn a little English!"

We all laughed, but my father suddenly seemed serious.

"It's an opportunity, daughter. To learn, to broaden your horizons, to think about the future. Europe also has a great, ancient culture, just like ours. You know, not many Uyghurs have a chance to travel now. You should take every advantage of being there."

"I'll do my best," I said.

"You always do." He kissed me on the forehead.

Kaisar hugged me, and I whispered in his ear, "Take care of them. They're not getting any younger."

A carefree smile I recognized from a long-gone time swept across his face. "Don't worry, Gul. I'll be the responsible one while you're gone. Promise."

My grandmother reached up to me from her wheelchair and held on to my wrist. "Gulchehra, come stay with me tonight, the way you did when you were young."

"Good," my mother said. "You take Grandma home and your brother will come home with us."

Once we got back to her house and had gotten ready for bed, my grandmother came into the little bedroom where I had spent countless nights as a girl. She had taken off her fancy silk hijab and had wrapped her old cotton headscarf over her hair. "Come kneel with me. Help me out of this chair."

She seemed as light as a little bird as I helped her out of the wheelchair and down onto a cushion on the floor. Her bones felt thin and fragile, like the slightest touch might injure her.

She began to pray, asking for my safe passage to Europe and that I might have a long and happy life ahead of me. "Gulchehra, you've always been my little angel. I might pass on to the next stage before you come back, but I don't want you to be too sad. There's nothing to worry about. I've had such a fortunate life. I'm ready to go."

I shook my head. "Grandma, you're not going anywhere. I need you!"

She smiled a little. Then she opened the Qur'an and began to read aloud. She read for a very long time. Her voice was reedy but still strong. Then she placed something in my palm and folded my fingers around it. It was an amulet for protection called a *tumar*. She had made it herself by writing prayers on a piece of paper, placing the paper inside a square of black leather and folding the leather diagonally so that it formed a small triangle about the length of a finger. She had sewn the edges together and attached a simple black cord so I could wear it around my neck.

"This will keep you safe from evil influences, my child. I've written all of my prayers for you in it." She squeezed my hand tightly. "Keep it with you. You'll need it in all the faraway places you're going to go."

When I left her house the next morning, we both cried as we said goodbye. I had spent so much of my childhood with her, eating lunch at her table when I was in elementary school, running to her when I had a problem or needed someone to talk to. She had always been there for me, and I felt that keenly as the taxi pulled away from her house. When I left, she was still crying into her sleeve like we'd never see each other again. I watched her from the taxi window for as long as I could, until she slowly faded from view.

PART IV

A NEW START AND A NEW LOW

Stepping out of the airport in Vienna, I was surrounded by unfamiliar languages, smells, and faces. It was my first time being so far from home, and I felt like I'd been dropped down a long chute that had hurled me into a completely new world. Elzat came to meet me, and we greeted each other like distant acquaintances. I was shocked at how thin he'd gotten. It looked as though he was skipping more meals than he was eating. We took the train to Wattens, a quiet old city near the Austrian border with Italy, where he was studying at the university. I had read that the headquarters of the Swarovski crystal company was there, and I tucked that away in the back of my head. Everyone would expect me to bring home presents.

We didn't talk much in the first few weeks. Elzat studied at the university for most of the day, and I was left alone in his apartment. I did wander some around Wattens, which has beautiful old European architecture and big open plazas. But not speaking any German or English, I couldn't communicate with anyone. I hated not being able to understand what people occasionally said to me on the street.

So I got into the habit of staying in the apartment most days. I quickly read through all of the books in Elzat's place—he wasn't much of a reader, aside from his studies—so I started surfing the Web. I'd never had access to a computer at home before, and I was completely shocked by what I discovered online.

When I searched in the Uyghur language, sites popped up that I had never come across back home. I didn't then fully understand the idea of a firewall or blocked websites, but it became obvious to me very quickly that the Chinese Web was not an open and unbiased source of information. The more I looked, the more I found. Activist websites detailing the abuses Uyghurs had suffered at the hands of Han policemen. Long explanations of the history of East Turkestan and how Chinese rule had only come about as recently as the 1700s, when the area was conquered by the hostile Qing Dynasty. That wasn't what we'd learned in school—we'd been taught that Xinjiang had always been part of China, and that we and our Han compatriots were all "brothers from the same womb." Of course, I'd known better from what my father had hinted. But now I knew there were limits to what he had felt safe telling me, even in the privacy of our own home. To see it all laid out so clearly and publicly came as a revelation.

When I was young, my father told me about the proud blue and white flag of East Turkestan but reminded me never to speak of it in front of others. And whenever I would visit him or my aunt at the Xinjiang Regional Museum, my father encouraged me to look at the exhibits and study our history.

"But don't believe the signs on the exhibits," he'd said in a low, serious voice. "They aren't accurate. If you're curious about something, come to me."

With this new, unfettered access to the world via the internet, I found things that shocked me to my core. Although I had a firsthand understanding of the difficulties the Uyghur people face in China, I had no idea about the range of atrocities that had been committed against them. Staring at the screen until my eyes ached, I read reports from Uyghur dissidents about their personal experiences and what they had suffered. Descriptions of brutality. Endless incarcerations. Rape. Executions. I devoured Western news reports about the Chinese government's violent suppression of freedom of religion and freedom of speech. It was all laid out in front of me, sometimes with horrific photographs as evidence.

Also, for the first time, I was able to freely listen to the Uyghur news broadcast of Radio Free Asia. Back home, huddled around the radio in a relative's house, I had heard one broadcast of RFA. But, because the station is blocked there, the sound was so badly distorted that it was hard to understand anything, and we only listened for about ten minutes before turning it off. There would have been serious consequences if we were discovered secretly tuning in to banned programs.

During the day, I read everything I could about the situation back home, and each night I lay awake, unable to stop thinking about what I'd just seen. Elzat was too involved in his studies to listen to me talk about it, and he didn't care about politics anymore. But I read about the East Turkestan Independence Movement, and everything I read made sense. The Chinese government had set out to systematically destroy Uyghur culture, along with anyone who tried to resist that oppression. As an authoritarian regime benefiting from the land and vast resources in the Uyghur region, the government wasn't just going to let us live the way we wanted to live. What else but independence could save my people and my culture?

Sitting in that cramped apartment near the university, I listened to the RFA Uyghur broadcast every afternoon. And afterward, I would often sit in complete silence, thinking about my life back home, asking myself the difficult questions that I hadn't before been equipped to ask, let alone answer. It wasn't just what was happening to my people; it was also my role in it.

For certain, I had been used by the Chinese government. My CCP minders at the TV station had promised that after I came back from Europe, I would be promoted. They would give me a role as a top presenter, and I would be the first at the station to experiment with livestreaming, which had a lot of potential for children's shows. They promised me additional training, a master's degree from the prestigious China Central Radio and Television University in Beijing—everything would be paid for by Xinjiang TV.

A few months earlier, I had still been enticed by those opportunities; now I knew it was all bribes to keep me under their thumb. They were providing an easy route to the top, and who knew how far I could go. But from the distance of thousands of miles away, I could see that my career goals, my progress up the ladder—it all had become the government's plan, not mine. The more skilled I was and the more famous I became, the more they could use me to further their goals.

Sitting in that apartment, I thought about my education at the Normal University, much of which had been geared toward teaching. I thought about Anargul and how much she and her family had sacrificed to put her brother through school. I thought about Abdul, and how he had never wavered from his commitment to go back to his small hometown and teach the local children.

I had started out that way too. I had wanted to give Uyghur children the gift of their own culture, to teach them our values, like honesty, like how to be a good citizen, like how to respect others and themselves. But the longer I was in TV, and paradoxically, the higher up in the hierarchy I went, the less freedom I had to teach any of those things. Instead, I had to parrot the CCP party line, telling Uyghur children that the Chinese Communist Party loves them like a father and that they must love it back. I had to teach them to be ashamed of their own language and to reject their own ancient music and books and stories. That Uyghur culture was backward; Chinese culture was the future. Every day when I went to work, I was being untruthful, not only to my viewers but also to myself. I couldn't look at myself in the mirror anymore. With my fake lipsticked smile and perfectly coiffed hair and blank eyes, I didn't even recognize the person I'd become.

There in that university apartment halfway across the world from my home, I spent a month peering into my own soul. I didn't like what I saw.

Elzat hardly knew what to do with me. I think he sensed that our life together was one of the lies that I just couldn't stand to perpetuate anymore. But he tried his best to please me. We took a bus to Paris for two nights—I had heard so much about it and wanted to see it for myself. Still, as we strolled along the Seine at dusk, what should have been a romantic moment was instead a strained effort. Neither of us had much of anything to say to each other.

I also traveled to Germany, but for that trip I had a very different purpose in mind. I wanted to visit an acquaintance from college who had moved to Munich right after graduation. I had heard vague rumors that he'd gotten involved in political issues, but of course back home, no one was willing, or perhaps able, to talk about it in any detail. I was determined to find out for myself. I sent him an email, and he responded by inviting us to visit for a few days.

But this time I went on my own. I didn't want Elzat's attitudes impinging on my ability to make my own decisions. I needed to be alone, to think, to experience, and to judge for myself. The second day there, my friend and his wife invited me to a protest that afternoon in the Marienplatz for Uyghur human rights. I was too curious to say no, but at the same time I felt terrified. A single photo could destroy everything I'd worked for. I had been trained my whole life to be cautious when expressing opinions that might be politically dangerous, and my caution had only increased the older I got and the more I understood. But this was my chance to see what the rest of the world had been doing while I was playing it safe.

That afternoon, I went to the square with my friends. A small crowd of Uyghurs had formed, with some of the women wearing the hijab and some dressed more like me. They were very orderly and calm, but when some signal came that I didn't hear, they all began to raise their placards and shout slogans in Uyghur, German, and English.

"Free East Turkestan!"

"Free the Uyghurs!"

"Stop the human rights abuses!"

My heart was pounding so hard I thought it might explode in my chest. I had never heard words like that spoken aloud before. I was on the other side of the square by a row of local shops, too afraid to get closer. But I could see the placards with slogans and some with photos of people who had been unjustly imprisoned or tortured by the government. So many stories, so much pain—it was all so horrifying to contemplate.

What kind of coward are you? I asked myself furiously. My brain and my stomach were both spinning. *Why aren't you out there with them?*

After seeing the bravery of those protesters, I knew I had to change everything. I couldn't just compartmentalize what I'd seen, return home to my apartment and my nice things, and go on spewing CCP propaganda to the very people those policies were destroying.

When I got back to Elzat's apartment in Wattens, I renewed my studies on the Uyghur condition with even more fervor. So much information was inaccessible to the people inside the Uyghur region, and I wanted to absorb as much of it as I possibly could. And then, after more than a month of painful soul-searching and internet searching, I unexpectedly came across a name I knew: Dolkun Kamberi.

Dolkun had been my father's colleague at the Xinjiang Regional Museum. He was also trained as an archaeologist, and he and my father had been close. Dolkun and his wife and daughter lived in the same apartment complex as my family when I was small. He'd left to study in America and had never returned. My father told me that he had gone to work for an American news agency. And here his name was, on the RFA website. And next to his name was a phone number.

I stared at that number for what felt like hours. It was like looking into a deep chasm with an unknowable bottom. I gently caught hold of the *tumar* hanging around my neck that my grandmother had given me. The comforting leather amulet felt warm against my skin, like my grandmother's hand. I heard the sound of her voice again, praying for my safety and happiness, asking Allah to bless me with wisdom and courage. I needed all of that now.

Taking a deep breath, I picked up the phone and dialed the number.

"Dr. Dolkun Kamberi?"

"Yes?" came the cautious reply.

"This is Gulchehra Hoja. Professor Abdulqeyyum Hoja's daughter."

There was a pause. He had left East Turkestan almost two decades before, perhaps he didn't remember me. And then, "Little Gul! How are you calling me? Where are you?"

My words came out in a rush, like I'd been waiting for years to speak. "I'm in Europe and I saw your name on the RFA website and now that I've listened to your program online, I just know that I have to work for you. That is, if you'll have me. I can't go back to the Uyghur region after everything I've learned. I feel so guilty about what I've been doing back home. I've had a successful career. But after listening to your program, I know I've just been parroting CCP propaganda. I loved my job. I love journalism. But I want to do something beneficial for my people, not teach them lies about themselves and their history. Of course I want to stay in journalism and do good work. But I can't see a future for myself back home anymore. I can't go back there."

"Gulchehra." Dolkun sounded shocked. "Listen, I know you're a big star right now back home. You've got family, you have all your fans, you have a life there. Are you sure you can give up everything to come here? Please, think about it carefully. It's a decision you won't be able to take back. Think once, and then think on it again."

"I've thought about nothing else for a month!" I cried. "I know my own mind."

He was silent for a moment. Then he said quietly, "Gul, you're your father's only daughter. I know how much they love you and how difficult it's going to be for them. Please, ask your father first before you make this decision."

My heart sank. "But if I ask him, of course he'll say no! He doesn't want me to go anywhere." I had to make Dolkun understand. "If I tell my father, and he says no, I wouldn't be able to do what I have to do. Please don't ask me to tell him. This is the first truly adult decision of my life. I have to make it myself."

He agreed to help me. He understood the gravity of the decision I was facing, and perhaps he didn't want to interfere in a moment that would change my life completely. He told me he would set up a meeting between me and the vice president of RFA.

When I told Elzat about the meeting, he scoffed at the idea that I could get a job in America.

"How are you going to work somewhere where you don't even speak the language?"

"I know it's an issue," I admitted. "But I have to give it my best shot."

"Gul, you're playing with fire," he said. "How on earth do you think this is all going to turn out?"

"I don't know," I told him quietly. I just knew that the course of my life was changing rapidly and I needed to swim as hard as I could to keep my head above water.

Two weeks later, I found myself in the lobby of a hotel in a nice neighborhood in Vienna. Elzat came with me, to help me navigate the train system. The HR director of RFA came down to the lobby to greet me and asked us up to his suite of rooms, where I sat at a little table by the window.

He had come to Europe just to meet with me, but when he started to speak to me in rapid-fire English, I couldn't keep up. I knew a tiny bit of the language by now, but not enough to have a conversation. I tried to use my travel dictionary to translate what he was saying, but it was impossible. And I couldn't express myself.

The HR director listened politely as I stumbled over a few phrases, but finally he told me, "If you don't know English, there's really nothing we can do. How can you live and work in America as a journalist if you don't know the language?"

I was desperate. My lack of English was a serious impediment, but I was good at languages. I had learned Chinese, and I figured I would be able to learn English as well. But since the HR director didn't speak Chinese, let alone Uyghur, it was beginning to look like I really had wasted everyone's time. I could feel Elzat's disapproving eyes on me.

But then I caught sight of a woman moving in the other room of the suite. She looked Han Chinese. I called to her. "Hi, can you speak Chinese?"

"Yes, of course," she said.

"Are you from the mainland?" I asked cautiously.

She smiled. "It's okay. I'm from Taiwan."

"Please," I said, "you've come all this way, and I just want to tell you why I want to work for RFA. Please just listen to me for five minutes. Will you translate for me?"

The woman, who turned out to be the wife of the HR director, was very kind and agreed to translate. In Chinese, I told her why I was so eager to work for RFA. I talked about government policy and what I had witnessed in the Uyghur region. I told her that I could no longer function in that repressive environment, but that I couldn't stop speaking for my people. I also told her how I wanted to develop the Uyghur broadcasts at RFA and what I thought could be improved. Everything I couldn't tell her husband in English, I described to her in Chinese.

She seemed taken aback by my intensity and translated quickly for her husband. His face changed and suddenly he seemed more interested.

"Okay," he said finally, "I'm going to give you a set of facts, and I want you to write up some news for me using them. I'll give you ten minutes to do the story."

His wife translated for him and rattled off a short list of items.

It took me two minutes to write a story on the hotel pad of paper. I was so used to producing programs quickly for Xinjiang TV that it didn't seem like a challenge at all.

The HR director seemed impressed. He pulled out a small recording device and handed me a Uyghur newspaper. "Okay, now I want you to read this article aloud for me, like you were doing it on a newscast. Don't worry, you can practice it a few times before I record. We just need to know how you sound on tape."

I took the paper and said, "I don't have to practice it. I'll just read it."

"Are you sure?"

I nodded and he started the recording. I read it through smoothly without any breaks or mistakes.

The HR director's eyebrows raised nearly to his hairline. "How many years have you been working in TV?" he asked me, through his wife.

Relief flooded through me. I smiled and said, "A few more than I'd like to admit."

He laughed. "Give us a few days, and we'll be in touch."

About a week later, I received an email with an official job offer from RFA. If I signed on, they would start the process to get me a visa to the United States. If I took this leap, I would never be able to go home. My grandmother, my parents, my brother, my cousins, all of my dearest friends—they would be as remote from me as the moon was from the earth. It was unimaginable. But it was also inconceivable that I would go back to my old life. That life—that me—didn't exist anymore.

First I had to tell Elzat. I had no idea what his reaction was going to be, but if I was really planning on turning our lives upside down, I had to give him a chance to tell me how he felt. I wasn't so naive as to think that my decision wouldn't affect him.

I broached the topic one night after a simple dinner, while I was sitting on the couch and he was at his desk studying. That was the way we had spent nearly all of the evenings since I'd gotten there—in the same room, but apart.

"Elzat, I have to talk to you."

"Mm," he said, still reading.

"No, I mean I really have to talk to you. It's serious."

He sighed and put down his pencil. "I know I've been very busy since you've gotten here. But I can't fall behind in my classes just because my wife is visiting. Other students have wives and they still get their work done."

"I won't take too much of your time," I said.

Something in my voice made him close his book and look at me.

"I'm not going back to Ürümchi."

"What do you mean, you're not going back?"

"I got the job. I'm going to America to work at RFA."

He sat back in his chair, stunned. "What do you mean, work in America? You don't know anything about America!"

"No, I don't know anything about America," I said calmly. "But I do know something about the Uyghur region. And I can't go back there the way things are."

"Gulchehra, I don't understand what I'm hearing."

I could hear the anger and panic rising in his voice. "I know this is hard for you. But I have to start living my life the way I need to. I can't just do what's expected of me anymore."

"And you have to go to America to do that?"

"Yes."

He shook his head disbelievingly. "I don't know what's gotten into you. Have you talked to your parents about this?"

"No." I felt a sharp pinch of alarm. "And they can't know anything until I get there. It isn't safe."

"Is this about all that stuff you've been reading on the internet? You've never been political before."

"Yes, I have. I just haven't been able to express it freely. Back home, everything is political—our language, our religion, our culture, even our dance! And I'm not going to be a puppet anymore, just saying the lines I'm supposed to say. I want to help our people, not try to hoodwink them!"

Elzat slowly lowered his head into his hands. He sat there without moving as the minutes ticked past. I felt like I was holding my breath. In the time I'd known him, he'd become less and less predictable to me. After the incident with the kitchen knife, I had no idea how he might respond.

"I can't force you to go back," he said slowly, his voice sounding rusty. "I can't force you to do anything now. But if you go to America, I'm coming with you."

"No!" the word exploded from my mouth before I knew what I was saying. "How can you come with me? You're in school here. You won't have a visa, and what about your family back home? It wouldn't make sense."

"You may not like it," he said wearily, "but I am still your husband. I can't let you go to some foreign country on your own. People will take advantage of you, or hurt you, or who knows what. I won't allow it."

I knew what he was offering to sacrifice for me and my eyes filled with tears. After everything, he still felt responsible for me. He still couldn't let go of his sense of duty. I didn't love him anymore, but I respected him for his sense of honor.

"Okay," I said, hearing a new steely note in my own voice, "if that's what you really want. We'll go together."

So it was decided: we would both go to the United States, carrying our broken hearts with us.

We spent the next month preparing. Neither of us had brought more to Europe than would fit in a suitcase. Objects were simple; the logistics were less so. I had to get in touch with RFA and ask them to apply for a spousal visa along with my work visa. Elzat had to deal with his surprised professor and the university red tape. He wouldn't be able to get a degree before he left, so it was as though all of his study in Austria had been wasted. But he didn't complain about that, or anything else. He had clearly resigned himself to letting me take the lead and make decisions for the both of us for the first time in our relationship. It must have cost him a lot. Perhaps part of him really did still love me.

We planned to leave in mid-September. My European visa expired on October 1, 2001, so it was a relief when our American visas were approved, pending a final interview. Most of our things were already packed and the apartment seemed to echo as we moved around it. Neither of us said anything to our families back home, or our friends. It was too much of a risk for anyone to know anything, and I had no idea how my parents would react. My mother would be devastated, I knew that much. I hadn't even gotten to say a real goodbye. And although I was hardly some high-level official defecting, there would be a price to pay for my decision not to go back to the Uyghur region. I had no idea the terror that was awaiting us, but I wasn't naive enough to think that the Chinese government would just let me go quietly.

Everything went smoothly until one day when I was watching the international news in English on TV, as I often did in the afternoon. I still couldn't understand any of it, but I was trying to get the sounds of the language into my head. I knew I had to start somewhere, and do it quickly. Suddenly, the broadcast cut away from the news anchor and to a live feed. I watched in disbelief and horror as totally unimaginable images played out in front of my eyes: smoke billowing out of skyscrapers, fire and exploding windows, terrified sobbing onlookers. Then a tower collapsing in an enormous cloud of dust and debris. I couldn't fathom what could possibly be happening. I switched the channel to a German news station, but it was like I'd never touched the remote; every channel had the same images, the same unbelievable footage.

I did the only thing I could think of, which was to call Dolkun Kamberi.

"What's happening there?" I blurted out as soon as he answered.

"No one knows," he said. He sounded frightened and harried. "We're getting the story now."

"Is the US under attack?"

"No one knows anything right now. They're saying it might be al-Qaeda."

"What's that?"

"Some terrorist group. We don't have any details."

"What can I do?" I asked. "There must be something."

"Not from over there." Dolkun spoke quickly, "Look, I can't talk now. Sit tight and wait for me to call you, okay?"

I put the phone down and sat staring at the wall above the TV. My already uncertain future had just turned even more chaotic. If America was at war, my personal problems were so tiny as to be insignificant. But it still meant that I'd be stranded illegally in Europe or be forced to go back to a life full of lies and increasing repression. My one avenue of escape had suddenly been closed off.

The next day, I read the coverage in Chinese on the CCTV website. Even if it wasn't unbiased news, at least I could get the gist of what was happening. The American government announced that all US embassies around the world would shut down for one month. One month! My visa would expire on October 1. That meant that in the best-case scenario, I would overstay my visa by two weeks or more. The thought frightened me. The last thing I wanted was to be stopped at the border and sent to China.

In the last week of my legal stay in Europe, I got my hair cut in a short bob. I wanted to look serious, and I thought longer hair made me look younger. I had the equivalent of only a few hundred dollars left, but I spent more than a hundred to buy myself a sleek Hugo Boss suit. It was black with a high-necked pale blue silk camisole, and it made me feel like an adult in a way I hadn't before in all the years I'd spent on camera working with kids. Then, I'd wanted to be approachable, friendly, warm, like a big sister. Now, I was preparing myself for a new challenge, and really the only thing I could control was how I appeared to the outside world.

After my visa expired, I didn't leave the apartment for fear of being stopped in the street and asked to show my papers. I didn't even know if that happened in Europe, but it certainly happened in the Uyghur region, and I couldn't risk it. I was terrified that somehow the Chinese government would know what I was up to and find me, even in the middle of a small town in Austria. I had no idea what they were capable of, and I didn't want to take any chances.

My appointment for the final visa interview had been scheduled for the middle of September. But I had to wait until the embassy reopened on October 11. When it did, Elzat and I were the first in line that morning. Everyone at the embassy seemed tense, but everything was moving efficiently, and before I knew it, we had our visas in hand.

The next morning, we went to a travel agency to buy tickets for twice the price we had expected. Elzat had to pay with the last of his student stipend. The following day, I found myself on a plane to Washington, DC, en route to my new life.

The morning after the flight, still dizzy from fatigue and jet lag, I went to work.

I made up my face carefully and made sure my bobbed hair was smooth and in place. I ironed my new suit until it draped perfectly on my body. Then I straightened my shoulders and took a deep breath. I was as ready as I'd ever be.

Dolkun was first to greet me, beaming at me with a warm smile. "Here's the gem we stole from the CCP!" he announced to the whole office.

I felt my face turning red. But everyone was friendly and introduced themselves. It was a relief to hear Uyghur spoken around me again, and I realized in a rush how lonely I had been the whole time I'd been in Europe.

Dolkun took me into the large, pleasant office of the vice president of RFA. A young Uyghur man in a sports jacket was also there, and he stood up when we came through the door.

"You know Arslan already, right?" Dolkun said.

I nodded. Arslan had picked us up at Washington Dulles Airport, took us to our hotel, and helped us get checked in.

"Well, as the administrative assistant for the Uyghur program," Dolkun continued, "he's really the one who's in charge around here. He'll help with things until you get settled in."

Arslan offered a quick, broad grin that lit up his handsome face. "Whatever it is, don't hesitate to ask."

I nodded shyly, surprised by my own reaction. I hadn't truly noticed another man since I'd gotten married, even though the marriage had been unhappy from the start. I'd been too tired at the airport to notice how attractive Arslan was. Still, I couldn't ignore the little thrill I felt during the meeting whenever he turned his serious dark eyes toward me.

"Gulchehra, it's wonderful to have you here at last!" the vice president said.

"I'm delighted to be here," I said. "It's like out of a dream." I meant it. Never in a thousand years could I have imagined I would be standing in the office of a radio station in America, preparing to start a new job. If I let myself stop and think for a single second, everything seemed so disorienting that I would begin to feel faint.

The vice president handed me a packet of information. "There's some paperwork in here for you, insurance, how you want your salary to be paid out, that sort of thing. Arslan can help you fill it all out."

I smiled and nodded briefly, hoping that my relief wasn't palpable to everyone. Before I arrived at the office, I had no idea whether I would even earn a real salary at RFA. I thought maybe the reporters were working for free as volunteers. I thought maybe I could work at a shop or have a side job. I knew few of the details at that time about the history of RFA, how it had been founded in the mid-1990s by an act of Congress, as a way of broadcasting news across Asia to counteract the propaganda efforts of the CCP. Modeled on Radio Free Europe, which broadcast behind the Iron Curtain during the Cold War, it promoted the values of free speech, democracy, and a free press by implementing those values itself. It first began broadcasting in 1996 in Mandarin and Tibetan, and soon expanded to include Burmese, Vietnamese, Korean, Cantonese, Lao, and Khmer. A Uyghur service was added in 1998, and by the time I joined, that program occupied its own section of the office and was considered an important part of the service.

After the quick meeting, Dolkun walked me back to my cubicle. "We really are glad you're here," he told me seriously. "We have some wonderful reporters on our team, but no one has as much experience in the media as you do. You're a real professional, and we can use your expertise."

"I wouldn't want to step on any toes," I said. "I mean, I don't even speak English yet."

"That will come in time. And don't worry about other people's feet, they should know to wear steel-toed boots by now! They understand that improving our programming is in everyone's best interest, especially for our Uyghur brothers and sisters back home and around the world."

"That's why I'm here," I said, meeting his eye. "I want to tell the truth to our listeners, and do it as compellingly as we can."

He gave me a smile. "Then you'll fit in here just fine."

I went back to my cubicle and stared at the blank notebook and the desktop computer and the empty file folders. This was my new life. I couldn't wrap my head around it.

"Everything okay?"

I looked up and saw Arslan staring at me intently.

"You looked a little lost."

"I . . . I need help with something. I haven't talked to my family yet and I need to tell them that I'm safe."

Arslan nodded. "Did they know you were coming to America in the first place?"

I shook my head.

"Gulchehra," he looked at me very seriously, "you know that once you call them, they'll be dragged in too. It won't be easy for them."

"It'll be worse for them not knowing what's happened to me, won't it?"

"We can get a message to them, if you want us to."

"I can't do that to them. They have to hear it from me."

Arslan nodded, his dark eyes grave. "Okay, you can do it from one of the studios." He showed me how to use one of the international phones used for work calls and left, closing the door behind him with a loud click. It sounded so sharp and final.

I stared at the phone, gathering my courage. I knew in my heart that my parents had to hear my voice to believe it, but I had no idea what their reaction would be. And the long-term ramifications of my actions were going to be serious, though I couldn't imagine just how severe they would be.

I finally picked up the phone and dialed. My mother's familiar voice answered. "Mom." My throat closed. It was unbearable.

"Gulchehra, is that you?"

"Yes, Mom. Listen. I don't know how to say this. I'm . . . I'm in America."

"After Europe you went to visit America?" she said, her voice confused. "We were worried when you didn't come back like you planned. But we didn't know how to get a hold of you."

I closed my eyes. "I know, Mom. I'm sorry. Can I talk to Dad?"

I heard her speaking to my father in the background as she handed the phone over.

"Daughter, what's going on?

"Daddy, forgive me. I made my first decision without your advice, and without your permission. I'm in America. I'm here with Dolkun Kamberi."

The line went so quiet that I thought we might have lost the connection. Then I heard my mother cry out.

"What's happening?" I exclaimed, but there was no response. Finally, I heard someone pick the phone back up.

"Call us later, Gulchehra," my mother said. It was the voice she used with her patients when she was writing them a prescription. "Your father's taken ill."

And then the phone went dead.

I sat there shaking for what felt like an hour. When I stood up, my legs were rubbery.

Arslan poked his head into the studio. "Are you okay?"

I shook myself, trying to wake myself from a daze. "I don't know." My eyes were filling with tears. "Something happened and the line went dead. I should call my aunt or—"

"It's the middle of the night there, Gul. Wait until tomorrow." Arslan's voice was low and calm. "There's nothing you can do now, okay?"

Then he tactfully closed the door as I began to cry.

The next morning I called my parents' house again. My mother answered the phone on the second ring.

"Your father went straight to the hospital," she told me, her voice strangely cool and impersonal. "They think it was a heart attack." I gasped, and she continued quickly. "Listen, what you have done is already done. You cannot fix this. You cannot help us now."

"Mom—"

"Listen to me, just be careful." Her voice softened slightly. "Your happiness is our happiness. We care about you no matter what. Just be safe over there. Don't worry about us. Your father will be all right. It was just a shock."

When we hung up, I called my aunt immediately. My heart was heavy with guilt and fear. I was worried my mother wasn't telling me what was really going on with them.

"Auntie, it's me."

"Oh, Gul, how could you do this? Your father's in the hospital! And your poor mother . . ." She started crying, or maybe she had been crying already when I called. "Every birthday, every wedding, every holiday starts with your singing and dancing. How can we live without you? How can your parents survive this?"

"Is my dad going to be okay?"

"Early this morning, your mother called a family meeting at her house. We were all there, except for you. You know what she told us? 'From now on, none of us is going to give bad news to Gul. Not about illnesses, or lost jobs, or problems, or jail. Nothing bad. She's in America now, and she's so alone there. I can't bear to think of her worrying about us back home.' She's the oldest sibling, so we listen to her." My aunt paused. Then she said, "Gul, your father will be fine. But . . . I have to tell you something."

My stomach turned sickeningly. "What is it?"

"Your grandmother passed away two days ago. You were always her favorite, you know. It was almost like she knew she'd never see you again and was ready to let go."

"But she can't be gone!" My voice ricocheted off the studio walls. "She was still so strong."

"We just have to accept what happens in life," my aunt said. "Take care of yourself. You're on your own now."

I sat there in tears, with the dial tone buzzing in my ear. My family had always been so strong and united. Any decisions that had to be made were made together. Now my grandmother was gone, the last of her generation. Now the decisions were being made without her, and without me.

Anguish rippled through me in unbearable waves. I had ripped a jagged hole in my family. The hole would slowly close, like a wound healing over time. But it would knit back together with me on the outside.

I began to work as many hours of the day as I could. It was the only thing I could do that made me forget the searing pain of being separated from everyone I loved. I didn't even know how my father was, whether my mother was spending all day at the hospital, whether my brother had finally found a job. I drove myself crazy imagining what was happening back home. RFA had booked us a hotel room for a week, and it was stifling to be there with Elzat. I dreaded going to bed next to him, lying there rigid as a board in my thick nightgown, hoping he wouldn't try to touch me. We hadn't been intimate since he'd left Ürümchi for Austria, and at night my whole body would tense up worrying about it, as though I could ward him off with my thoughts.

Fortunately, it was a thrill to go in to the office. I felt like for the first time I was among serious journalists, people committed to uncovering the truth and reporting it. They were working on weighty stories—people who had been arrested without cause, human rights abuses, crackdowns on religious expression as simple as going to pray at a mosque or wearing a hijab. It felt like a real news organization as opposed to Xinjiang TV.

Still, because the Chinese government invests a lot in propaganda, a lot of money had been floating around the Xinjiang TV station. We'd had the most advanced technology—everything was brand-new and high tech. I thought RFA would have the best of everything, too, but I quickly learned that wasn't the case. At RFA, the equipment was well used and sometimes hard to work. Instead of separate offices, we all worked from cubicles set around a big open floor plan. And the studios for recording and broadcasting were worn instead of shiny and new.

But another major difference was that the RFA offices were in an open building. Anyone could just walk in and ask to see someone. In contrast, a phalanx of officers guarded Xinjiang TV, and military police patrolled the grounds around the building. No one could get in without an official badge or a verified appointment. Although RFA was only a few blocks from the White House, no guards or personnel blocked the entryway. Our office, taking up two floors in an eight-story building, was manned by only one reception desk downstairs. I could feel the trust and the sense of freedom immediately, and that seemed to extend out to the larger society I found myself in.

Now that I was finally able to tell the stories that mattered, I called local officials and anyone willing to talk to me back home and scoured the internet for stories posted on bulletin boards. One story that I followed closely was the family-planning policies that had been imposed in the Uyghur region and that were being implemented with startling brutality. Sources described women having IUDs implanted in their wombs without their knowledge, which led to health issues, and others forced to abort pregnancies against their will. Other families buckled under the fines and fees levied against them in punishment for having more children than they were allowed. I was determined to report on these things as they were happening.

While I was useful at work, making use of contacts back in the Uyghur region that no one else had, it was painful feeling like an infant in the rest of my new life. It was such a stark contrast to back home, where I was as independent as a young woman could be. In the United States, I couldn't understand anything that anyone said. I couldn't even shop for myself or see the doctor or rent an apartment.

I could say hello and goodbye, but for everything else I needed a Uyghur–English interpreter.

And for the first several months, Arslan was my guide to this new world. As the Uyghur service's administrative assistant, he was responsible for helping new staff adjust to their new lives. When our week at the hotel was up, Aslan even cosigned on an apartment for Elzat and me in his building—above and beyond his duty. Our tiny studio was on the fifth floor of an older but tidy building just a few blocks away from the White House. On the day we moved in, with just our suitcases in hand, Arslan, who lived on the floor above us, was there to welcome us with some pastries from the bakery down the street. He and Elzat were polite, but I could tell they'd taken an instant dislike to each other.

The studio was completely empty when we arrived, and we spent the first night on the floor with a few blankets Arslan loaned us. Luckily, a family was moving out of the building that week, and we bought a double bed and a sofa from them for less than fifty dollars. We didn't have enough money for anything else but a few cheap basics to get us started: utensils, towels, a handful of pots and pans. We were building a new life from the ground up.

The Saturday after we moved in, Elzat went out early to try to find a job. He was looking for restaurant work, which was a huge step down from being a physics instructor. But he spoke only a little bit more English than I did, and a job in a kitchen where he didn't have to speak to anyone or in a restaurant where he could speak Chinese seemed like the only real option.

A few hours after he left, I heard a quiet knock on the door. My hands turned clammy at the sound and my heart started pounding. A rush of fear overtook me as I imagined the Chinese police had found me and were there to take me back. I had only been in America for a week, but every moment I wasn't sleeping or concentrating on work, I was worrying. I hadn't even called my family again because I was afraid the call would be monitored, and I didn't want them to be targeted. I was also afraid of what they would say to me, their disappointment and betrayal.

The person knocked again, and I tiptoed to the door and looked through the peephole. I almost laughed aloud in relief. I pulled open the door. "Oh, it's you," I said, trying to hide my pleasure.

Arslan flashed his bright grin. He wasn't especially tall, but he was as solidly built as a football player, with broad shoulders and a muscular chest.

"Sorry if I'm interrupting."

"You're not. Elzat just went out."

"Well, I was wondering . . . can you ride a bicycle?" When I nodded, he continued, "I saw a bicycle for sale in the neighborhood for twenty dollars. Would you like it?"

"Yes!" I said eagerly.

"Good, because I already bought it for you."

"But I—"

"You've been here for a week, and how much of the city have you seen?"

"None," I admitted.

"I thought so. Do you want to go for a ride?"

I thought for a second. "Let me go get changed."

That was the first of many long bike rides we took together around DC, and I began to feel like I had really arrived in America. In the first few days, all I'd seen were the stretch of street between the apartment and the RFA building and the inside of the offices. Arslan took me to different neighborhoods around the city. We rode to the Potomac River and visited all of the monuments. We toured the White House and spent a morning at the National Mall. We stopped nearby and ate a bite of lunch together, and I watched the squirrels playing. I was shocked by how many there were. I'd seen a rare squirrel in the Tengri Tagh Mountains, where it's special just to catch sight of one. Behind the Mall, they practically climbed into my hands, hoping to get fed. We spent many lunch hours biking through the city, and little by little I came to feel like I belonged.

I also started to get to know Arslan better. He was the only person I had to talk to, and I came to look forward to hearing his voice every day and the little jokes he would sprinkle into our conversations. And it helped to have an ally at work, where I quickly learned that the office politics could get very complicated.

Dolkun had meant it when he asked me for suggestions on how to improve the service. In my first few weeks there, I studied how the reporters worked and how each hour-long broadcast was put together. By the time he called a staff meeting with all ten of our journalists, I was ready with a lot of recommendations.

I came into the meeting prepared and launched right in. "First, I'd like to address the structure of the show. We just give story after story, without any introductions. Listeners need a way to orient themselves and we need to make them want to tune in. I think we need a brief introduction for each show by an anchor so that listeners know what the headlines are. And we need theme music and a Uyghur-language introduction. I also think . . ." I paused for just a second, "I think that the news could be read a bit more smoothly. The delivery matters. Even if it's hard-hitting, groundbreaking news, if it isn't delivered in a compelling way, people aren't going to listen. We need to make sure we can get through a whole story without any breaks or mistakes."

Dolkun nodded thoughtfully. "I like it. A little more polish to the program. Why don't you come up with a format and we'll see how it goes?"

I heard two of the other reporters whispering, but I paid no attention. I wasn't afraid I'd overstepped. It was natural for there to be resistance to change. And coming from Xinjiang TV, my standards were exacting. I'd been working as a media professional for years, and I wasn't prepared to compromise. Instead, I wanted to help bring my colleagues up to the highest level we could achieve.

"And are you ready to get on air?"

"Yes," I said crisply. "I've been working on a story about bilingual education and how it is a form of cultural assimilation. Our kids are losing their own culture and sense of belonging."

"Good. Have you thought about your on-air name?"

"My on-air name?"

"Each of us has a name we use on air so we can limit our exposure," one of the reporters said. "It's not just friends who listen to the show, you know."

My back stiffened. I was young and female and new to the station, but that didn't mean I needed a lecture on the basics. "I know the Chinese government is monitoring everything we do. But I'm going to use my own name."

There was a momentary silence and then everyone started talking at once.

"You can't do that, Gul. It's too dangerous. For you and maybe for us too."

"Do you want them to start looking for us?"

"We've got families, you know. Even if you don't."

"I do have a family," I cried. "My whole family is back home. I know it's dangerous, but I've just come from the Uyghur region. Everyone there knows my voice. What's the point of trying to pretend it isn't me? And what about the next generation? Do we want them to be so afraid too? We need to sacrifice for them, for the freedom that we want to have and want them to have too. I'm here so I can teach through my actions."

"Don't be so foolish!"

"That's enough." Dolkun held up his hand. "If Gul wants to use her real name, then that's her right. And it doesn't reflect badly on anyone else for making a different decision."

I looked around the room at my colleagues, feeling their fear and their resentment. I didn't want to show them up or imply that they were weak. But I also hadn't taken this huge risk just to keep hiding and pretending.

That afternoon after the meeting, I called my parents. I had waited for weeks, and it had gotten to the point where I couldn't stand not knowing what was going on with them. I didn't even know if my father had recovered enough to leave the hospital.

But the voice that came over the line was my father's.

"Dad, it's Gul. I miss you so much! Are you all right?"

"We're fine, darling. Everything's okay. I'm home now."

There was an artificial pause and I wondered if my mother—or someone else—was gesturing to him, telling him what to say and what not to say. It was crushing to feel so remote from him and everything that was happening back home.

"Gulchehra," my father lowered his voice almost to a whisper, "after your last call, four policemen came to the house. They asked a lot of questions, and we didn't know any answers. They asked if you had a plan to go to America before you left China. They asked whether you'd come under the influence of anyone. They made us write down a list of all of your friends, anyone who might have put ideas in your head. Then they took my passport away."

"What?" I said, horrified.

"They told us not to leave Ürümchi. Daughter, you can't come home. No matter what happens to us, you'll never be able to come home now. Don't ever forget that."

I heard a bit of static on the line and then my mother came on the phone.

"Your father's tired," she said. "Listen, Gul, I'm only going to say this once. You've made the authorities very unhappy. You mustn't call anyone else in the family, or any of your friends. They're all being questioned and you'll only get them into trouble. They've already taken your show off the air, and all of those commercials you made are gone. We can't even see your face on the TV anymore."

Her voice broke and I could hear her begin to cry.

"Mom—"

"We understand your choice, Gulchehra. But please be very careful."

The line went dead and I stared at the phone in my hand. I couldn't call my family, couldn't talk to my friends. Everyone I knew and loved was being harassed by the authorities, and I was completely cut off. My long nightmare had already begun.

When I came to the United States, I lost so much, above all my family. But I also lost the ability to get by in even the most mundane situations. It was humiliating to have to depend on others for everything. The simplest tasks became terrifying; I was afraid to go into a store on my own because I might not be able to communicate what I wanted. I was so helpless in English that when I had to undergo a medical examination for my new health insurance at RFA, I had to bring an interpreter along. To my great consternation, Dolkun told me that Arslan would be the one accompanying me.

"Don't worry," Dolkun reassured me. "He's very discreet."

Arslan and I took a taxi together from the RFA office to the doctor's office. I could feel my blood pressure rising. We were friends by this time, but back in the Uyghur region, it would be unthinkable for a man to accompany a woman to a medical appointment unless he were her husband. When we got to the waiting room, a bored-looking receptionist handed me a clipboard with a thick sheaf of pages.

"It's just a medical history form," Arslan told me. "I'll help you fill it out."

He began to read out the questions to me—name, address, age, marital status—and when I answered, he would fill it in in English. Then suddenly he stopped. He looked down at the page, his face reddening. "Sorry . . . I don't mean any offense. But the next question is about . . . your time of the month."

I immediately felt my face flush. I'd never spoken about that openly with any man, not even Elzat.

"When does it usually come, and how long does it last?"

I tried to imagine that I was talking directly to the doctor. "It usually comes at the beginning of the month and lasts for five or six days."

He was scribbling down my answers assiduously. "And, um . . ."

"Yes?"

He didn't lift his eyes from the paper. "Forgive me. How many men have you had relations with?"

"What kind of question is that?" I asked indignantly. "I'm a married woman."

"Yes, yes, of course," he said hastily. "They have to ask about your . . . history."

I lifted my eyes to heaven. "Well, I've only had one husband, so you do the math."

He gave a little snort of laughter and wiped a hand across his sweaty forehead. "This isn't usually so hard," he mumbled.

"It's never been this hard for me either!" I was giggling like a girl.

He turned the page over with relief. "Thank Allah, the next part is about deadly diseases."

I started laughing and he joined in. My cheeks were still bright red, but my heart felt as buoyant as air.

After that, I decided I had to get serious about learning English. I held the key to my own independence. I had learned Chinese, so I was confident I could learn a third language too. All it would take was time and hard work, and I was ready to give both of those to learning English well enough not only to survive but also to thrive in my new environment. It turned out that learning English would be more painful than I thought, but not because of verb tenses or prepositions.

In my second month after arriving in the United States, Radio Free Asia hired a professor from George Washington University to come into the office to teach us English and computer research skills, which we needed for our jobs. Because the Uyghur channel at RFA had been established only a few years earlier, most of us in the Uyghur service were new to the United States, and our English-language skills were very limited. We didn't get much practice around the office, either, because we all just spoke Uyghur together. The professor was extremely patient and taught me beginning with the ABCs. Most importantly, she was very encouraging. She would say things like, "This country is for you! We were all in the same boat when we came here." She was from Venezuela and had come to the United States thirty years before, and eventually became a professor. She truly believed that if *she* could do it, we could too.

During that period, I used the dictionary every day to teach myself something new. I was picking up words little by little, but I was still too shy to speak. I learned to read English fairly quickly, but I was still scared to communicate.

Arslan tried to help, telling me, "I'll teach you a new word each day. You can just speak with me in English. There's nothing to be nervous about. Ready? *One, two, three* . . ."

But that wasn't enough to bring my language level up to proficiency. So I paid one thousand dollars, which was a lot of money for me, for a three-month course at a language school in nearby Arlington. My intention was to learn how to speak, and the class, with its American teacher who spoke with an accent that was easy to understand, really helped.

By the beginning of the third month, we all had improved considerably. There were only nine students in my class, all of us from different countries. Our language skills had gotten to the point that the teacher started each class with a student presentation in which each student had the chance to introduce themselves.

The teacher called me up last, saying cheerfully, "Gulchehra, it's your turn. Please tell us where you're from, what language you speak, something about your culture, why you came to this country. Whatever you'd like us to know."

I went up to the blackboard, feeling a quiver of pride and anticipation.

"I am Uyghur," I began. I wrote a few Arabic letters on the blackboard. "This is our script. In English, some people spell Uyghur with an *i*, but we prefer to spell it with a *y*, because that comes closer to the way it sounds in the Uyghur language. I was born in the capital city of Ürümchi, in my country of East Turkestan."

I paused and drew a rough map on the board. "This is Central Asia. East Turkestan borders on eight countries, see? We are occupied right now by China, and the Chinese call our area Xinjiang, but the name of my country is East Turkestan."

Every time I said the words, a thrill went through me. For so many years, saying those words was forbidden because the Chinese government had become so paranoid about "splittists" and the separatist movement. Even my father wouldn't say such things in public. If anyone heard me talking this way back home, I would be labeled a separatist and thrown in jail, or something much worse. Now, in the safe confines of this small classroom, I could finally express myself fully without fear of horrible repercussions.

"Please, Gulchehra," the teacher interrupted, "you're going to confuse the other students. What you've drawn on the map is part of China, right? You are Chinese."

In an instant, my heart iced over. "I am *Uyghur*," I said carefully. I held her gaze as I continued, "My country might be considered part of China right now, but my people call it East Turkestan. We're very different from the Han Chinese. Many people don't know the history of the region, and that's why I'm telling you this."

"You can't say your nationality is East Turkestani," she scoffed. "We can't find that on a map."

"I just drew you a map." I gestured at the blackboard. "This is why I'm here, in this country. I want to show the world where my country is and why I'm proud to be Uyghur. I left everything behind in my country. It's a beautiful country, and rich in so many ways. Can't I be proud of where I come from?"

"Your passport is from China, isn't it? You should at least begin by saying you're Chinese."

I was trying to hold back my anger as best I could. How dare she try to tell me where I was from! I swallowed hard. "I came here so that I would have the freedom to speak out. Freedom of speech is my whole goal! That's why I left everything behind."

The other students had been sitting there in shocked silence, but when they heard those words, they slowly began to clap. A man from Honduras, a woman from the Czech Republic, another from Somalia. They understood.

But the teacher couldn't hear me. She was so consumed by the idea that the words on your passport always represent the truth that she wasn't willing to let me speak.

Suddenly, I couldn't take it any longer. I hadn't abandoned everything I'd ever known just to be forced to repeat lies halfway across the world. I went back to my seat, grabbed my jacket and purse, and left the classroom.

"Gulchehra!" the teacher called after me.

But I headed straight to the office and asked for my money back from the secretary.

"I can't continue with these classes. Besides," I added, my fury starting to fade a bit, "I think my English skills have a gotten a lot better if I can talk back to my teacher!"

The teacher was waiting for me in the hallway.

"I'm sorry, Gulchehra. Please just come back to class and we'll forget it all happened."

I shook my head. She must have been worried that I was going to complain to her bosses. But I had no interest in getting her in trouble.

"Please remember that you're a teacher," I said. "Students need to be encouraged. We're not just learning English here. We're learning to survive. We're learning how to be free. You're not just teaching us language. You're teaching us how to be human in a new place."

After that, I went back to my dictionaries. I learned from TV and radio, I read the newspaper every single day, and I practiced with Arslan on our bike rides. It was a struggle, but slowly I became more comfortable in English. It was about more than getting by. It was essential that I be able to have little conversations in the market or in restaurants. Since I couldn't contact anyone I was close to back home for fear of endangering them, I felt an overwhelming loneliness that seemed to hover over everything. It colored every day and every night; it seemed as inescapable as my own face.

Adding to that pressure, I felt a tremendous responsibility to make something of myself, to ferret out the important news stories and expose to the world what was going on in the Uyghur region. Otherwise, none of this would have been worth it. I put everything I had into my work. Because my children's program for Xinjiang TV had been so popular, I came up with the idea of doing a children's segment for the RFA broadcast. I pitched it to Dolkun.

"Why not a kids' segment? We need to teach them how to speak freely, think freely. The Chinese government wants to assimilate them, control them, even control their thoughts. We can teach them about humanity and democracy and real freedom. I had a huge following back home. I know our program is blocked by the Chinese authorities and most of our listeners come from outside the Uyghur region, but maybe some people back home will be able to find our program and listen to me again. I hate that they must feel abandoned by me."

Dolkun thought for moment. "It's an intriguing idea. But I don't know if it's a good one. Think about it, Gul. It's illegal to listen to our program back in the Uyghur region. People are punished for even tuning in to our show. If we start targeting kids and they want to listen, who knows what the government will do to them. And their parents will get in trouble too. We don't want to put them at risk."

My heart sank. Of course he was right. The last thing I wanted to do was endanger the kids I was so passionate about helping. I couldn't do anything to help them now. I pushed back a quick rush of tears and said, "I'll keep doing news then. Investigative reporting, the hardest-hitting stuff."

"Okay, we'll give you that chance." Then he said, his voice deadly serious, "If you do this, you're going to be putting sources at risk, not to mention yourself. Make every report count."

I lived by that edict. My first report centered on a boy who had gotten into trouble over the new flag-raising policy. I had heard a rumor from an online source that the principal of a school in Kashgar had begun making the students come into school every morning at six to raise the Chinese flag. One ninth-grader there wrote an anonymous letter to the principal saying: *This is too much. If you keep forcing us to do this, I'm going to raise the East Turkestan flag instead.* The author of the note had been discovered. The police had come and pulled him out of class to arrest him.

The story made my blood boil. The first thing I did was call the Kashgar Ministry of Education and ask questions: Why has this child been arrested? How is he being treated? Has he really committed a crime by writing this letter? What crime is it, exactly? All I got were evasive answers and an eventual curt goodbye.

Then I called the Kashgar chief of police, with whom I'd been on friendly terms during my days at Xinjiang TV. He had helped me do a few TV segments in and around Kashgar and had been delighted at the positive publicity for his city. "This is Gulchehra Hoja, from Radio Free Asia."

"From where? Gul, is that you? We heard you left. What on earth were you thinking?"

I brushed away his questions and answered with some of my own. "I'm calling about the child who was arrested over flag-raising. Is this really a matter for the law? What crime has he committed?"

There was a brief pause. Then the chief said, "Oh, Gulchehra, these are difficult questions. I don't know how to answer you." His voice sounded vaguely embarrassed.

"I know you care about the kids there," I said. "What is going on?"

"Our hands are tied. Everything's getting . . ." He stopped. "Look, I'll do what I can," he told me, and hung up.

I aired my story, and a few days later, I heard from my source that the boy had returned home and could go back to school. I was under no illusions that my reporting alone had forced his release, but the pressure might have helped.

One thing I had brought from home was the list of phone numbers in my cellphone. And I was going to make good use of every contact I had.

Once I started broadcasting again, some of my old excitement came back. I finally felt useful again. Although I was working all the time, it was so much easier than it had been at Xinjiang TV. Back home, everything was scripted. Everything had to pass through stage after stage of censorship before it could go on air. At Radio Free Asia, I could just write my copy and read it on the news. We had editors, but I could say what I knew to be the truth. That was real journalism. It was the first time I felt like I was a real journalist and not just a parrot repeating what it had been taught. I worked very late at the office, doing research and writing my story for the next day.

I was following several important stories, above all what was going on in the wake of September 11. The Chinese government had picked up on the US rhetoric of the War on Terror and was subverting it to its own ends. Suddenly, anyone who supported Uyghur independence or the recognition of East Turkestan was no longer just a "splittist" but now also a "terrorist." The change in nomenclature was significant. It meant that the CCP could harass and arrest Muslims while claiming to be merely protecting Chinese national security against outside jihadist influences, even though there was scant evidence of any significant presence of religious extremists in the Uyghur region. But the CCP took the opportunity to increase its campaign of surveillance, pressure, and punishment, including the summary execution of some Uyghur activists.

In the evening, when I was too tired to keep working, I would try to learn a little English or practice reading copy in the studio. It helped that Arslan also liked to work late, and we'd pop into each other's cubicles for a brief chat or just to say something to see the other smile. Often, we'd leave the office together and he would walk me back to the small apartment to which I dreaded returning.

One night after I got back after nine, Elzat was waiting, sitting on the couch in the dim light. Usually he was in bed by the time I got home, so instantly I was on my guard. Could he have seen me walking home with Arslan? Everything was completely chaste between us. We were just friends, and I had nothing to feel guilty about. But a deeper part of me knew that I was forming an attachment to Arslan that Elzat wouldn't like.

"Home so late?"

"Working," I said casually. "I'm going to take a shower."

"Wait. Sit down."

I sat down obediently on the edge of the couch, as far from him as I could.

"I spoke to my parents today."

My heart skipped a beat. "Are they okay? Did something happen?"

"They're fine. But they know what you've been up to."

"What do you mean?"

"Your reporting. All of the political stuff. They got a visit from the police today and were questioned like criminals about whether they'd had contact with you. It scared them half to death. Gul, you've got to stop this. My parents think that I haven't been a husband to you, that I've been letting you run wild here. Maybe they're right."

I was silent as I tried to keep my head cool. I couldn't believe what I was hearing.

"I've tried to be patient, but this has gone too far," he said. "You're picking the worst news to report, the most sensitive issues, and then you're calling officials back home! You've got to start mending your ways."

"Mending my ways?" My voice was low and tight. "You sound like some CCP official."

"This isn't just about you and your family, you know. My mother is terrified. She had some choice words about you."

"Your mother—" I stopped myself. "Listen, I've given up everything for this. You didn't have to come with me. But now we're here, and all I have is my work. I'm a real journalist now and I won't let you put limits on what I can and can't do."

"I'm not putting limits on you! These aren't my rules, are they? Look, you can't ever go back home. We both know that. It's a huge sacrifice. But I can't do the same thing. I'm the oldest son in my family. I have to go back someday and take care of my parents. I can't risk it all just for your work. If you do this, you'll involve my family members as well. The government won't let any of them live in peace ever again."

"Then leave me," I said. "There's your answer."

"Never."

"Then stop trying to control me!" I leapt up from the couch, feeling like a caged animal in the confines of our tiny studio apartment. I just wanted out, out from all of it. "You think you can go back? As my husband? How naive are you? The Chinese government already knows everything."

I went into the bathroom and locked the door. Elzat's hope of going home was useless. He had tied his fate to mine. And my fate, whether I wanted it or not at this point, was to stay here.

As much as I felt trapped in the apartment, I found a sense of freedom biking around DC with Arslan. He was so different from the men I'd known back home. He'd grown up in Kazakhstan, where the society was much more open, and where people weren't constantly on guard, worried about what they could and couldn't say. I felt comfortable around him, as though some buried part of myself I'd been holding back was slowly emerging.

Elzat eventually found a job working in a Turkish restaurant downtown, leaving me to my own devices on the weekends. It was a huge relief to have time to myself that wasn't in the office.

One Saturday afternoon, Arslan and I took a bike ride to a park in DC where we'd never been before. It was early spring and still chilly out. The air stung my cheeks as we rode, and it felt invigorating to be outside. As we approached the park, I spotted something that I recognized.

"*Pekos*!" I cried out to Arslan.

He grinned. "Pretty, aren't they?"

We slowed our bikes and got off at the edge of the park.

"They're called magnolia trees in English." He glanced at me. "Hey, hey. What's wrong?"

I felt my cheeks with my fingers and found tears. It was so cold that I hadn't felt them falling. "My father has one of these back home, in a huge pot. He wipes the leaves down when they get wet or dusty.

In the winter, he moves the pot away from the radiators so it doesn't get too hot. In the summer, he moves it in front of the window so it gets the best sun. It's his treasure." I smiled, although now I was crying in earnest. "He treats it like his own child."

Arslan patted my shoulder very briefly, a gentle, respectful tap. Then he wheeled our bikes over to a bench in the sun and we sat in silence for a long time.

"I know it's terrible for you and for your family to be separated," he said finally. "But I want you to know that I'm very glad you're here."

I wiped my face and gave him a small smile. "Thanks for saying that."

"I remember how excited Dolkun was when you contacted him. He knew your father very well, didn't he?"

I nodded.

"And he knew your work too. He asked me if I knew who you were. I told him I grew up in Kazakhstan, I don't know anything about Xinjiang TV. You know what he told me? 'Oh, she's a celebrity back home. She beautiful, she's talented. And if we get her, it will be amazing. She'll bring our broadcasting to another level.'"

I felt myself blushing. "Quit trying to make me like you."

"I know you like me," Arslan said, his voice suddenly serious.

I ducked my head, not knowing how to respond.

"And you like it here, too, right?"

"Yes," I said. "You know what DC seems like to me? One great big park. Like this place." I waved my arm at the trees just coming into bud around us. "In China, a place like this would be called People's Park, but people wouldn't be able to just go in. Back there, you always have to pay some admission fee or buy a ticket, even for a little park like this. There's the 'people's government,' but you can't get anywhere near any government buildings, let alone have a say in policy. Or, take Chinese money even. It's called the 'people's currency,' but it definitely doesn't belong to us. Nothing labeled 'people' actually belongs to the people!"

Arslan laughed his loud, infectious laugh. "You should use that on the show," he said. "Come on, I'll buy you lunch."

That night, lying on the couch to avoid joining Elzat in bed, I thought about Arslan and how grateful I was to have his company. Back in Ürümchi, I was rarely alone. I'd had three different cellphones: one for work, one for friends, one for family. I spent each day in the lap of my extended family, surrounded by friends and by fans. I spent time with children every day for the show. I made a good living as a TV personality. Now, at least I had my work and Arslan, because otherwise, I had next to nothing, and all I could think about was basic survival. Not just mine, but my family's back home.

Uyghur family members rarely say *I love you.* We cook for each other, give gifts, hug and kiss. At home, I'd never once said *I love you* to my dad. But, lying there, I realized that now, apart from everyone, the only way I had to show my love was through my words.

I hadn't called my family for a long time because I was afraid of the consequences for them, but that Monday, I went into one of the studios and called my parents' house. If they couldn't talk to me, they could hang up without saying anything. But I couldn't bear the idea that they might believe I didn't think about them every single day.

When my mother answered, I said, "Mom, it's me. I called to tell you . . . to tell you how much I love you."

There was a long pause.

"We know, my child," she said. I could hear the tears in her voice. "We know."

"I don't know when I'll be able to hug you again," I told her. I was crying too. I still couldn't accept that she was across the world from me.

"Your father was just talking about what you were like as a little girl, all of the funny things you did. Do you remember the time you came flying into the house and told him that you'd taken a taxi and didn't have any cash in your bag? You'd just started your job, and it was the first time you'd asked for money from him since you were little. He said to me, 'Qimangul, I'm so stupid. I'm such a fool. She asked me for twenty yuan for the taxi. Why didn't I give her two hundred? Why didn't I give her two thousand?'"

My mother's voice broke.

"Is it okay if I call every now and then?" I asked her. "I feel so . . . alone here."

"It's okay. Call us! It's too hard not to be in touch. We can handle whatever happens on our end."

During those rare phone calls, my parents always told me little anecdotes about my childhood or things they remembered me doing. Before I left, we never seemed to have time to really sit down and tell each other how important we are to each other. Now there was a huge physical distance between us, yet emotionally we got even closer, even though there was so much we couldn't say.

We all assumed our conversations were being listened to, so we couldn't talk about politics. But from my contacts and reporting, I knew that the situation in the Uyghur region had gotten rapidly worse since I'd left. After September 11 handed the CCP the convenient label of "terrorist" to apply to anyone who objected to government policies, the authorities had tightened the screws on religious and educational activities, especially in the more rural southern areas. They punished anyone who was found with "unofficial information," including religious materials, information about East Turkestan or Uyghur history, or anything that didn't align with the party line. Mosques near schools were razed, since they might act as a bad influence on students. Teachers who taught anything suspect were rounded up to be reeducated or imprisoned.

Not for the first time, I wondered about Abdul in his village of roses and what he might be going through. Had he married his childhood sweetheart? Did they have children? Was he still able to teach the Uyghur language? Had he been rounded up, thrown in jail, beaten? I couldn't protect my friends and I couldn't even find out details about how they were doing because even making contact could put them in danger. It was bad enough that the police were keeping such close tabs on my family; I couldn't do that to Mehray or Abdul or any of the other friends I missed.

Since I couldn't maintain my ties, my parents kept them for me. In those early months and years after I left, whenever close friends came to visit, my parents would give them something from the objects they had salvaged from my house. Of course, many things had been taken away by the police—my diaries, most of my photographs, books, anything I'd written, tapes of the TV shows I'd been in. They had confiscated anything with my picture or voice. But other things—my clothing and trinkets I'd collected and little gifts fans had given me—were left behind. My parents gave my friends objects to remember me by, reminders to keep at least the memory of those friendships alive. When they asked me if that was okay, I told them to give away everything.

I'd come to the United States with one suitcase, and I had no illusions that I would be able to go back for any of my things. My parents had trouble mailing anything to me, but finally they did manage to send me a package, in care of RFA. In it, they'd packed one of my photograph albums, wonderful pictures mostly of my childhood and early adulthood. They also sent me some foods that they knew I wouldn't be able to find easily in the United States, like a few pieces of nan from our neighborhood stall. Nan is our staple, our daily bread, and it's sacred; if a piece is dropped on the floor, it must be picked up and kissed in repentance. I've moved seven times since I received that package of nan, but I still have it in my freezer as a keepsake. To my delight, they also sent me bags of *kishmish*, a kind of long, green desert raisin from Turpan; *badham*, almonds in the shell from Kashgar; and *khaq*, dried apricots that taste of honey.

One other unusual object my father set quickly became one of my greatest treasures.

It's a simple stone, about the size of my palm, flecked with dark gray and traced with very fine lines, almost like the impressions of fossils. I'd never seen it before. I lifted it to my face to get a better look, and all of a sudden, I caught a whiff of the rich, familiar scent of Ürümchi after a good rain. My hometown flooded back to me and it was almost as though I were there again, standing in front of my parents' house. I couldn't stop the tears that welled up.

The next time I spoke with my father, I asked him about it. "Dad, I don't know why you sent me that stone, but it smells like home!"

"Yes," he said. "I picked it up from our yard. It's just a random stone, but it's still from home. Remember our expression, a stone is most precious where it belongs? Everything from your homeland, even a rock from the garden, is so precious. I thought you might need it now."

The stone held the scent of Ürümchi in a way that seemed magical. During that lonely, frightening time, I started to sleep with it by my bedside each night. It was the only thing that gave me comfort. I could smell its faint scent and be home again. It was a lesson: when you're separated from everyone you love, every memory, every reminder of your family, every hint of your country, is a precious gift.

At the same time, my makeshift family in the United States brought me very little comfort. Elzat and I barely talked, avoiding each other as we went about our daily routines. I had started to make some friends in the small Uyghur community in DC, but it was hard to build mutual trust, and those relationships stayed casual. And despite knowing it was wrong, I was also forming a closer and closer attachment to Arslan. The more time I spent with him, the less I could deny my feelings.

One evening with Elzat after a silent dinner of takeout he'd brought home from the restaurant, everything boiled over. I just couldn't keep my emotions hidden anymore.

"Elzat, I'm not happy and I know you're not happy either. I need to tell you something. I have feelings for someone else."

"Feelings? What kind of feelings?" He half rose from the table, then sank back down into his chair. "Stop this. I don't want to hear any of it."

There was something surprising in his voice. Instead of anger, I heard resignation. It was as though he'd known for some time. He still didn't want to hear it. As though if it remained unspoken, it wouldn't be real. But things had gone much too far for that.

"I can't stay here anymore. I can't. Not when I feel this way for someone else."

All of a sudden he was screaming. "Why are you saying this? What are people going to think of you? The things they're going to say about you!"

"I'm telling you I have feelings for another man, and this is your response?" I couldn't help but raise my own voice too. "What are they going to say? What do I care? All that matters is how we feel, how things are between the two of us. All you care about is what other people think!"

"I can't live without you, Gul. I'm warning you." Then he broke down into sobs that wracked his body so hard that he could no longer speak.

A few days later, Arslan asked me to have lunch with him. As I sat there picking at my salad, he said quietly, "I can tell something's wrong. What's going on?"

I shook my head. "I'm okay."

"You're not okay, and I hate seeing you this way!"

It was the first time I'd heard Arslan sound impatient, and it startled me so much that I put my fork down and looked at him.

"I'm sorry." He sighed. "Look, I need to just tell you something. I know that you're married, I know that this is a traumatic time for you, I know the last thing you need is another emotional burden. And I don't mean for this to be a burden. But, Gul, I care for you. Not just as a friend, but as something more."

"Don't tell me this," I said, holding up my hands as though to physically hold him back. "I can't handle it right now."

"I wish I could change the way I feel, but I can't."

"I'm married!"

"Tell me you love your husband and that you're happy with him, and I'll never say anything about this again."

I avoided his eyes, but I couldn't lie to him. Of course I wasn't happy. He knew that as well as I did. I'd told him a little bit about the situation with Elzat, not the gritty details but enough for him to draw conclusions.

"Gul—"

"You're so much younger than I am. How many years—"

"Four. Who cares."

"It will never work out. It's too complicated!"

I tossed my salad into the garbage and hurried the couple of blocks back to the office on my own, with only my painful ambivalence for company.

The next day, Arslan called to me from the doorway of one of the studios. "Gul, could you give me a hand with something?"

I was sitting at my desk in my cubicle, and I couldn't ignore him or our colleagues would wonder what was up. They were already noticing the number of times we had lunch together. They also seemed to pay attention to whether we sat next to each other at meetings or smiled at each other in the hallway. I didn't want to give any more fodder for gossip.

Reluctantly, I got up and went into the studio where he was waiting, the phone in one hand. He shut the door and handed me the receiver.

"Talk to my father, please."

"What?" I was so shocked that the phone slipped from my hand and banged against the side of the desk.

He patiently picked it up and handed it to me again. "My father. He'd like to say a few words to you. You don't have to say anything if you don't want to. Just listen."

"Assalamyu aleykum," I said shyly into the receiver. *Peace be with you*, our polite greeting.

"Aleykum assalam, kizim," a pleasantly sonorous voice answered. *Peace be with you, daughter*. The phone connection to Kazakhstan was much better than the one I usually had to East Turkestan. "You must be Gulchehra Hoja. I'm Arslan's father. He told me about your . . . complicated situation. I've spoken to his mother about it, and we both agree that if you love my son and he loves you, there's nothing to stop you from being together. Love is more powerful than many obstacles. My son feels strongly about you and we trust him to do the right thing. I think you'd be very happy with him."

I couldn't think of what to say, so I simply handed the phone back to Arslan. He said goodbye to his father and turned back to me.

"I just wanted you to know that my family has no objections. They know everything, and they support us."

"What do you mean, 'us'?"

"I want to marry you, Gul. You're the one I've been waiting for. There's no question in my mind. After all the time we've spent together, after everything you've told me, I'm absolutely certain that we're going to be man and wife."

"Is this . . . are you serious about this? You know how our community feels about divorced women."

"I've never been more serious about anything in my life."

He held my gaze and I felt my legs go weak.

"I'm going back to Kazakhstan tomorrow to see my family. They'll give me their blessing in person. When I come back, I need an answer from you. The time has come to make a decision. Can you do that?"

"I'll try," I said in a small voice. "It's going to take time."

"As long as it takes. I'd wait until the end of time for you." Arslan handed me a small key ring. "Here, these are the keys to my new condo. It's bigger than the old one, and in a better building. I haven't moved in yet, so it's empty. But if you need a place to go while I'm away, you have a place. Whether you decide to be with me or not. I just want you to be safe."

I hesitated for a long moment. Then I took the keys and slipped them into my pocket.

Over the next two weeks while Arslan was away, I thought through everything over and over again, my brain working wildly like a car spinning out on ice. The way I found myself walking only reluctantly back to my studio apartment, the constant avoidance of my husband's touch, sleeping on the couch to avoid his nearness. It all added up to an unavoidable conclusion. I couldn't live like that for the rest of my life. I had known it for a long time but had been too afraid to confront it directly. We'd already spent so much time apart, yet here I found myself, still trapped in the narrow cage of my old life in the middle of an enormous open country with possibilities I hadn't even begun to imagine yet. I had to take the final step to my freedom.

On my walk to and from work each day, I turned it over obsessively in my head. I would take Arslan's keys out of my purse and hold them in my hand, feeling their slight weight and the pinch of their zigzagged shapes against my fingers. If I went to Arslan's condo, it would be like a promise to him. My ambivalence was like a constant pain in my side, distracting me from work, from meals, from everything.

It was obvious to me that I couldn't take the next step all on my own. It felt like jumping off of a cliff into a chasm whose bottom I couldn't see. I decided to take a risk and call my parents' house from the studio.

My brother answered. I hadn't spoken to him since I'd left Ürümchi.

"Salaam, sister!" he said. "I've missed your voice. Are things okay?"

"I miss you too, Kaisar, so much. And everything's okay. I just need to tell you something." I took a deep breath and dove in. "While you were in jail, I was in another kind of prison. My marriage has been a sham from the beginning."

"Oh, Gul." He sounded distant and sad.

"I know it's wrong, but I'm going to leave him. I can't take it any longer."

"You don't deserve to be unhappy. If you feel that the right thing to do is to get divorced, then that's what you should do. I won't let anyone say anything about you here."

"Kaisar, I'm sorry. I'm sorry I left you all like this." My voice was thin and weak. Guilt was like a collar always threatening to tighten around my throat.

"While I was in jail, you had to be both a daughter and a son to our parents. I know all of the sacrifices you made back then. Well, now it's my turn. I'll be the son and the daughter. Don't blame yourself. We all understand why you did what you did." He lowered his voice until I could barely understand what he was saying. "Things aren't good here, Gul. Even our books could get us thrown in jail now."

"Our books?" I said, confused.

"In Kashgar, they've been burning books, thousands of them. Even Turghun Almas's histories! Dad's put his history books behind some Chinese dictionaries, but if they start looking . . ."

"Tell Dad to get rid of them," I said, whispering too, speaking very quickly like we used to when we were kids, in the hopes that if anyone else was listening in, they would only understand a bit of what we were saying.

"You know how he is. I'm glad you're not here, Gul. Things are only going to get much, much worse."

Then there was a click and a dial tone, and my brother was gone again.

That Saturday, when Elzat left for his job at the restaurant, I took a long, hot shower. Every familiar movement felt alien, like my body was out of joint. I was worried about my family, worried about my homeland, and worried about my future. But now I knew what I was going to do. With Kaisar's blessing, I finally felt I had some kind of permission to act, to follow my own happiness as best I could. Really, I was giving myself permission.

I sat down on the couch and wrote Elzat a short note.

> We haven't loved each other for a very long time. Neither of us should have to live this way. I won't divorce you until you get your own visa here. But I can't live with you anymore.

My hands were shaking so badly that it didn't even look like my handwriting. I left it on the couch where he would find it as soon as he came through the door. Then I packed the same suitcase I'd come to the United States with, leaving the few household items we'd collected but taking everything my parents had sent me from home. Now those bits and pieces—my one photo album, the stone from our yard, the nan I couldn't bear to eat—were the only things I had left of my old life.

As I packed, I thought about how I'd grown up, surrounded by family, by our traditions and language and music and dance. I thought about the page of a middle school Chinese textbook a source had sent me for a story. It had a conversation for Uyghur students to study:

"We are Chinese."

"I am Chinese too."

"I love China, our motherland."

"I love China too."

The home I'd known was being destroyed, and the marriage I'd relied on was over. It was almost too much to bear.

But I was more fortunate than my relatives and friends back home. At least I had safety. At least no one was knocking on my door in the middle of the night. At least I could speak the truth. At least I wasn't being held somewhere, frightened and alone.

At RFA I was working on a story about a group of Uyghurs who had been captured in Pakistan and who were being detained in a holding center at Guantanamo Bay. The claim was that they had been undergoing some kind of training in Afghanistan. Their detention made no sense to me. No Uyghur I had ever spoken to had ever expressed hostility toward the United States; if anything, Uyghur freedom fighters looked to the United States as a vital counterbalance to China's power. I couldn't believe that these detained Uyghurs could have been involved in any way in what had happened to the Twin Towers. I had started to make contact with some people around these men, and I was gathering as much information as I could about what had really happened. I suspected that they were just devout Muslims who had gotten caught up in something they didn't understand. Time would prove me right, when several years later they were finally released from Guantanamo without ever being charged with a crime.

No matter what I was facing, I was among the lucky ones.

My eyes were dry as I left the studio apartment for the last time and rode the bus across town to Arslan's new condo. I couldn't stay there for long; I was still married, and I wouldn't live with him until after my divorce came through. But at least it was a safe place where I could be alone for a few days while I figured out what to do.

As I entered the silent, empty condo and dropped my suitcase in the middle of the floor, the bare walls echoed back the sound. I thought to myself: *You are about to enter the loneliest time in your life*. It was the lowest I had ever been, and it would take me a long time to pick myself back up.

PART V

A SENSE OF PURPOSE

It took a year and a half to finalize our divorce. The interim was painful. For much of it, I rented a room from a woman I knew through Arslan. I didn't want to move in with any of my Uyghur friends because of the trouble it might cause them. The CCP seemed to know everything, and I didn't want to risk their families back home being harassed because their relatives in America had given me shelter. My parents sometimes mentioned in half-code on the phone that my old friends from my TV station days still occasionally got visits from the Chinese police, checking to see whether they'd had any contact with me. I was considered an official enemy of the Chinese state, and that meant that anyone who got close to me was fair game. I wasn't the only one. In my time at RFA, I'd also witnessed the harassment and abuse of the family members of my close colleagues. We lived with that pain every single day.

But the pain was invigorating, too, as I lived alone waiting for the divorce to come through. It motivated me to work even harder to better myself and my situation. After the failure of my marriage, I was newly aware of my own autonomy and dignity, and not just my ability to survive in a new place and at a new job. In the evenings alone in my small room, I studied English constantly, I cultivated my sources and professional contacts online, I made sure I got enough exercise. I explored new boundaries and interests.

When I'd first arrived in the United States, I was very curious and I tried every kind of cuisine I could find. But more often than not, it just gave me a stomachache. Sometimes I missed home so badly that the only thing that could soothe it a little was Uyghur food. But there were no Uyghur restaurants in DC then, so I had to learn to cook what I wanted myself. Back home in Ürümchi, my mom cooked for the family and the rest of the time I ate out with friends or at work dinners. I'd never bothered to really learn how to cook, aside from a few simple dishes my mom had taught me. But after I came to the United States and had to take care of myself, I found pleasure in cooking. Before, at home, if I was happy, I'd dance. After I moved to the West, I'd cook foods from many different cuisines and experiment with different spices and techniques.

I also started practicing Islam seriously for the first time in my life. I had been around some form of Islamic culture and tradition my whole life, but aside from my grandmother, no one close to me was openly religious. But Arslan had grown up in Kazakhstan, where people could practice their religion openly, and he had a strong faith. When we got engaged, he introduced me to the local mosque, and I started to go there to pray when I was feeling lonely or afraid. I began to understand that although I had left all of my closest friends behind, the only friend I truly needed was Allah. He was there when I was struggling, and when I was happy. I could always turn to him for anything. That feeling brought me great comfort, and I would need it soon enough when times got dark again.

A few months after my divorce, Arslan and I signed the paperwork to be legally married in March 2004. We hadn't had the ceremony yet, but in the eyes of the law and Allah, I was finally married to the man I was completely, hopelessly in love with. Not long after, by some miracle, my mother managed to get a visa to come to the United States. We had expected to host Arslan's parents and not mine, but in an inexplicable reversal, his parents were denied visas. After September 11, travel from any Islamic country like Kazakhstan was uncertain. My father's passport had been confiscated after I left East Turkestan, so he couldn't even apply for a visa. But somehow my mother was granted travel papers, and after three long years of painful separation and unending longing, she arrived in the United States in April of 2004.

We drove to Washington Dulles to meet her. When she appeared through the international terminal exit doors, I burst into tears. We were both crying so hard that we could barely greet each other. We just hugged as tightly as we could, kissing each other's cheeks and breathing in the familiar scent of the other. It was like she had brought back the whole of my childhood with her.

Over the next week, I spent every moment with her. We took walks around the neighborhood and saw all of the tourist sites in DC. I took pleasure in showing her every little aspect of my new life in America—the grocery store and our local pharmacy, the park near my apartment, the RFA office. She told me all of the gossip from back home, describing my cousin's growing family and my aunt's recent surgeries. We talked about my father and how he was spending more and more time in the garden. My brother was trying to rebuild his life after being released from jail.

"Kaisar should find a girl and get married," I told my mom. "He should have a normal life."

She shrugged. "He says he doesn't want to."

"He's not young. When is he going to start a family, if not now?"

"He thinks no girl will have him. Not with everything that's happened to him, and to our family. A lot of our neighbors avoid us now."

I felt suddenly stricken with guilt. Even three years later, my decision to leave the Uyghur region was still affecting their daily lives.

That night, I convinced my mother to let me cook for her, the first time she had ever tasted my cooking. I made *laghman*, her favorite meal. It took me forever, but I made the dough for homemade noodles, rolled them out to just the right thickness, and stretched them until they were tender and a little chewy. I sautéed ground lamb with onions, tomato, green pepper, and celery until it cooked down to savory perfection.

"I can't believe my little Gul can cook like this!" my mother marveled as she ate. "Arslan is a very lucky man."

"And he knows it too," I told her with a laugh. "Believe me."

Sometimes while we ate, I would catch her watching me carefully, the way a mother watches a very young child, as though rediscovering the contours of my face.

"How does it feel to fall in love with me again, Mom?" I joked.

"I never didn't love you, my child," she said seriously.

I picked up her hand and kissed it lightly. The skin was paler and more papery than I remembered. "I know, Mom, I know."

Her face suddenly turned tense, like a shadow had passed over her.

"What is it?"

"Gul, you're our only daughter. We've missed you so much. Your father . . ." She swallowed, tears starting to roll down her cheeks. "Allah has given us so much, but it's so hard to be without you."

I lowered my head. "I know. I know I've caused the whole family a lot of pain."

"What really pains me is to see you here, like this."

I looked up at her, shocked. "What do you mean?"

She waved a hand around my tiny apartment. "You were the princess of our family. You were a princess of our whole community! And to see you in this dingy . . ." She stopped abruptly. "Gul, you're becoming someone else. Not the person you set out to be, who we raised you to be. I've come to take you back home. Back where you belong."

My head reared back. I couldn't believe what I was hearing and a haze descended over my senses. Confusion overtook everything. I knelt down on the floor beside her and took her hand. "Forgive me, Mom. I can't go back again. I'm free here, and I'm able to be the woman and the reporter that I've always wanted to be. This is my home now. Arslan is my home."

"If Arslan really loves you, he'll come back with you."

"Why would he go live under the thumb of the Communist Party?"

Tears were streaming down her face. "They promised you would both be safe!"

An icy sensation slid down my back. "What do you mean, *they*?"

"That was the only way they'd let me come." My mother's voice dropped to a whisper. "They told me that they understand you were weak and ideologically still raw. You came under evil influences in the West. If you come back, they'll let you have your old job, they'll let you have your old life back! Isn't that what you want? To be with us again? Just go along with it, and everything will be okay again."

My throat closed around what felt like a hard, bitter stone. I couldn't speak. I got up slowly and turned away from my mother. I couldn't bear to look at her face. Suddenly, I felt like I would suffocate if I didn't get out of the apartment right away. Without another word, I picked up my coat and went out into the hallway. I ran downstairs and blindly headed toward the office. I didn't know where I was going.

"Gul!" It was Arslan's voice. He was just coming home from work and caught me by the elbow on the sidewalk. "What's happened?"

Haltingly, choking on my own tears, I told him what my mother had said.

He was silent for a moment. Then he sighed deeply and looked up toward the sky. His eyes were rimmed in red. "My love, I know how much you gave up to come to the United States. I see the pain in your face every single day. You live here, but part of you is always back there, with your parents, with your family. I was afraid one day your mother would ask you this. If you feel you need to go back, I would never blame you."

I looked up at him in amazement. "How can you even think that? Yes, it is painful to be here, and yes, I miss my family every single day. But I made that decision almost four years ago. And now we have a life together here. How could I ever leave you?"

Arslan drew me into a tight hug and I could feel his heart beating hard in his chest. His face and voice never revealed any fear, but I knew that he didn't want to lose me. I felt his warmth and solidity, and for a moment, everything seemed normal again.

"Come on, let's go up." He took my hand and led me back to our apartment.

When we got inside, my mother was cooking.

"You're back!" she cried. She held her arms wide open and hugged both of us at once. She kissed us both on the forehead, holding our faces in her shaking hands. "I wish you every happiness," she whispered.

Arslan looked at her with concern. "Are you all right?"

My mother dropped into a chair and put a hand over her heart. Her face had turned a mottled, chalky hue. "I think so."

He glanced at me. "Come on, we're going to the hospital."

We spent an anxious night at the hospital while the doctors worked to bring my mother's blood pressure down. Before my brother's incarceration, she had never had any health issues. But since then, and especially after I had left, her health had seemingly gotten more and more fragile.

When my mother had rested and recovered, we decided to take her on a little road trip, visiting some scenic spots on the way to Niagara Falls. She and Arslan clearly enjoyed each other's company, even after hours spent in the car, and she said nothing more about me going back to Ürümchi and resuming my old life. I knew that she had been pressured by the government to try to convince me to go back. After our conversation, she told me that it had been a condition of getting her passport back from the authorities. She was supposed to bring me back with her, but she now understood that that was impossible.

Seventeen days before she was to fly back home, my mother cooked a delicious meal of handmade *laghman* with tomato, green pepper, and lamb. The way she made the peppery, fragrant noodle dish tasted so much like home that I found myself fighting back tears on my first bite.

After dinner the three of us settled on the couch to drink tea and chat.

"Daughter," my mother said, "I'm so happy you've found a good man like Arslan."

Arslan squeezed my hand.

"I know you haven't set a date for your wedding ceremony yet, and I know this is a big request. I want to be there for your wedding." She paused. "I don't know . . . when I'll be able to come back to America."

Arslan and I looked at each other.

"We'll make it happen before you go," he told her. "Nothing would make us happier than to have you there."

That night, we started making phone calls, telling our friends that we were going to have our wedding celebration as soon as we could. Arslan's friends were thrilled and promised that they would help with the preparations. With all of their excitement and energy, it felt like we had a whole phalanx of helpers behind us and it didn't seem so daunting. But Arslan and I hadn't even really had a chance to discuss what kind of wedding we wanted.

"I can't pretend to be the blushing new bride," I told him. "Let's just keep things simple."

He cupped my face gently in his hands. "I want this to be the most memorable day of our lives. You know I don't care about what happened in your life before you met me. All that matters is our future together. I want to show your mom how much I love you and how well I'm going to take care of you. Let's make this a celebration to last a lifetime."

I hugged him tightly and knew in my bones that I had never been so loved in my life.

The next day, I went to a bridal boutique with three of my closest friends from the small group of Uyghurs living in DC, many of whom had escaped the Chinese regime like me. With our common experience, we understood each other in ways others couldn't, and I finally felt I had genuine friendships again. They bustled me into the shop and told the first salesgirl we saw, "Our friend is getting married in less than fifteen days. She needs a dress!"

A woman in a chic purple sheath dress came over to us. She was clearly in charge of the shop. "Are you the bride?"

I nodded.

"And you have fifteen days before your wedding date?"

I nodded again.

"The shop is closed for the next two hours," the manager called loudly to the handful of other customers. "We've got a bridal emergency here!"

My friends helped me try on the different dresses—long and short, beaded and covered in lace, simple and flouncy. All of the different choices were overwhelming, but finally I chose an elegant creamy off-white dress with spaghetti straps that showed off my figure. My friends couldn't stop singing its praises, and I knew that I would look stylish and modern. But as we left the store, the dress safely in the hands of the in-house tailor, I felt a twinge of regret that I wouldn't be wearing a Uyghur wedding dress. I suddenly remembered the costume I'd worn while filming the movie about Amanisahan, all of the traditional ornaments and veils and delicate gold embroidery. I'd never have been able to find any of that in DC even if I did have the time to look.

But I couldn't feel sad for too long because there were so many arrangements to make and people to call and details to sort out. We booked the main ballroom of a Hyatt Hotel and arranged the meals, flowers, transportation, and specifics of the service all within two weeks.

Then, seemingly in the blink of an eye, Arslan was stepping out of a white Hummer limousine that had pulled up to the curb outside the apartment building. He looked fit and handsome in his sharp white tuxedo, and his friends from Uzbekistan, Tajikistan, Russia, and Kazakhstan sat in the back of the limo, dressed in matching black tuxes. All together, they could have been from an ad in a fashion magazine.

As he helped me into the back, he leaned down and said to me, "You don't have to worry about anything anymore. You're mine now and I'll always be here for you."

We had a traditional Islamic wedding ceremony with our local imam, and as we said our vows, I could see my mom in the front row weeping into a handkerchief. My heart was so full just having her be part of the day. I wished that my father and brother and cousins and aunts and uncles could be there too; I would never be rid of that emptiness. But I knew that she would go back to Ürümchi and tell the rest of the family all of the details of our magical day. It was the polar opposite of my first wedding, where I'd been surrounded by my entire family, yet had never felt so desolate in my life.

After the dinner, Arslan and I took to the dance floor for our first dance as a married couple. Our more than three hundred guests surrounded us, and I felt buoyed by all of the support and generosity they had shown. Everyone knew it was my second marriage, but that day, there were no whispers or side glances. I had pledged myself to Arslan and he had pledged himself to me, and we had done it without any misgivings or second thoughts. We were now inseparable in the eyes of Allah.

As the music started, I heard a sudden gasp from the guests and a light shone over our heads. A huge screen had descended over the back wall of the ballroom, and a slideshow was being projected: us dancing, laughing together, out on the town, clowning around in various parks in the city over the time we'd known each other. From over Arslan's shoulder, I saw my mom crying tears of joy. It was the happiest I'd seen her in years.

The very next day, we took my mom to the airport and bid her farewell. I clutched her hands and cried, reluctant to let her go. I had no idea when—or if—I would see her again.

"Give my love to everyone, Dad, Kaisar, my cousin . . ."

"I will, I will. They know you love them. And they love you." My mother kissed me on the cheek and held me close, our tears mingling. Then she pulled away and dried her cheeks impatiently with her handkerchief. "And don't forget, daughter. You're not getting any younger." She shot a meaningful glance at Arslan. "You should be thinking about starting your own family now."

As though her words were prophetic, before we knew it, we had started our own family. I wanted my home with Arslan to be full of laughter and love and constant motion, and a few months into our marriage, I found I was pregnant. The first thing I did was call my mother and let her know. She let out a little shout of joy, and then told me she would be there to help with the birth. She had received a multiple-entrance visa the first time she'd traveled to the United States, and it was still valid. As long as she wasn't stopped at the airport, she would be at my side.

Sure enough, when my daughter was born, my mother was there with me to help with the birth and the exhausting days that followed.

She was able to stay for three months, and her help and wealth of experience were the only things that kept me going. Arslan was there as much as he could be, but with our busy jobs, after my mom left I struggled to manage all of the demands on my time.

I didn't want to tell my mom how much I needed her because she couldn't come back. When she'd returned home, the authorities confiscated her passport. There was no explanation and no means of appealing the decision. I didn't know how long it would be before I'd be able to see her again, feel her comforting presence, and taste her expert cooking that brought me straight back to my childhood with a single bite.

But slowly Arslan and I fell into a rhythm with the baby and found a new routine, with friends and babysitters helping out. When I found out I was pregnant again two years later, we just dug in and managed. We were lucky to get a lot of support from our friends, especially after I went back to work.

As our family was expanding and our happiness with it, at work I lived in a world that couldn't have been more different, reporting on the cruelties visited upon my fellow Uyghurs back home. I got a tip-off that local authorities in Hotan, a particularly religious area, were offering free lunches at workplaces during the month of Ramadan. Like many Chinese government policies, to an outsider, it looked like a slightly odd gesture of generosity. But during the month of Ramadan, Muslims fast during the day. Offering free meals, and observing who took them, was a way of determining who was following the religious proscription against eating before sundown during this sacred month. I spoke to several Uyghur low-level government workers who had been forced to sign a "letter of responsibility" promising not to fast or abstain from cigarettes during Ramadan. If they refused the free meals, they'd be fired.

The US State Department's annual report on religious freedom in 2008 described China's human rights situation as worsening, which was putting it mildly. I could hear the increasing tension in the voices of the people I spoke to in my reporting. East Turkestan was a pressure cooker, and the Chinese government kept turning up the heat. The work gave me purpose, but I was haunted by the feeling that the worst was yet to come.

Not long after my third child was born a few years later in December 2009, I got a phone call.

"Gul? Is that you? Finally, I found you!"

I recognized the voice right away.

"Mehray! I can't believe I'm hearing your voice."

We had lost touch after I came to the United States and she had moved to Malaysia to go to school. Now she had ended up in Switzerland, for reasons I didn't know. She had finally gotten in touch with my parents through mutual friends and got my cellphone number from them.

"I have a surprise for you, Gul. I'm coming to the US to do an English-language course. I could visit you in DC before it starts."

My heart leapt at the thought of seeing my old friend again. "Fantastic! You can stay with us for as long as you want."

I didn't give a thought to how busy I was at work. I had been reporting furiously for half a year on the aftermath of a massacre that had happened in my hometown in July 2009. It had kicked off when people took to the streets of Ürümchi to protest the beatings and murders of Uyghur workers by their Han coworkers at a toy factory in faraway Shaoguan, a town in southern China. A few Uyghurs were accused of sexual assault by a disgruntled Han employee who had been fired, a claim that was later discredited. Things were already tense at the factory because the Han workers resented the Uyghurs for taking away jobs and many of the Uyghur men and women had been sent to work in the factory against their will.

Forced labor was one of the main threads I was following in my reporting. I had documented specific cases in which people from East Turkestan were compelled to leave their homes for Chinese cities to work in deplorable conditions at factories, construction sites, and other places of manual labor. Many of the Uyghur workers at the Shaoguan toy factory were there because they had been threatened with jail time or enormous fines if they refused. When I found out that some workers were from Opal, the town where I had met Anargul, my heart sank. For all I knew, she could have been there in the factory.

In response to the false accusation of sexual assault, a mob of Han workers in Shaoguan attacked their Uyghur coworkers in their dorm in the middle of the night. They used knives and metal rods to beat the Uyghurs, killing at least two—probably many more, though with the coverup that followed, few facts could be corroborated—and injuring more than a hundred. It was a horrific incident, but the Chinese authorities were slow to act. The police didn't even show up to the scene for four or five hours. And in the end, more Uyghur men were arrested for "brawling" than Han men were arrested for murder.

When we heard about what happened, I immediately used the Chinese search engine Baidu to look up the phone number of the factory in Shaoguan. When I reached someone there, I said I was calling with important news for a friend and asked to speak to Anargul. I had no idea if she was actually working there, but hers was such a common Uyghur name that I expected someone would come to the phone.

Soon a young woman's voice came on the line.

I told her I was a reporter with RFA and asked her if she was willing to speak to me. When she hesitantly agreed, I asked her if she'd witnessed the violence.

"No," she said, her voice barely louder than a whisper. "But there were so many people hurt. And for no reason at all!"

I tried to keep my voice calm. "Did anyone die?"

"Yes, but I don't know how many. A lot more than they're saying."

And then she was gone, the line buzzing emptily.

So few details were available in the first several months, especially in East Turkestan itself, that the frustration soon boiled over. The protest in Ürümchi began as a way to demand that the Chinese authorities arrest and punish those responsible for the violence against the Uyghur factory workers, and to demand an accurate accounting of how many had been injured and killed. But the protest met with harsh police response and quickly devolved into violence as people's frustrations finally exploded. Anger at all the oppression, the state violence, the unjust application of laws, the inability to live freely—it all came out. The authorities immediately cracked down, sending in military police to regain control swiftly and brutally.

But what happened after that was worse: police conducted citywide sweeps, arresting anyone suspected of having participated in the protests. They cut off telephone and internet access to the entire region, essentially depriving the citizens of any means of outside communication. When my son was born six months later, those communication restrictions were still in place.

That meant that it was virtually impossible to speak to anyone in Ürümchi, including my family. But I kept scouring government websites for information about what was happening. Because my Chinese was still excellent, I could read the documents easily and even download PDFs of official statements. I learned that more than four hundred people had been charged with crimes in connection to the protests, nine of whom were executed that fall. By the time Mehray came to visit, the number of executions had risen to close to thirty.

I tried to put work out of my mind when I went to Reagan Airport to meet Mehray's flight from the UAE. I stood outside the gates at the international terminal, watching for her, a big bouquet of flowers in my arms. After such a long time of feeling cut off from my past, my history, my culture—especially now that any news from Ürümchi was harder than ever to get—I couldn't wait to reminisce with my old friend.

I waited and waited as people streamed through the gates and walked right past me. Then a young woman in a headscarf stopped right in front of me. I moved a bit so she could get by, but she stayed where she was, smiling. I glanced at her again, and my eyes widened.

"Mehray?"

She was standing right next to me, but I hadn't seen her. I was waiting for someone else, someone from the past. We hugged tightly for what felt like a very long time, ignoring the hubbub around us.

"Look at you! You're such a stylish professional woman now." She held me at arm's length as though to get a good look at me.

"And you're wearing a hijab!" I blurted out. Like me, she had never been particularly religious.

"My ex-husband was very devout," she said with a smile. "And I have to say, starting to wear the hijab has been one of the best decisions I've made in my life."

"Ex-husband?" I was surprised. She had lived a lot of life while we'd been out of touch. I tucked my elbow under hers. "I want to hear all about it. But first let me take you home and introduce you to my family."

Mehray stayed with us for two weeks. Each day, she and I took the kids for a walk, my five-year-old and three-year-old walking with us and the baby happily riding along in the stroller. They fell in love with Mehray immediately and would cling to her sleeve and beg her to play whatever crazy game they had just invented. With Mehray there, I suddenly remembered all sorts of little things from my own childhood that I had forgotten. We even played "Blackbird," with Mehray swooping in as the eagle and my kids shrieking with excitement as they scattered to avoid her marauding beak.

While the kids napped or played on their own nearby, we got caught up on the events of our lives. I told her how Arslan and I had fallen in love as easily as breathing, and how our children had arrived one after another like little miracles.

"They are little miracles," Mehray said, her usually glowing face growing serious. "I can't have any, you know."

"No! But why? I'm so sorry, Mehray."

She shrugged delicately underneath the elegant folds of her hijab. "I've gotten used to it, I guess. I had to have an operation before I left China. You know what the standards of care are like for people like us. For all I know, it was deliberate."

I nodded. Uyghurs were frequently offered substandard medical care, treated like disposable bodies. And I had spoken to many women who were sterilized unknowingly or against their will, as part of the policy to reduce Uyghur birthrates. As far as the CCP was concerned, a woman simply didn't have the right to control her own body.

"Anyway, something happened and . . . and that's that."

"Can it be corrected?" I asked tentatively.

"I've seen so many doctors now. There's nothing they can do. It's the will of Allah."

I put a hand on her forearm and squeezed gently. After years of vowing to stay childless with Elzat, I already couldn't imagine my life without my children, all of the happy, noisy chaos, their smiles in the morning when I woke them up with a kiss on the nose.

"The worst was my ex-husband." She sighed deeply. "He wanted to take another wife. Of course he's allowed to, under Islamic law, if the first wife is infertile. But I couldn't stand the idea. So I left him. That's how I ended up in Switzerland. I asked for asylum there."

"You did the right thing," I told her. "Sometimes divorce is unavoidable."

"And sometimes it's right. Look at your beautiful family, a loving husband and three wonderful children. I always wanted all that, and I'll never have it. I hope you get down on your knees and thank Allah every day."

As soon as she spoke the words, I had an image of my grandmother, down on her knees praying. I could almost remember the exact words she had used the night before I left for Austria, the last time I'd ever seen her. The memory was like a gentle touch on my cheek, warm and familiar.

"You know what else I'm thankful to Allah for? For you."

Mehray laughed, her eyes turning bright again.

"I mean it. You were always so loyal. You taught me about courage and what real friendship is. I'll never forget when you dropped your dance costume on the floor of the cafeteria while the school officials looked on. I thought they were going to pass out!"

We dissolved into giggles, just like college girls again, until my kids came running over wanting to know what was so funny.

Each night when we'd put the kids to bed and I was lying comfortably next to Arslan, I thought about Mehray. She had transformed from a young, tempestuous girl into a humble and religious woman. I saw her pray several times a day, and I saw the comfort it gave her. She'd gone through so much, much more than I had, but she could always rely on Allah. I felt envious of that pure, unwavering consolation.

On her last day staying with us, I took a day off from work and got a babysitter for the kids. We went sightseeing around DC, taking photos, doing a bit of shopping, just enjoying each other's company before we had to part again. It was chilly out, so I was wearing a thin cashmere scarf around my neck. Mehray had on a silky white hijab that contrasted nicely with her dark coat.

"I listened to your broadcast yesterday," Mehray said as we strolled through the Botanic Garden, enjoying the early spring greenery. She'd always loved flowers, so it was the best place I could think of to give her a good send-off. "I can't believe how bad it's gotten back home."

I nodded. I had just reported a story about a woman who had been refused entry to a public library in East Turkestan for wearing a hijab. "They're targeting women for all kinds of religious expression. Men too. We've done stories about men being forced to shave their beards. I've heard of women having their headscarves ripped off their heads by policemen, just to prove a point."

Mehray touched her hijab delicately. "They're trying to shame them," she said. "And it works."

"Would you feel ashamed if you showed your hair?" I asked her. "I mean, we showed our hair off all through college."

She smiled. "We were so young then, weren't we. I cover my hair now for modesty. But it's also about my commitment to my faith, and my devotion to Allah. It has a lot of meaning for me. Now that I'm used to it, I wouldn't dream of leaving the house without it. I just feel terrible for our sisters back home who have the same feeling but can't express it. It's just another form of oppression."

As we walked, I mulled it over. Here in the United States, I was living in a free country. People didn't care about my religion or my ethnicity or what I believed. I had a right to think and believe whatever I wanted, unlike back in China where everything that could be controlled was. Here, no one even cast Mehray a sideways glance, and everywhere we went there were women with their heads covered or bare, wearing every type of clothing from full coverage to extra-mini miniskirts. I thought about what it cost women back home to wear the hijab and how here it wouldn't cost me anything to express what was deep in my heart. After all, Allah was the best friend someone could have. Hadn't he given me so many blessings?

"Remember my grandmother and that old cotton hijab she always used to wear?" I asked Mehray.

She laughed. "Oh, she was the sweetest woman. But thank goodness Muslim fashion has evolved a little since then!"

I laughed with her, thinking how much I wished I could feel my grandmother's thin arms around me again.

"Tell me something," I said. "What does wearing the hijab mean to you?"

"It means dignity," she answered seriously. "It's not just a piece of cloth. It represents my commitment to my faith, to my community, and to Allah. It represents my efforts to be a good person, to be a moral person, every single day. And it means that I stand up for justice and for the right of women everywhere to dress as they want to and do what they want to."

I was silent, letting all of that sink in.

"Hey, let's take a photo together here," Mehray said, stopping on a small bridge. "I never want to forget this day."

"Before we do," I said, "I want to ask you a favor."

"Anything."

"I want you to give me my first hijab."

She stopped in surprise. "Are you sure, Gul?"

"I don't want to be afraid anymore," I told her. "I need Allah's help for that, to deal with all of the pressures. I'm constantly afraid for my family back home, I worry about my children growing up healthy and strong, there are so many pressures. But you've taught me that I should be grateful and appreciate everything I have, including the ability to freely express my faith."

Mehray had started to cry happy tears. "After all these years, Allah has given us an opportunity to reunite with each other. And now you've given me the most precious gift you could ever give me. If I give you your first hijab, Allah will reward me."

She found a few extra safety pins in her handbag, and I handed her my scarf. She wrapped it carefully over my hair so it framed my face. Then she pinned the fabric under my chin and wrapped the remaining scarf over my head. The folds draped gracefully over my neck and upper chest.

She stepped back and admired her work. "You look so beautiful, Gul." And then she gave me a strong, warm hug. "You're going to love wearing the hijab. Trust me."

And I did feel happy and comfortable wearing the hijab from that very first day. It was a pure expression of my faith, and Arslan was unconditionally supportive of my decision.

Of course, I got mixed reactions from others. At the office, one male journalist pulled me aside in the hallway and said, "The Chinese government calls us terrorists and says all Uyghurs are extremists who want to force their religious views on everyone else. How can you play into that by wearing the hijab? Uyghurs are modern Muslims, you know that. Why on earth would you bow to the old ways?"

"Modern Muslims make their own decisions," I said tartly. "Isn't that the whole point?"

"And are you going to wear hijab in your video segments?"

I paused. After the Ürümchi protests and crackdown, I had filmed a few news segments on my own initiative, because I felt a purely radio format was too limiting. I was used to TV, and I knew how to make it work. When I showed the segments to my bosses, they liked them so much that they gave me the go-ahead to make a weekly news bulletin that would be uploaded to the RFA website and to YouTube. But in all those videos, my hair had been in full view, lustrous and cut stylishly, like a Western network anchor. Was I really going to change my image that much?

But the next time I had coffee with my friend from Uzbekistan, she told me that she appreciated my decision to wear the hijab. "I'd be too nervous to wear it myself," she said. "But I think it's a good message to the Chinese government. The Uyghurs are a free people who have the right to do whatever they choose to do. It's a show of courage for you to practice your religion so openly, like other Muslims around the world can."

I didn't feel nervous wearing the hijab on the street, but I did hesitate before wearing it on air for the first time. I asked Dolkun for his advice, and he simply responded that I was free to do as I pleased. It didn't make any difference to RFA one way or another.

So I went on the show in my hijab. The reaction was immediate from some of the Uyghur community who watched our video segments. I received a lot of email in support of the decision from Uyghur women. Most of the negative responses came from men, who thought it was "backward" or too extreme. That was easy to ignore.

What was not easy to ignore was what my family told me the next time I called them.

"We got another visit," my father said wearily. That was how he told me the police had been to their house. Over the years, the police visited regularly, an unpleasant reminder that they were always watching and that nothing my parents or I did would escape their notice.

"What did they say this time?"

"Well, before you were labeled a dissident. Then they called you a separatist. Now, apparently, you're a religious extremist. Watch out or you'll be upgraded to being a terrorist!"

We were both laughing, because that was all we could do. They could label me whatever they wanted, and we had no recourse against any of their propaganda.

Then my mother came on the line. She was not laughing. "The police said you've been infected by extremist ideology."

"Mom, you know that's ridiculous."

"But in our family, nobody wears a hijab anymore. That was for your grandmother's generation. I'm seventy years old and I've never worn one. Besides, it's too early for you to cover your head. You're still a beautiful woman."

"It's not too early for me, Mom," I said gently. "I'm not a little girl anymore. I have a husband and three children and my own life to lead. Here in America, we have the freedom to wear whatever we want to wear, to believe whatever we want to believe. It's a different world from China."

"Are you telling me the American government doesn't give you a hard time for wearing the hijab?" She was skeptical, and given her experiences, I couldn't blame her.

"Of course not. The government here doesn't care what you put on your head. This country stands for freedom and liberty. It's not perfect here—nowhere is. But the First Amendment allows everyone freedom of religion. And I'm practicing my religion."

She sighed. "You don't sound like our little Gul anymore."

"I'm a proud American now," I told her, swallowing a lump in my throat the size of a boulder. "But I'll never stop being your little Gul."

I understood why my mother was afraid. In my research I had heard increasingly disturbing stories about the suppression of religious activities. In the countryside, where people tended to be more devout, the local CCP committees had quietly started banning hijabs and "overly modest" dress for women, along with facial hair for men. Even these simple, deeply personal expressions of faith were considered signs of religious extremism. Stations were even set up at the entrance to the outdoor bazaars, where rural women still did their daily shopping, to inspect their dress and whether it seemed "modern" enough. Police would even cut skirts that were deemed too long by some arbitrary standard—while the women were wearing them.

I reported on one woman who had resisted having her clothing cut away from her legs. She was arrested and taken to one of the local police stations in Kashgar by Han policemen. When her relatives heard about it, they were enraged. It's a deep insult for a devoutly Muslim woman to be touched, let alone manhandled, by a man who is not her husband. The woman's husband and several of his brothers went to the police station to demand her release. In response, the police arrested the men too.

I found the telephone number for the local police station using Baidu and called. When I identified myself in Mandarin as a reporter, the Han desk clerk confirmed that they had arrested several Uyghur men and that "charges were pending." He made it clear that they would not be back with their families for a long time.

Although this was all happening across the world from me, I felt like these people were still my neighbors. Even if I couldn't speak to my family, I was speaking to Uyghurs around the world every day for my reports. And I was always thinking of what effect my reporting on these stories might have on my family members. Often after one of my stories appeared, whether about forced labor or the so-called bilingual education system that had by that time proved to be a monolingual Mandarin education system, my parents would get a visit from local Han policemen. It was predictable but still terrifying for them. One day, those policemen might not just leave after having tea and an intimidating conversation. Part of my mind was always back there, in that apartment with my parents, amid my father's books and the fragrance of my mother's cooking. From the day I started working at RFA, I had kept two clocks on my desk, one with the DC time, and one with the time in Ürümchi. While I often had no idea whether it was going to rain that day in Washington, I always knew the weather back home in the Uyghur region. I couldn't detach myself from any of it, even though each day in front of me was frantically busy.

In DC, our family kept to the same daily routine, just to make sure everything happened that needed to happen. I would wake at five a.m. to pray. When I was done, I would prepare quick lunches for the kids and make breakfast. Then it was time to wake the kids, help them pick out their clothes, and send them off to school or preschool. Arslan and I would drive to work together, and often this was the only time all day we'd have to talk alone. At the office, I'd choose a topic for an article and then conduct research and interviews. I'd make a cup of tea or coffee and make phone calls and write emails and messages, collecting information about what was happening back home or to Uyghurs elsewhere in the world. Everyone had started using WeChat and other messaging services, so it was getting easier to ferret out details of stories happening across the globe. At ten o'clock, we'd have an editorial meeting where we talked about our daily articles and bounced ideas around. Then we'd get down to writing, editing, and recording the stories. I loved going to the office. It was like a separate little Uyghur town, where I could speak Uyghur and feel completely comfortable.

Just when we had the household running smoothly and all of our bases were covered, I learned I was pregnant again. Although I knew four children would throw us back into happy chaos, I was delighted and so was Arslan. I wanted to share the news with my family back home, but I knew that they would be concerned about me. With three children and no extended family to help us, my mother would surely worry about my health and whether I was going to be overwhelmed with both work and the household responsibilities. With that in mind, I decided not to tell anyone back home until after the first trimester.

More than a decade had passed since I'd left home—gone, as though with a single blink. By then, all of my relatives were sending around messages and photos and videos of their kids on my family's WeChat group. I had at first been reluctant to join the group, for fear that the government would monitor it more closely. But my parents assured me that it was all innocuous family gossip, so I joined and was able to get all of the news firsthand. From the group, I learned that my parents had bought a little house in the countryside outside Ghulja so that my father could do some gardening after he retired. They had decided to spend the summers there and go back to Ürümchi for the winters. My parents liked to post photos of the lush garden my father had planted and the tomatoes as fat as little pumpkins that he produced for my mother to cook with.

I tried not to send too many messages over WeChat because the Chinese government watched everything I did. But when I learned that the child I was carrying was a boy, our second, I was just bursting to tell my family the good news. I sent my mother a message on WeChat saying that I had something to tell her. When I didn't get a response after several hours, I messaged my father. Again, nothing. Finally, I messaged my brother.

Call me when you can, he wrote back.

When I got hold of my brother on his cellphone, he told me that my father had had a stroke at their house in Ghulja. He'd just collapsed one afternoon in the garden and my mother hadn't been able to revive him. Because the medical care in the countryside was subpar, they'd moved him back to Ürümchi. He was still in the hospital, and the doctors weren't yet sure what his prospects for recovery were. My mother hadn't left his side the whole time.

My heart dropped out of my ribs. This wasn't the time to say anything to him about my news. I said a quick goodbye to Kaisar, making him promise to keep me up to date on everything, and I ran to the bathroom to vomit. I hadn't had much morning sickness, but now it hit me full force.

I was terrified that my father would die without me seeing him again. All I could do was cry and get down on my knees and pray to Allah. I felt terrible that I couldn't be with him, couldn't help him at all. I felt the distance between us so keenly that it was like a knife in my ribs.

I dragged myself through each day, forcing myself to eat, to work, to try to sleep. The only thing I found pleasure in was hugging my children so tightly that they eventually complained and wriggled away.

After a month, I went to the doctor's office for a checkup. Right away, the nurses began to act strangely. They sent me from room to room, running different kinds of tests and noting things down on my chart. No one told me anything, but I knew something was wrong. They sent me in for an MRI, and as I lay there on the frigid table, terror that I would lose the baby at the same time I might be losing my father swept over me.

Finally, a doctor came into the room where I had gotten dressed again.

"I'm afraid I have some bad news for you," she said. "The fetus you're carrying has a range of developmental issues. The heart is enlarged, and that means that the lungs can't develop properly."

"How . . . serious is it?"

"There's a very high likelihood that the baby won't make it."

I was crying silently, trying to hold myself together as the tears dripped into the folds of my hijab. "What can I do?"

"In cases like this, it's not uncommon to end the pregnancy," the doctor said gently. "It's completely legal and very often leads to better health outcomes for the mother. Of course, it's entirely your decision."

I couldn't even speak. A terrible refrain thrummed through my head. *It's my fault. It's my fault. It's my fault.*

"But you should know," the doctor continued, "that if the fetus dies in utero, there can be very serious complications for the mother, including possibly fatal ones. You need to be aware of the risks before you make any decisions."

I sleepwalked through the next few days, feeling like a ghost in my own house. Finally, Arslan sat me down on the couch while the kids were at a friend's house.

"You can't keep this up. We have to make a decision."

"I know," I said dully, my head throbbing. I hadn't been able to keep food down for days. It was as though my entire body was rebelling.

"You can't blame yourself," he said.

"But I do blame myself!" I burst out. "I've been so worried about my father that I can't eat, I can't sleep, I can't take care of myself at all. Of course the baby is suffering."

"How can you think that?" His shock was apparent in his voice. "Gul, this child is a gift from Allah. He gave you this baby, and He has given you this decision. You're not to blame for the circumstances of your life. What happens to your parents is out of your control, you know that. What you can control are your own actions."

"But how can I make a decision like this?" I whispered. The doctors had made the risks of the pregnancy very explicit to me. But how could I end a pregnancy that had been given to me by Allah? I wanted another child to join our warm, loving family, to learn from his brother and sisters, and to teach them in return. The world is so harsh and unforgiving, and my children were without their aunts and uncles and cousins. Even their grandparents were across the world from them. The more siblings they had, the more support they would have throughout their lives. And I had so much more love to offer.

Arslan took my hand. "I talked to our imam at the mosque. He says there's a panel of imams we can ask about things like this. They can give us guidance that the doctors can't. I think we should do it."

Once again, I put my trust in my faith and felt a burden lifting from my shoulders. "Let's see what they say."

We wrote a letter to the imams, telling them the situation and describing my condition. We sent them copies of my medical information and all of the documents we'd gotten from the doctors. After a few weeks, they wrote back:

> In this case, we believe what the American doctors say. The child will not live. In such a case, it is permissible under Islamic law to terminate the baby. You will not be punished

under the tenets of Islam. You and your husband have already been blessed with three children who must be cared for. Beyond that, the decision is yours. We suggest you pray for guidance from Allah.

I spent the next day fasting and praying. It was the beginning of Ramadan, and so the whole family was fasting from morning until night. Unlike Uyghurs back home, I could practice my faith freely and openly. I read from the Qur'an and spent time in our bedroom in quiet contemplation. It was a relief to know that, from a religious point of view, it wouldn't be wrong to end the pregnancy. Given the risks, the choice seemed obvious.

As I said the prayers, I pictured my soul being cleansed of all of my sadness, my guilt, my anger. All of the thoughts that had led me down wrong paths, all of the unkind words and deeds. I focused on concentrating my whole being on the great might of Allah, on His beauty and strength. My life, my pain, my suffering were infinitesimal before His pity and compassion. I could give myself over completely and trust in Him.

When I came out of the bedroom that evening to prepare our evening meal, the iftar, I felt calmer than I had in weeks.

Arslan was already in the kitchen setting out dates and tea we would eat to break our fast.

"I'm going to carry our son to term," I told Arslan. "I believe that a miracle is possible."

He hugged me tightly against his chest, as strong and comforting as ever. "You are a very brave woman, Gul. The bravest."

The doctors gave me the best possible care over the following months. I had appointment after appointment and so many tests that I couldn't keep track of them all. I did everything they told me to do, tried every supplement they suggested, ate all of the foods they told me to eat, and didn't touch what they told me to avoid. I wanted to give my son every chance of survival.

Every day I put a hand over my stomach and felt for my son, making sure he was still with me. Each kick against my abdomen was a little gift. Every time he turned or I felt an elbow in my ribs, I felt a surge of joy. He was still there, still fighting.

And I was still fighting, too, reporting on those things that mattered. I was following a story about forced medical examinations being perpetrated against the Uyghur population throughout East Turkestan. People were being stopped on the street or taken from work or school and compelled to submit to tests, including blood draws, DNA swipes, and urine samples, and to have electrocardiograms, X-rays, and ultrasounds done on their bodies. They were told that these were routine medical examinations, but it seemed to me that the CCP was building an enormous database of Uyghur biometrics.

I spoke with someone at the Human Rights Watch in New York who told me that samples from forty-four million people had been collected without oversight or consideration for the right to privacy, and that a national database was being built with the information. It was a terrifying prospect—the Chinese government would literally know how to identify every single Uyghur in the Uyghur area. The Orwellian consequences were horrifying to contemplate, ones that could be extended to all Chinese citizens, or potentially around the world.

Throughout all of the work stress and fear for my son inside my body, I told my family in Ürümchi nothing. That was the hardest part, feeling that I had to hide all of my pain and joy from them and the sense of separation that came from that. But my father was still very ill. After the stroke, he'd lost the ability to walk and to say more than the simplest sentences. He was having to learn the basics of functioning in the world again from scratch. My mother and brother had everything they could handle trying to take care of him, traveling back and forth from the hospital, making sure he had everything he needed. I couldn't burden them with what was happing in my life, all the way across the globe.

When my water broke, I was very calm. I had done everything I possibly could over those nine months. And I had learned so much about myself and about how to take responsibility for something beyond myself. And ultimately, how to hand over what I couldn't control to a far greater power than any human agency.

My son was born after a short labor. An hour later, he passed away, snuggling against my chest. His lungs hadn't developed properly and he couldn't breathe on his own. There was nothing the doctors could do to save him. The room was crowded with medical personnel, just waiting with us. I was very grateful for that; although there was no human intervention that would make a difference, they stayed with us. After he stopped breathing, a nurse gently took him from me. My body and heart felt emptier than I ever imagined possible.

It is the hardest thing in the world to say goodbye to your child.

When I woke up a few hours later, a nurse was adjusting my IV and the room was quiet.

"Where is my son?" I asked the nurse. "The imam will come in the morning to give him a blessing and take him for the burial preparations."

"We've done some last tests," she said. "He's being refrigerated until he's taken away."

I couldn't bear the thought of my baby being cold and alone, away from the comforting warmth of his mother's body. Every muscle in my body ached and I barely had enough energy to lift myself up on my elbows. But I raised myself up and begged the nurse to bring my son back.

"I know he's gone," I told her. "I'm not delusional. But I have to keep him warm. Please."

She laid a hand softly on my shoulder. "I'll talk to the doctor."

When she came back, she was carrying my son in her arms. They had wrapped him in a warm blanket, and when she handed him to me it was as though he were just asleep. His face above the blanket was perfect: a tiny button nose, delicate fringes of eyelashes, a thin silken coating of dark hair on his unblemished head. I cradled him against my chest as I had my other perfect children.

Every hour over the course of the night, the nurse came back with a new warm blanket. I will never forget her kindness. I wrapped my son in the warmth, kissing his forehead again and again, rocking him and telling him how much we loved him. That he would always be loved.

Finally, as dawn was breaking, the imam came into my room. My baby's skin had developed a terrifying bluish tint, but his face was still so beautiful. As I gazed down at him in the early light, I realized that he looked just like my father. The resemblance was disconcerting, it was so exact.

The imam stood over the bed and looked down at me somberly. "Gulchehra, I have come here to say the du'a prayers for your baby. But I will not say one for you."

"But, Imam, please, I need you to pray for me," I said, starting to cry again. My whole head hurt from crying all night, my eyes and temples throbbing. The rest of my body felt like it had been beaten to a pulp.

"Sister, you have suffered greatly for your son. Not everyone would have carried this child to term. This is perhaps the greatest test of your life. Why are you crying? You have shown your strength and your goodness. Allah gave you the opportunity to carry this child, and in so doing, you have learned so much. We all will die someday, and if you do nothing else good in your life, this is enough. You carried him into this world and eased his passage out of it. For this, you will be welcomed into Jannah, where nothing will ever hurt you again. You should be rejoicing, sister."

As he began the prayer for my son, I felt the pain in my heart ease like a cramped muscle gradually loosening. I thought, *I am not the Creator. I did my best as his mother. I can give him back to Allah now.* I listened to the imam praying and closed my eyes, saying goodbye to the son I'd held for the briefest of moments on earth.

When I got home from the hospital, I didn't know what to tell my three children—who were still so innocent at only nine, six, and five years old—about what had happened to their baby brother. My heart was completely raw, and I didn't know if I could even talk about it. But Arslan had already prepared them.

"Remember what I said?" Arslan asked, crouching down so he could look into their dark, serious eyes. "Your mom gave birth to a little brother. But he wasn't born an ordinary human like us. He was born an angel. That's why he had to go right away back to Allah. Allah created him for your mommy to carry and for us to love, but now he has to go back to Allah. We did our best and we'll always love him. And after we die, he'll be there to open the doors to Jannah for us."

The children were crying, and so were we, but I could tell that they understood. That evening, as I lay in the bedroom recovering, they tiptoed up to the bed in a little group. My eldest daughter shyly handed over three pieces of paper. They'd each drawn a picture of their little brother flying up to heaven. I reached out to hug them, pulling them close and holding them for as long as they would let me, breathing in their sweet shampoo scent. I could feel my love for them expanding into the empty space their brother had left behind. Part of that emptiness would always remain, but the gaping wound would slowly heal.

A few days later, when I felt strong enough, I called my mother and told her briefly what had happened. We cried together, and my mother told me that she'd never forgotten about my older brother who hadn't made it.

"The pain fades, but it never fully goes away."

"I know," I said. "I blamed myself while it was happening, but now I think I have a deeper understanding. As long as we have love, we have everything we need. I know that now."

"And now you know the full experience of womanhood," my mother said sadly. "It isn't easy."

"Mom, I need to know how Dad is. I know you've been protecting me by not telling me everything. But you can tell me now how bad it really is." I felt I could take anything. My heart had been pummeled, but I had picked myself up. I braced myself for anything she might say.

"Oh, Gulchehra," my mother said. "Darling, we have good news. Really. Your dad has started to walk again. Your brother has been a miracle worker with him."

She told me that my brother had quit his job to focus on taking care of our father. After all of his medical training and the experience he'd gained taking care of other prisoners in jail, he was highly skilled and had managed to get my dad walking and talking again.

All of this had happened without me. I didn't know how to help. I couldn't be there in person of course, and any time I tried to send money, it was immediately returned. The Chinese government had put a block on my account and monitored my family's bank accounts for any unexplained deposits. While I was pregnant, I had tried to talk to my dad a few times on the phone, but he would just start crying and

I couldn't understand a word he said. I felt so guilty for not being there for him.

But at least now there was a little bit of good news that I could focus on as I gradually built my strength back up and returned to normal life.

When I returned to work, my colleagues treated me gently, taking over some deadlines so that I could have more time. But after a few months, I was ready to get back to the usual pace of research and interviewing, writing and presenting, and then doing the whole thing again the next day.

And I was working on an explosive story, maybe the biggest I'd ever found, if it was what it seemed to be. I had begun to uncover a system of reeducation that had been building slowly for years. I had heard of people being sent for fifteen days or a month to "Party schools," centers staffed by CCP members meant to teach people Marxism and inculcate them with a love for the Chinese Communist Party. These schools taught that any religious belief was superstition and only CCP ideology represented truth. People were held there for minor infractions—going to the mosque, refusing to sing the Chinese anthem, dressing "too modestly," refusing alcohol—and forced to recite communist propaganda, swear their loyalty to the Communist Party, and promise not to engage in "religious extremism."

When I called around to find out whether this was true, I used a two-pronged strategy. I dug into my research and got names and phone numbers for so-called schools off official Chinese websites. Then I would call and identify myself as a reporter from RFA, speaking in fluent Mandarin. If the person on the other end of the line was Han, they would often be caught totally off guard, thinking that I must be from some official Chinese outlet. They would tell me things like how many people they had held in the last six months and for how long. They would sometimes brag about making sure their "students" barely had enough to eat so they would be motivated to learn. From these conversations, I built a picture of a rapidly expanding, punitive system of forced reeducation.

If I got a Uyghur person on the line, I would immediately switch to my mother tongue. Usually, Uyghur workers at these so-called schools were more reticent. They knew that they were being watched and what they said was being noted. But often they were very clever and told me what I needed to know without really saying it.

"I heard a rumor that an entire half of the population of one village in the south was sent to be educated," one told me. "That's a lot of people, you know! But, of course, we don't believe that."

Even with all the restrictions and fear, our people managed to get the information out. We all knew it was a matter of survival.

When I was reporting on the situation in East Turkestan or interviewing Uyghurs around the world, that was when I felt closest to my family back home. I couldn't be there to help my father stand up and walk again or to ease the burden on my brother or to comfort my mother who was still trying to work while worrying about my father. But I could try to make the situation better for all of our people, one story at a time.

Still, work couldn't numb the pain of having lost a child. That fall, Arslan and I took our children to visit their little brother at the cemetery where he was buried. They brought flowers and a few little toys to place at his graveside. I cried with them, standing there together, even with the knowledge that he was looking down at us from above. Arslan picked up our son as I held my daughters' hands tightly, feeling the warmth of their bodies, their vitality and spirit.

As we slowly walked away from the grave, I felt I was saying goodbye to a part of my body that had been severed and buried there in the ground. I was leaving a piece of myself behind forever. Then, surrounded by my husband and my children, suddenly I was filled with gratitude like a little burst of sunlight. I had so much. And my son would wait for us in heaven, where he would never be lost. In the meantime, I could visit his grave there, in that quiet little cemetery, to rejoice in the brief spark of life he'd been given.

In 2015, a year after the death of my son, RFA sent me to Turkey to interview some two hundred Uyghur refugees who had fled there by way of Southeast Asia. Thailand was sending the Uyghurs back to China against their will, where they were imprisoned and often tortured. The Turkish government, though, had agreed to take the women and children who had made it to Thailand, but the men had to stay behind and face their fate. Since their husbands weren't with them, the women would only agree to speak to a female journalist, preferably a hijabi Muslim like themselves. And they would only talk face-to-face.

It was my first big reporting job in some time, and I was looking forward to the challenge. I also had another objective in mind. Mehray had moved from Switzerland to Istanbul to work as an interpreter. Her birthday was that week, and although I didn't have her address, I was hoping to figure out where she lived and surprise her with a visit. We hadn't been very good at staying in touch over the phone, and I was eager to see her familiar face again.

Just as my plane descended over Istanbul, it began to snow. By the time I took a taxi to my hotel near the city center, the roads were a slushy mess. Overhead was the worst snowstorm Istanbul had seen in twenty years.

The next morning, more than a foot of snow had fallen. Everything was covered in white: the narrow, hilly streets, the monuments, the colorful roofs and minarets. The buses had stopped running, and no one dared to take a car into the blowing snowdrifts. The only things that seemed to be moving in the entire city were the many city pigeons darting back and forth, trying to find food amid the snowbanks.

Without public transportation or taxis, I was stuck in my hotel room. I had to think of another way to get to the women I was supposed to be interviewing. I had scheduled five days for my trip, and I was on a tight budget. I couldn't just sit and wait for the snow to stop falling.

I went down to the lobby and found the concierge. "Please, I need a taxi."

"I'm sorry, madam, the taxis aren't running yet." He turned back to his paperwork.

"A car, then. Something. Anything!"

He looked at me. "My brother-in-law has a car-for-hire business. But I don't think they're sending their drivers out right now."

"Please, will you call him and ask him? Tell him I'll be sure to make it worth his while."

The concierge nodded and made a few phone calls. An hour or so later, an SUV appeared outside the door to the hotel.

I climbed in and noted with relief that the driver was a smiling, friendly young man. "I need your help," I told him as I gave him the address I had for the camp.

A frown floated over his face. "It's pretty far . . ."

"Please," I said. "It's very important. I can pay one hundred dollars a day."

He nodded and we took off, slipping and sliding over the slick roads despite his careful handling.

The camp was gray and grim, with low cement buildings and a vague stench hanging in the air. But at least it didn't seem inhumanely run. The women there told me that the camp where they had been held in Thailand was much worse, with garbage strewn about, overcrowding, and limited sanitary facilities. The Turkish facility, in contrast, was fairly clean and the women at least had some privacy for themselves and their children. They all agreed that the food was more to their taste as well.

The women I spoke to were nervous and insisted that I not use their real names, for fear of reprisals by the Chinese government. They had all fled their homes because of pressure from the Chinese. One woman's husband had been blacklisted by the government for participating in religious services and for refusing to eat pork, as a practicing Muslim, at his work canteen. Another woman had fled because she was pregnant with her third child, in violation of the strict family-planning regulations designed to drastically reduce the Uyghur population. Another woman had gotten in trouble simply because she was a Uyghur-language teacher and had insisted on teaching her class in Uyghur rather than in Chinese.

All of the stories were horrific, and the women seemed beaten down, frightened, unmoored. But my spirits sunk the lowest when I talked to the Uyghur teacher. I suddenly thought of Abdul and his cheerful, shy smile. He had gone home to his rose-scented village to teach the Uyghur language after college. Had he now been disappeared into the penal system too? How could someone as gentle and sensitive as him survive in such harsh conditions? How could anyone?

I cried with the women as they told me their stories, and at the same time I was also crying for everyone I knew back home. It was so hard to leave them there to their unknown fates.

Exhausted and emotionally drained after three long days interviewing the women, I was still determined to spend my last full day trying to find Mehray. The roads were just beginning to be cleared of the snow, and beneath my window, a few buses roared past, splattering slush everywhere.

When my driver arrived as usual that morning, I climbed into the car and told him we were going somewhere different that day. "But I don't have the address. I just have a phone number."

He looked at me, confused.

"It's an old friend of mine. Can you please call her and tell her that her friend Gulchehra has sent her flowers, and you don't know where to deliver them. Hopefully, she'll give you her address."

He laughed and said, "Okay, well, I'll try." He called the number on his cellphone and spoke in Turkish. Because Uyghur is a Turkic language, I could understand some of what he said. "I'm holding an order of flowers for you," he told her. "Where should I deliver them?"

She gave him her address and off we went. On the snowy roads, it took us nearly two hours to get there, especially since I had the driver stop so I could actually get flowers and a small honey cake along the way. I also popped into a small grocery store and picked up some groceries. I tipped him generously as I got out of the SUV, my arms filled with the gifts for Mehray.

"Will you pick me up tomorrow?" I asked the driver. "My friend and I have a lot of catching up to do."

When Mehray opened the door and found me standing there, she took a full step backward in surprise. Then she was laughing and hugging me and pulling me into her simple but comfortable apartment. She looked thinner and she had lost some of the bounce in her step, but otherwise she was the same girl I'd known since eighth grade.

"I only have one night left," I told her, after I explained what had brought me to Istanbul. "So let's make the most of it. Where's your kitchen?"

"Why? We can just order something in."

I laughed, buoyant from the pleasure of seeing her and hearing her familiar voice. "I know you hate to cook. So I'm going to cook all night for you so you can have a taste of home after I'm gone."

"How much can one woman eat?" she exclaimed as she took in all of the groceries I had brought.

"That's what freezers are for," I replied.

We stayed up the whole night, cooking and drinking tea and talking. She cooed over the photos of my children, and I thought about all of the Uyghur women who couldn't have children because of botched forced abortions or forced sterilizations. I was one of the very lucky ones who had managed to get out of China with my body and mind still intact.

I asked her if she was lonely and she thought for a moment.

"There's a nice Uyghur community here, so in some ways, no, I'm not. I do have friends here. But they're not like the friends I had back home."

"I know exactly how you feel. In America, people feel like they're taking a risk being friendly with me. They don't want to be associated with me, since they or their families might become a target too."

I told her about a recent occasion when Arslan and I had been invited to the home of some Uyghur friends in DC. The guests also included another friend and her parents, who had just arrived from Kashgar to visit her. Arslan and I came a bit late to the dinner, and arrived as others were already eating. As soon as the woman's parents caught sight of me, fear came over their faces. After a moment or two, the woman's mother said she felt sick and asked to go back home. They left without even finishing their meal.

"I thought you said she was your friend?"

I shrugged. "She called me the next day and apologized. She told me, 'My parents have to go back to Kashgar. They'll go back to China and they know that the Chinese government treats you like an enemy. There's so much propaganda about you there. They're afraid. Being friends with you is like sitting on the point of a needle. It's dangerous. I respect you, but I don't have the courage to get close to you.'"

Mehray sighed heavily.

"What is it?"

"I didn't want to tell you, Gul."

My heart was sinking.

"My parents have been harassed too. After I went to America to visit you, they started to get visits from the police. That's why I haven't been in close touch since then. Like you said, you just never know when people are watching."

I felt a stab of pain flash and shut my eyes briefly.

"I'm so sorry, Mehray. Please apologize to your parents for me too."

She caught my arms tightly. "Gulchehra, don't you ever say that again. You have nothing—nothing!—to apologize for."

I hugged her as hard as I could. But inside me was a cold, hard nugget of guilt and fear that would never go away.

A few months after I returned home, I called my parents to check up on them. With all of the strain of working and caring for my father, my mother had developed high blood pressure and had painful varicose veins in her feet. I was increasingly worried about all of them. I didn't know how they'd manage if something happened to my brother, the only young, healthy one among them.

When I called, my mother's voice sounded strange. I begged her to tell me what was going on.

She lowered her voice and started to whisper. "They took your brother."

I immediately felt sick to my stomach, the fear pressing against my esophagus. "Why, what happened?"

"He was driving me to a doctor's appointment, for laser surgery for the varicose veins. He stopped at a gas station to get gas. He had to show his ID."

I had heard that now in order even to buy gas, Uyghurs had to show ID and look into the cameras mounted above the cashier's desk. Other minorities like Kazakhs and Tajiks might get hassled a bit, too, but Han residents could just pay for their gas and go. A fully two-tiered society had been imposed, one tier facing a technologically advanced surveillance state.

"He was supposed to have gone to check in at the police station the day before. But because of my surgery and the preparations, he decided to wait for a day. But they came and picked him up as soon as he went into the gas station. I had to take the bus home. I don't know when we'll be able to do the surgery now."

"But why are they targeting him?" I said, trying to keep my voice low and calm.

"The police told me it's because of you." My mother's voice was flat. "Your reporting. Your troublemaking. They're very angry about your story on the medical examinations. They say it's for our own good, to make sure we're healthy."

I swallowed hard and put a hand over my eyes, where a pulsing pain lashed my forehead. "Listen, give me the details of what happened to Kaisar and I'll write it up and put it in tomorrow's broadcast. The only thing that might help is the pressure of publicizing this abuse of power."

"No!" The word was as sharp as a driven nail. "I've already lost one child to another country. I don't want to lose another one to endless jail."

There was nothing I could say to that, and no way to comfort her.

And there was nothing I could do but continue my work. I looked for stories of people being taken off the street, summarily arrested for no discernable crime. I found more cases than I could report. Almost overnight, young men had begun being disappeared right and left, and no one knew where they were being taken. The government seemed to be targeting anyone with ties to a religious institution and anyone who had an arrest warrant. They also pulled in people who were in contact with Uyghurs abroad. My brother fit their profile.

This was connected to the network of reeducation centers that I had been reporting on for several years. And while my own brother was being dragged into the system himself, I had a breakthrough in my research. I discovered through a Taiwanese newspaper report that a new jail had been constructed just outside of Ürümchi that could hold over three hundred thousand people. It was a mind-boggling number, but it made sense to me. If the Chinese government was preparing to incarcerate huge numbers of Uyghur civilians, they would need somewhere to keep them all.

I called every number I could find for the Ürümchi jails. Sometimes I got no answer, as though the phones had been cut off. Finally, I reached a prison official who would speak to me anonymously. He told me that eight jails in the city had been combined into an enormous "jail city." It was exactly what had been reported in the Taiwanese press. More than seven hundred people had been hired as guards for the system, along with one hundred administrators to make the whole monstrosity run.

"More are being built too," he added casually, "all around the region. There's going to be a lot of work to go around."

"Who's going to be held there?" I asked.

"Who knows for sure? All we've been told is that there will be ordinary criminals and political criminals too."

With me in the United States and working as a reporter, my family were de facto among those "political criminals." And with my brother gone—we didn't even know which jail he was in, and whether it was this "jail city"—my mother had to take care of my father alone. But her feet were in worse and worse shape, and she didn't dare leave my father's side long enough to get treatment. The neighbors helped out when they could, but everyone was too afraid to get involved with our family. The police were always at our door, my brother was in jail, and the government was still issuing propaganda saying that I was a separatist.

Finally, my mother managed to hire a man who had moved to Ürümchi from one of the southern villages. He didn't know much about our situation and needed the money. He was a good man, and tried to help, but he had no medical training and couldn't handle everything that my brother had been doing for our parents. And a few months after he'd arrived, my father fell in the kitchen, breaking his shoulder and his hip in several places. He spent months in the hospital, in and out of consciousness. I called the hospital several times a week, asking the nurses about his condition and trying to make sure he had what he needed. My mother tried to hold everything together, but all she could really do was cling to the hope that my brother would be released soon.

I knew it wasn't likely. In the course of many months of research, I learned that people were simply disappearing without a trace. Most families, like ours, had no idea what had happened to their loved ones. And it wasn't only young men who were being held for no cause. Through a Kazakh human rights activist I knew, I got in contact with a middle-aged Uyghur businessman named Omir Bekali, who had just been released from what he said was a massive internment camp for men near Karamay, about four hours northwest of Ürümchi. He'd grown up in Turpan and moved to Kazakhstan, where he eventually opened a travel agency. He went back to China for a business meeting and was arrested for no reason he'd ever been told. In the camp, he experienced constant hunger, sleep deprivation, and physical torture. After eight agonizing months, his wife and friends back in Kazakhstan had managed to get him released by going through diplomatic channels. When he went to the camp, Omir had weighed 190 pounds, and when he got out, he weighed barely 100. He told me, crying on the phone, that his children hadn't even recognized him.

I wrote up Omir's story, and the whole time I was thinking about what my brother must be experiencing. I pictured him in a camp like that, held without dignity and without the basic things human beings need to live: food, water, warmth. That prison official I had spoken to was right. Lots of camps were being built all across East Turkestan, and they had already started pulling in large numbers of people. Although they were called "reeducation camps," or sometimes just jails, in fact they constituted a terrifying, enormous system of internment camps.

I had been working at RFA for fifteen years at this point, and I had never reported a story as big as this one. It wasn't just my story, or a Uyghur story. It was clear to me that this was the biggest story the world was facing: the mass internment of people simply because of their ethnicity, culture, and religious beliefs. I convinced the businessman to go on the record. He was the first survivor of the Chinese government camps in East Turkestan to come forward and speak publicly about his experience. Although many in the Uyghur community knew basically what was happening, the story was finally coming out to the rest of the world, and I was determined to be part of revealing the truth, regardless of the risks.

At the beginning of 2018, a few days after my story about Omir and the camps aired, I got a call from a close Uyghur friend. She was living in the United States, but like me, she had left all of her family behind in Ürümchi.

"Gulchehra, please don't cry when I say this. I hate to give you bad news, but you need to know."

"Okay," I said quickly, "just tell me. What happened to you?"

There was a small pause. "It's not me. It's about your family back home."

Immediately, my heart felt like it was going to explode in my chest. Fear flowed through me. Tears pricked the corners of my eyes. I knew that my dad had just had a stroke and was still in the ICU. And my closest aunt was recovering at home from heart surgery. I prepared myself for the worst.

"I'm ready," I said, taking a deep, steadying breath. "Tell me."

"My mom sent me a text. Gul, your whole family's been taken. Twenty-four people. All of them, arrested in one night."

"My mom and dad?"

"They were taken too."

My hands started shaking. I couldn't put together a single thought. I let the phone drop onto my desk.

Arslan was working at the desk next to mine as usual. "Gul, what is it? What's happened?"

"We have to call my family. Now."

We both started calling everyone we could think of. My father and mother first. Then my aunts and uncles and cousins. But no one answered their phones. No one returned a text. It was as though they'd been swallowed up by a huge void. My panic grew with each unanswered call. My hands were sweating so badly I could barely dial the numbers, but at the same time my body was numb.

Finally, my aunt who was recovering at home from heart surgery picked up the phone.

"What happened?" I said, barely able to get the words out. "Why isn't anyone answering the phone?"

"My child," she said carefully. "Don't worry about us. Don't worry about your family. We're going to be okay. Just . . . don't call again. Please, don't call again for a while."

I knew then it was real. My aunt was the bravest of my family members. She had always told me I could call anytime, that she wasn't afraid. *What, we can't say hello to each other?* she used to scoff.

Now she sounded terrified. Her son and her son-in-law had been taken in the same night and no one knew where they were.

Panic overwhelmed me.

My husband guided me gently into a chair and took hold of my hands.

"How can I bear it?" I whispered. "They're being punished because of me. They didn't do anything!"

"Gul—"

"Dad's still in the ICU. They're going to kill him!"

I pulled away from Arslan and went back to the phone. I called the hospital where my father had been for months and got a nurse whose voice I recognized. We'd spoken only a few days before. I asked her to put me through to my father.

"We don't have a patient by that name here." Her voice sounded different, stilted.

"What do you mean? He's been there for months."

"I can't help you."

"Please," I let my desperation show. "Please."

"I'm sorry." Her voice lowered, and there was a hint of sympathy. "All I can tell you is that we don't have a patient by that name in the hospital anymore."

When she hung up the phone, I turned back to Arslan. "Tell me they haven't killed him. Tell me. He can't have left the hospital. He can't even stand up on his own!"

Pressure was building inside my chest and thoughts raced chaotically through my head. This had to be retribution for the reporting I'd done on the camps. There was no other possible answer.

"I have to go back," I told Arslan. "Let them have me! But they have to let my family go. They can't suffer like this for what I've done."

"The time has come, Gul. You knew it was coming. You have to be strong now. You're the only one who can help them, and you can only do that from here."

I dropped my head into my hands. I couldn't bear it.

He gripped my hands fiercely. "If I have to let you go, I will. But how do you know that they'll free your family, even if you do go back? Or are they just going to arrest you along with the others? And what about our children? Think about it, Gul. Do you want the Chinese government to finish off our entire family?" He pulled me into his chest. "I'm with you. You're not alone now. We'll do absolutely everything we can to help them."

I couldn't sleep for three days. I kept thinking about what was happening to my loved ones. I didn't have any information at all, just my own terrified imagination.

Then, finally, with the exhaustion and fear and guilt overtaking me, I managed to pray. Haltingly, tearfully, I prayed until I felt the tiniest spark of courage. Even in the depths of my despair, as the days passed, it grew into a weak flame. I imagined myself cupping my hands around it, to protect it so it could become stronger.

Things were coming apart at the seams. At home, I was trying my hardest to pretend everything was okay. I forced smiles and cooked and tried to act normal and keep to our routines. I didn't want my kids to know what was happening and to worry too. But children know. They feel everything.

One evening, I was standing at the sink washing dishes. My youngest son crept up behind me. He caught me around the waist in a hug.

"What is it, sweetheart?"

"Mom, did I do something to make you angry?"

I frowned. "No, of course not. Why?"

"You haven't smiled at me the way you used to for months. I know you're mad at me."

I sank down to my knees and hugged him tightly. "No, no." The guilt was like a knife stabbing into my chest. "You haven't done anything. I'm so sorry, sweetheart. None of this is your fault."

At eight years old, his arms still felt thin as he squeezed me. "Don't be sad, Mommy. I'm going to change. I'm going to get better."

My heart constricted and I knew I had to get help. I was changing, and my children could feel it. I had to do something to take care of myself or we all would go down like a sinking ship.

I called a friend who's a psychologist and told her, "I'm not normal right now. I look in the mirror and I don't see my own face."

"You can't collapse," she told me firmly. "Thousands of Uyghurs look to you for courage, for information, for strength. We can't lose you, Gul."

"What do I do?" I said, my voice shaking. I had no strength left.

"You have to speak out. The worst has already happened. Only if you speak out will you start to feel better."

I was terrified, but deep inside, I knew she was right. I had to be strong for my family, and the only way to help them was to do the unthinkable: publicly confront the actions of the Chinese government.

The next day, I went to speak to the director of RFA.

"I've been working here for many years," I said, "finding other people's stories, helping others in any way I can. But now I need help. I'm not just a journalist. I'm a daughter. I'm a sister. I'm a niece. I have a duty to help my family too. I can't continue this way."

The director immediately responded, "Of course we'll help. Take all the time off you need—"

"No!" I broke in. "I can't just go home and do nothing! Everything is gone, and nothing means anything anymore. The only thing keeping me sane is my kids. I'm a mom, I have to keep myself together. Sometimes I want to scream out loud, but I don't want to scare my kids. I have to *do* something."

He nodded, and I could see he truly understood. "We're here for you, Gul. Whatever you need."

That very day, I wrote and taped an open letter to the Chinese government. In all of my experience as a journalist, it was the hardest piece I've ever had to produce. I had to record and rerecord over and over again. By the second sentence, everything would rush up at me, and my voice would start changing, tears slipping through my resolve.

But I couldn't show my weakness, my terror. I was just one person facing the largest country in the world. I had to make it clear that I wasn't giving up. I had the right to speak. I had the right to know where my family was. I drew on every ounce of strength I had.

I edited the recording painstakingly, until it sounded the way I needed it to. Then I sent it everywhere I could think of. I sent it to my friends, my colleagues, human rights organizations, even the Chinese embassies in the United States. I put it up on Facebook, too, just trying to reach the largest audience I could. I was determined to get my family released, no matter the cost.

I talked to anyone who asked me to, anyone in the media or the government who would listen, in my halting English. I didn't care how I sounded. I just needed to get my family's situation out there, and everywhere I went I spoke from the heart.

Finally, my story reached the right ears, and in July of 2018, I was startled to find myself invited to speak at a hearing of the Congressional-Executive Commission on China about human rights abuses in the Uyghur region.

I prepared my speech meticulously and arrived in tasteful makeup, a somber gray suit, and my finest white silk hijab. I was one of four speakers, including the professor of Uyghur history Rian Thum; Jessica Batke, a senior editor at ChinaFile and former researcher at the Department of State; and Ambassador Kelley Currie. It was very distinguished company, and my heart was beating so hard as I began to speak that I was sure the members of Congress could hear it.

> As is well known, Chinese authorities have even resorted to threatening my colleagues and me at Radio Free Asia, even though we are based in the United States and most of us are US citizens. They do this by targeting our China-based relatives. I am among six journalists with RFA's Uyghur Service whose family members have been jailed, detained, or forcibly disappeared, often in connection with, if not as a direct result of, our work for RFA. One of my colleagues has two brothers, sisters-in-law, and an elderly mother in detention. Another has three brothers in jail. Two more

> each have a brother in detention. I have about two dozen relatives of extended family who have been detained, almost all taken on the same day. The sad thing is we cannot be too sure about our families' well-being or their fate, since attempts at contacting them carry serious risks.

My voice threatened to break, but I continued, relying on all of my professional training and experience to get me through.

> I know and my colleagues know that our work is important. After we began reporting on the events unfolding in Xinjiang, journalists in Western media have investigated and confirmed many details that were first reported by RFA. The *Wall Street Journal*, the *New York Times*, *Washington Post*, the *Financial Times*, BuzzFeed, BBC, CNN, CBS, the *Economist*, Human Rights Watch, Amnesty International, France 24, and many other reputable organizations and media have done outstanding work as well. Knowing that so many of our peers turn to RFA as a trusted source is very encouraging. But the cruel irony doesn't escape my colleagues and me that, although we have journalistic insight about so many events happening in Xinjiang, we are often the last to know if our mothers, our fathers, our brothers, our sisters, and our children living there are in prison or not. If they face sentencing or punishment. If they are in need of help or medical care. If they are still alive. That is the fear we live with, every day and every hour. But there is one greater fear that urges us on: that if we stopped doing our duty as journalists, if we were silent, the world would simply forget.

Whether it was because of my speaking out or some behind-the-scenes political machinations of which I knew nothing, my mom was released from prison on March 10. The first thing she did was call me. In addition to her time spent in a cell with many others, she had also been kept chained to a drainpipe in the Ürümchi Women's Prison for nine days. This, despite being seventy-three years old and in poor health. The instant I heard her voice, I started crying.

"We're alive," she said, sounding tired and hoarse. "I have to tell you that I'm alive, because of you."

"What happened? Tell me." I didn't want to hear any of it, didn't want my fears to be affirmed, but I knew for her sake as well as mine that she had to speak.

She told me that the police had pounded on the door late at night while she was alone in the house, my father in the hospital and my brother in prison despite there being no charges against him. She told me about being driven to a holding cell with her face hooded and her hands tied tightly behind her. She told me about being chained to a pipe in a cell with thirty other women and having to go to the bathroom in a bucket. It was like a brutal kidnapping, except the kidnappers were the Chinese authorities.

Then she told me that she'd made friends with the Chinese guard. I gave a little bark of laughter in disbelief, but really it didn't come as a surprise. My mother could make friends with almost anyone. She'd slowly developed a rapport with the guard, a Han woman in her thirties. At first, the guard would tell my mother to shut up. But my mother would just calmly suggest that the guard needed to eat better or get more exercise or sleep better.

"I told her her color wasn't good. She spent too much time inside. I said, 'We have to be in here, but you're not trapped in here. Go take a walk!' Then one day she called me *kanjuk*. No one had ever talked to me like that in my life! Well, I just started laughing. The guard got mad, of course, and asked me what I was laughing about. I said, 'Do you know what that word means?' She said, 'They told us it means whore.' I said, 'It means Mongol,' so calling me that is pretty insulting to our neighbors to the east.' And we laughed together. After that, she seemed calmer around me. I could tell her when one of the other women was sick and she'd pay attention. I think she started to respect me a little."

And perhaps that was why, when my mom collapsed on the bare cement floor of the cell, the guard rushed in and unshackled her. She called in to the guard station and asked for a special medical transfer to the hospital. That guard had surely saved my mother's life.

"I was the oldest woman in that cell," she said. "I've already had a good long life. But there were so many young girls in the cell, beautiful just like you. My heart bled for them. They had done nothing, nothing at all. When I asked them why they were there, it was because they'd called a friend in a foreign country. Or posted something religious online. They weren't real criminals at all."

Each day, she was given a single steamed bun to eat and nothing else. Sometimes the bun was stuffed with rotten meat or gristly bits of what she thought could have been rat.

"Gul," my mother told me calmly, "because of you, I'm alive. I told myself, 'Eat! You have to eat this, you have to stay alive.' I ate because of you."

I pressed the phone to my ear, shaking with guilt and grief. I was on the other side of the world and couldn't even comfort her.

"Do you remember what I said to you last year? When your brother was taken away by the police? I told you that the police had said it was because of you. Because of what you're doing there in America. I've felt terrible about that every day since. None of this is your fault. It isn't your fault we're being persecuted. I had to survive, to make it out of prison so I could tell you that."

"Mom . . ." I was crying too hard to tell her how much I loved her and how desperately I wished I could protect her.

"No, my daughter, don't cry. I'm all right. Really. Just hug your children more. Breathe deeply. Appreciate everything, even plain water. Because everything's beautiful, the sun in the sky, the moon, everything!" She paused and added, "If you're alive, everything is possible. Everything."

Epilogue

As far as I know, my parents and brother are all back home now. I can't be certain, because calling them is much too dangerous for them now. I've been officially designated a "terrorist" and a "separatist" by the Chinese government and put on their Most Wanted List. At the same time, my family members have been forced to go on camera to denounce me. On-screen, their eyes look dead as they speak. Now, any information I get about my family is through secondhand sources—old neighbors, the rare in-the-know visitor from Ürümchi. I can't even be certain that my cousins are out of the camps. For the time being, I don't dare call my aunt to ask.

The nightmare for them, and for the rest of East Turkestan, is far from over. Along with the establishment of the internment camps, the Chinese authorities have gone into overdrive to monitor and control the population. Sophisticated electronic surveillance systems have been put into place with facial recognition that can identify Uyghur faces from afar. There are cameras installed on every street corner, as well as in many private homes. To get inside your own house, you have to scan the QR code on the door to get in, which transmits all of your information to the authorities. If a Uyghur is caught by facial recognition on a camera outside of their own neighborhood, they can be taken to the camps. If a Uyghur doesn't have an ID on them, they can be taken to the camps. If a Uyghur sends a text to someone in a foreign country, they can be taken to the camps. If a Uyghur tries to visit a friend's home after that person has been accused of a crime, they can be taken to the camps.

Many people have been held in these camps for years, with no end in sight to their unjust incarceration. Chinese authorities have started calling them "vocational training centers," but that so-called training merely feeds into the system of forced labor, which sends people across mainland China to work in sweatshops, where half of their already abysmal salary is deducted from the paycheck to pay for their previous incarceration.

If and when someone gets out of the camps and is allowed to go back home, they are given a "scorecard" on which points are tallied according to whether they behave well or badly. Behaving well might be going to a Marxist study group. Behaving badly might be watching a contraband Turkish TV soap opera, speaking in Uyghur instead of Mandarin to their own kids, or saying a prayer at night. All of this is recorded by a camera installed in their living room or observed by a Han "family member" who has been sent to live in their house and report on their behavior. Every month, the scores are tallied, and if the points are too low, they are taken back to the camps. In this Orwellian system of authoritarianism, with its complete lack of privacy and its swift, brutal racialized state violence, my beautiful homeland has been turned into one enormous open-air jail.

Sometimes it gets to be too much, and I want to scream out loud, but I don't want to scare my children. I close the door and cry. I just want to give them a normal life, but I've long since forgotten what it feels like to be a normal person.

My work at RFA helps with that feeling, at least. I can connect with my people, feel the same happiness and pain and hope. I feel like I'm part of the Uyghur experience, even though I'm not there. Since China began to pursue a policy of genocide against the Uyghurs, we have had to unite more completely. Our common suffering and persecutions have made us understand that we are one nation, united by a common ancestry and a common destiny. As my father taught me back when I was a starry-eyed girl in Ürümchi, the word *Uyghur* originally meant "to join together," and today, that is truer than ever.

Not long after my family was disappeared and imprisoned, I was contacted by a woman on Facebook. She sent me a few messages saying that she had grown up watching me on Xinjiang TV and that she wanted to connect with me. Her messages made her sound very young, full of cute emojis and smiley faces. But then she mentioned that she had three children. I did a bit of research and discovered that she was in Egypt. The Chinese government had recently been pressuring the Egyptian government to arrest Uyghurs living there and to send them back to East Turkestan, where most of them were disappeared into the camps. When Mihrigul sent me her phone number in a message, I decided to call her. She told me a horrifying story.

She had been living in Egypt with her husband and had given birth to healthy triplets. With no friends or family to help care for them, she decided to go back home while her husband stayed behind in Egypt for his job. When she arrived in Ürümchi, however, she was pulled from the customs line and interrogated for hours. Her tiny babies were taken from her, and she was taken away to a holding facility. They put a hood over her head, just like they did to my mother.

When she was released weeks later on "parole"—although she'd never been told why she was being held, let alone been charged with any crime—she discovered that one of her infant sons had mysteriously died in the hospital. The other two triplets were ailing, having difficulty eating and suffering from a range of physical issues. No one would tell her anything about what had happened to her babies.

As we spoke, I heard children playing in the background. "Are those your children?"

"Yes," she said. "At least they're able to play now. For a long time after I got them back, they were so listless you'd have thought they were dolls."

"Will you tell me about the camps?" I asked her.

"Yes." Her voice sounded very far away.

"Wait. What phone are you using?"

"A Xiaomi phone I bought in Beijing before I flew back to Egypt. Why?"

"Don't tell me anything," I said. "You have to get a new phone. They can monitor everything through those phones. There are so many backdoors into your information."

"I don't have the money to buy another one," she said quietly. "To be honest, I can barely buy groceries. I know the government is probably listening in, but what can I do?"

"You can protect yourself. You have to protect yourself." I looked around my living room at my kids' toys and all the happy chaos of our lives, and it took me one second to come to a decision. "I'll wire you the money. And then we can talk."

When Mihrigul had a new phone, she described her experiences to me in the "reeducation" camps.

"They wanted to interrogate me about what kinds of things I did in Egypt. I was unable to return to Egypt before this detention because all of my documents were in the hands of the authorities, and I had been blacklisted. The camps were terrible. Everyone in there was just an ordinary person who'd been pulled in for some false offense, like going to the mosque. I was tortured for seven days and nights when

I first got there. They kept me awake the whole time. They gave me some sort of 'medical examination' that was humiliating and painful, and then they shaved my head. I started having seizures and losing consciousness, and I guess they were afraid I was going to die in there, so they released me to my father's care. He told me to take my children and get out, to take the train to Beijing and fly back to Egypt from there. He didn't care what the consequences for him or the family would be. They just wanted me to be safe."

The echoes of my own family situation were so painful that I had to end the conversation there to cope with the flood of emotions. When it comes to the work I do, the line between journalist and activist can be thin. I was always very careful to identify myself as a journalist to anyone I spoke to, and my editors at RFA made sure we all met the highest standards in our reporting. But the moment the Chinese government took my family away, I couldn't just report on the story anymore. I had become part of the story itself.

In that moment, I was extremely concerned for Mihrigul's safety. She would never be secure as long as she was in Egypt, so I went straight to the China Desk at the State Department. I was helping them collect information about the dire situation in East Turkestan. When I told them about Mihrigul's plight and the condition of her children, the official gears began to grind. Several months later, after Mihrigul had spoken to US government officials, she and her children were given a special emergency visa, and they were able to safely fly to the United States.

Helping Mihrigul fight her way out of a desperate situation lifted some of the burden I was carrying. I could do so little to help my own family, but I could do something to help others. Here in the United States, I'm free. But I know what's happening back home in East Turkestan. It's always with me. Not an hour passes without me thinking about it. Any person in my situation would do the same. If your family members were carted off in the middle of the night, brutally punished, wouldn't you speak out?

That need to speak out has consumed the better part of my life. There have been moments of desperation and times when I felt like none of it made any difference. After my family was taken, I experienced real moments of darkness. But there have also been bright sparks, and support has come from unexpected corners.

After I publicized the fact that my family members had been rounded up, I received an invitation to speak at the 2019 Women in the World summit being held in New York City that April. It was a whirlwind few days of meetings and interviews and listening to other women speak about their experiences, aspirations, and accomplishments. Part of me was starstruck—Oprah was there!—but the bigger part of me was deeply inspired. I felt buoyed by the bravery of the women, many of whom were fighting tirelessly for causes like ending child poverty across the world. I spoke about the horrors being visited upon the Uyghur population, but I also spoke about our strength. I quoted a Uyghur saying: *Women rock the cradle with one hand, and rock the world with the other.* And when Tina Brown, the founder of Women in the World, echoed my words in her closing speech by saying, "Let's rock the world together!" I felt in my heart that people were finally beginning to listen. Later I would feel that again when I was invited to speak about the mass internment camps in East Turkestan at the Oslo Freedom Forum, where I received so much support for our cause. These experiences convinced me that there is still hope left in the world.

Even a chance encounter in a DC carpool gave me an opportunity to bring the plight of the Uyghur people to a much bigger audience.

One day Arslan came home from work in a state of excitement. He'd carpooled with a man named Tim Nelson.

"He works for the State Department," Arslan said. "We got to talking. He asked me where I was from and I told him I'm a Uyghur, born and raised in Kazakhstan. I told him about the genocide going on in East Turkestan. Then I told him about you and how you work at RFA and how you've been targeted by the Chinese government. I told him we cover all of the Uyghur issues, but we also have become the story ourselves."

I nodded.

"He was very interested, and I think he might want to help."

We got to know Tim and became friends with him and his wife. It quickly became apparent that Tim had connections to some powerful people, and not just inside the US government. He also knew Bill Browder, the force behind the Magnitsky Act that allows the US government to impose targeted sanctions against people who perpetrate human rights abuses.

Tim set up a meeting with Bill, and when Arslan and I met him, I could tell that he was a true champion of human rights; Bill fought for the life of his lawyer and friend Sergei Magnitsky, who died in a Russian prison, and he was now trying to make sure others wouldn't suffer the same fate. He listened to my story carefully, his liquid brown eyes filled with compassion and understanding. Although I spoke about the plight of the Uyghurs all the time, I wasn't used to telling the details of my personal experience; it was too painful to recount casually, and usually I would just outline the facts for anyone who expressed interest.

But Bill asked questions few others did, like about my parents' medical conditions and whether they'd been denied care while in detention. He asked how many Uyghurs were being held in the camps, and I told him that because of the CCP secrecy there were no definite numbers, but we believed more than 1.8 million people were being held in over one thousand camps. The statistics are hard to take in, but I felt that he could see the faces behind those inconceivable numbers. I saw a rare kindness in him and an impression of real empathy. For him, all those people were real flesh-and-blood humans, not just numbers. I left the meeting buoyed by the sense that at least a few people were listening, at least a few people really cared. He made me feel like I wasn't so alone.

Several months later, I got an unexpected email from Bill. I read it over several times before I fully absorbed the message. Bill had nominated me for the Magnitsky Human Rights Award Board, and they had chosen me as that year's recipient of the Award for Outstanding Human Rights Activist. I was to fly to London that fall to speak at the ceremony, along with defenders of human rights, free speech, and social justice from around the world. I felt humbled to be placed among them.

After telling Arslan and my superiors at RFA, I immediately started to plan an acceptance speech. The Magnitsky Act, which Bill had helped create, was the only legal tool that the United States had against individual CCP officials to punish them for their civil rights offenses. It could be used to sanction them, freeze their overseas assets, and refuse them entry to the United States. My hope was that in speaking out, such tools would start to be used against specific Chinese officials who had targeted my family and the families of others. And even if that took time to happen, whatever I said in my acceptance speech would reach many more people than my Uyghur broadcasts did. This was my chance to speak to the world about what was happening. I had to find a way to make people understand exactly what was at stake.

The ceremony was held at the palatial Central Hall Westminster. I chose my outfit very carefully. I wore a purple and white etles print jacket to represent the Uyghur people. Etles is a kind of Uyghur silk produced by the atlas moth, dyed in intricate patterns and woven into delicate cloth. Traditionally, every Uyghur woman would have at least one special etles dress that she would wear on important occasions. I did my makeup carefully, and then covered my head with a pale pink hijab with a silver chain printed across it. If everyone could remember how interconnected we are, interlinked by our basic humanity like one long chain extending out across the entire earth, perhaps all kinds of atrocities would become impossible.

In the excited hubbub before everything began, Bill managed to find me backstage. He sat down next to me and asked me how I was doing.

"I'm frightened," I confessed.

"You're a pro," he said. "This is nothing."

"It isn't stage fright." I lowered my voice. "I don't know if I should say what I came here to say."

Bill took my hand gently. "Gul, we're here for you. Whatever you want to say, just say it. Your message is so important. We are all here to listen to you."

I squared my shoulders. It was time for me to speak up for all Uyghurs.

Bill introduced me and amid the warm applause, I made my way onto the stage. My whole body was trembling. As I began to speak, I heard my voice shaking too. Because of this speech, my parents could be punished, my brother rearrested, my distant relatives harassed. There was no telling what the Chinese government's reaction would be, and yet again, my actions could lead to the suffering of those I loved the most. But I heard Bill's words echoing in my head and I knew I had to do it. Not many people had a chance to speak on a global stage like this one. I strengthened my voice to deliver the closing I'd rehearsed so many times:

> The Chinese Communist Party is taking hostages by the millions, not only inflicting pain directly on those it puts into its concentration camps, but even delivering illegal threats individually to relatives abroad. The world's silence has only encouraged China to expand its concentration camps to hold millions of people. And those outside the camps suffer under the world's worst Orwellian mass surveillance police state.

I was speaking slowly, trying to make sure every word carried the weight that it should.

> I only hope the world remembers its commitments and laws and finally voices with meaningful actions the words we each must have the courage to demand: *Never Again!*

As I said those words, making clear that what was happening to the Uyghur people was a genocide, the purposeful destruction of a people and a culture, I felt a new kind of freedom. I had finally said it. The stakes could not be higher.

The audience was on its feet, and the applause sounded as though it were coming from far away. I had traveled such a distance—from my beloved hometown of Ürümchi to DC and now to an international awards ceremony in London—and had lost so much along the way. I suddenly thought of that stone my father had sent me from our garden, the one that still smelled like the Ürümchi earth, like my childhood, and a wave of unbearable sadness came over me. The Chinese government had taken from me everything that it could take. It took my culture, my language, my friends, my family, the dignity of my people. I lived with the pain and guilt every single day of knowing that they had suffered because of me. My father taught me that a stone is most precious where it belongs, and though I still longed for my home, I was where I was meant to be now, where I belonged.

My father would have no way of ever knowing I'd stood up on this stage and spoken for him, for my family, for my community, for my people. But he'd given me the courage to do it. He taught me how to speak the truth, and now I could be certain of one thing: I would never stop using my voice to speak up for the voiceless.

Acknowledgments

First and foremost, I would like to thank my family and friends in the Uyghur region. They have never given up on me and have provided a constant source of support, no matter what they themselves were going through. I would also like to thank the viewers of my children's program, who took me into their hearts and homes. Even years later, many of them still remember me, and it gives me great joy to have touched their lives in that way. They've encouraged me to become the person I am. This book is a culmination of everything I've learned from the many trials my family has faced and from my years living in exile. Countless people opened their arms to me and showed incredible generosity, above all, of course, my husband and children, without whom I would be lost. Thank you also to those individuals who believed in my story and helped bring this book to fruition. Finally, I would like to thank all of the people around the world who have paid a terrible price for their family, homeland, peace, freedom, love, friendship, pride, or whatever they know to be sacred. They inspire me, and I hope this book inspires them.